Longings and Belongings

LONGINGS AND BELONGINGS

ESSAYS BY NANCY HUSTON

McArthur & Company

First published in Canada in 2005 by
McArthur & Company
322 King St., West, Suite 402
Toronto, Ontario
M5V 1J2
www.mcarthur-co.com

Copyright © 2005 Nancy Huston

All rights reserved.

The use of any part of this publication reproduced, transmitted in any form or by any means, electronic, mechanical, photocopying, recording or otherwise stored in a retrieval system, without
the expressed written consent of the publisher, is an infringement of the copyright law.

Library and Archives Canada Cataloguing in Publication

Huston, Nancy, 1953-
    Longings and belongings / Nancy Huston.

ISBN 1-55278-547-5
    I. Title.

PS8565.U8255L66 2005   C844'.54   C2005-905278-3

The publisher would like to acknowledge the financial support of the Government of Canada through the Book Publishing Industry Development Program, The Canada Council for the Arts, and the Ontario Arts Council for our publishing activities. We also acknowledge the Government of Ontario through the Ontario Media Development Corporation Ontario Book Initiative.

Some of the pieces in the present collection were previously published in English in a slightly different form:

"A Tongue Called Mother," *Raritan*, New Brunswick, N.J., Winter 1990; in *Vancouver Review* n° 12, Fall 1993.
"Towards A Patriotism of Ambiguity," as "A Bucking Nightmare" (emphatically not my title) in *Saturday Night*, Toronto, June 1997.
"Erotic Literature in Post-War France," in *Raritan*, New Brunswick, N.J., Summer 1992.
"On Being Beautiful," under various titles, in *Salmagundi* n° 106-107 Saratoga Springs, N.Y., Spring/Summer 1995; *Harper's Magazine*, New York, October 1995; *Brick, A Literary Journal*, Toronto, n° 52, 1995.
"Novels and Navels", in *Critical Inquiry*, Summer 1995.
"Three Men and a Cradle: Bobin, Kundera, Handke," in *Salmagundi* n° 112, Saratoga Springs, N.Y. Fall 1996.
"Good Faith, Bad Conscience: Tolstoy and Sartre" in *Salmagundi* n° 128-129, Saratoga Springs, N.Y., Fall 2000.
"Destroy, She Said : Elfriede Jelinek" in *Salmagundi* n° 148, Saratoga Springs, N.Y., Fall 2005.

Cover design and composition: Tania Craan
Printed in Canada by Friesen Printers

10 9 8 7 6 5 4 3 2 1

To Sacha, Léa and Boris

TABLE OF CONTENTS

Foreword 1

LONGINGS

SIMONE DE BEAUVOIR'S CHILDREN   5

TWO STARS, POLARIZED
Sylvia Plath and Ted Hughes   19

A TONGUE CALLED MOTHER   47

NOVELS AND NAVELS   61

LETTER TO SIMONE WEIL, WITH PASSAGES OF TIME   85

EROTIC LITERATURE IN POST-WAR FRANCE   109

THREE MEN AND A CRADLE
Kundera, Bobin, Handke   133

THE LIMITS OF THE ABSOLUTE
Marguerite Duras   155

GOOD FAITH, BAD CONSCIENCE
Tolstoy and Sartre   169

DESTROY, SHE SAID
Elfriede Jelinek   197

BELONGINGS

REASSURING STRANGENESS   223

REASSURING STRANGENESS REVISITED   233

CALGARY, FRANCE   239

SINGING THE PLAINS   245

TOWARDS A PATRIOTISM OF AMBIGUITY   257

ON BEING BEAUTIFUL   281

THE GOSPEL ACCORDING TO SAINT MATTHEW   301

THE DECLINE OF "IDENTITY"?   313

KNOWLEDGE UPROOTED   331

THE FOREIGN MOTHER   351

Bibliography   357

Foreword

These are the musings of a young, then less young woman, spanning the past quarter of a century.

Flipping through her files and disks, I see that this woman wrote a rather staggering number of pages, changing styles from one text to the next, trying out different voices, now serious, now lyrical, now painstakingly researched and now free-flowing and rather funny — never, though, at least I hope never, purely academic. As she went about looking for herself in her new language, in the Old World, she was part chameleon, part parrot.... In the final analysis, however, she was remarkably consistent in her obsessions — she basically wanted to talk about a single subject: *the relationship between mind and body.* (This was perhaps because people often expected her to be all one or all the other, and she could not put up with this mutilating alternative.) But to discuss the "mind-body" is also to deal with the themes of passing time, mortality, existential anguish and the attempt to overcome it through creation or destruction... So she gave a great deal of thought to how different people dealt with these themes — men and women, mothers and fathers, Christians and adepts of voodoo, the French and the Americans. Artists, warriors and prostitutes....And she also gave some thought to the good and bad things that happen to a body, and to a mind, when it is uprooted, expatriated, caught up in a permanent misunderstanding about identity.

The twenty texts collected here, despite their imperfections and their occasional clumsiness, continue to move me and matter to me. What I can say about these pieces taken as a whole is that the young woman who wrote them was looking for new ways of articulating desire and reality. That pair is a bit like mind and body — of course they're different, but at the same time they're inseparable; if you divide them radically from one another, or allow one to dominate the other, the results can be damaging not to say disastrous. We all know that it is silly to mistake one's desires for reality, and tragic to give up one's desires in the name of reality, and pointless to count on all of one's desires becoming reality...so the question is, what sorts of bridges can be built between these two worlds?

Nancy Huston, April 2005

N.B. This collection contains pieces from two different volumes of essays published in French by Actes Sud (Arles) and Leméac (Montréal): *Désirs et réalités* (1995) and *Ames et corps* (2004).

Longings

Simone de Beauvoir's Children

The "ideal" image which I had for so many years of Simone de Beauvoir was just that — an idea. It was an idea made up of everything that is commonly known about this uncommon woman — that she'd lived an incredibly full life, blessed with not only intelligence but energy, the physical and moral stamina her intelligence needed to blossom; that she'd travelled to the farthest corners of the earth, had famous friends and defended great political causes; that she'd been honoured, praised, translated, read and admired the world over.... And then, of course, there was the extraordinary couple she had formed with Jean-Paul Sartre — two geniuses who had loved and respected one another for fifty years, even if he took advantage more often than she did of the sexual freedom that was part of their "pact" from its inception....

Over the past few years, however, as I have explored the novels and autobiographical writings of the author of *The Second Sex* and tried to grasp something of the woman's reality, my *idea* of her has gradually been belied, or at least thrown into question. I have found it disturbing, and what I shall try to transcribe here is a bit of this disturbance. My intention is by no means to "burn my idol" (to "murder the mother"), but rather to gently remove her from her pedestal and bring her down to earth.

Between 1949, the year in which *The Second Sex* was published, and 1970, which marked the rebirth of the women's movement in France, Beauvoir changed her mind about feminism. Most importantly, in her later years she no longer believed that it should be subordinated to the class struggle, and that socialism would automatically put an end to sexism. On certain points, however, she remained staunchly faithful to her original choices and stances. In a recent interview, for instance, she declared (I quote from memory): "Neo-feminism isn't dead at all; it's doing just fine. It wandered off into the impasse of 'difference' for a while, but now it has emerged from it again."

What the word "difference" refers to in this declaration is a current of French feminism including thinkers such as Luce Irigaray, Hélène Cixous, Annie Leclerc and others, who attempted to explore and revalue a certain female *specificity*, which generally revolved around the female body (and its possible effects on what that body wrote): menstruation, pregnancy, giving birth, a cyclical sense of time; a different relationship to "the other" because women receive "the other" in their bodies, and fabricate other bodies within their own — a possibly different relationship, therefore, to nature, culture, and language. In these texts, the themes of excess, splurging and squandering, chattering, giving, flowing, the ungraspable, the emotional — weeping, laughing, thumbing one's nose at Reason — were often shown in a positive rather than a negative light.

This could scarcely have enchanted Simone de Beauvoir who, in the opening chapter to *The Second Sex*,

"Biological Givens," had listed all the disadvantages encountered by a mind that was forced to inhabit a female body — ten pages that make your hair stand on end, so frightening is their evocation of the oestrus cycle that "takes place every month in pain and in blood," the "exhausting work" of gestation and the mortal dangers of delivery, culminating in the depressing conclusion that women are "the most profoundly alienated of all female mammals, and the ones who reject their alienation most violently."

Women's alienation, says de Beauvoir, is her subordination to the species. "Since her entire organism is oriented towards the perpetuation of the species, it is through motherhood that woman integrally fulfills her physiological destiny…"; "woman, like man, *is* her body; but her body is something other than herself." Is it possible that these facts have *no effect at all* on the ways in which women perceive reality, enter into interaction with other people, conceive the passage of time? Are they mere handicaps and nothing else — so many obstacles on the path to women's humanisation?

"The impasse of 'difference'"…. It so happens that motherhood — that "destiny," that "orientation," that "alienation" of the "female mammal" — was exactly what Simone de Beauvoir had rejected for herself. Here is the reason she gives for this decision (which of course no woman should ever need to *justify*): "If I decided not to have children, it was because I wanted to have only *chosen* relationships, with *chosen* people." Thus, according to her personal system of values, the individual must always win out over the species, the mind over the body, choice over contingency, necessity over gratuitousness, or — to return to the now-outdated terminology of existentialism that was guiding de Beauvoir's thinking back in 1949 — transcendence over immanence.

"I've never regretted not having had children," declared de Beauvoir in another interview, "given that what I wanted to do was write." And to those who might drag out the tired cliché according to which a woman's books are a substitute for the children she didn't have, Beauvoir correctly retorts, in *The Second Sex*, that for many women, children are a substitute for the books they didn't write or the professional goals they didn't reach.

In the first volume of her autobiography, *Mémoires d'une jeune fille rangée*, de Beauvoir tells us that her decision not to have children dates back to her early childhood. As a little girl, she noticed that "a mother always has a husband in tow; she is weighed down by a thousand tedious chores. When I thought about my future, these constraints seemed so burdensome that I renounced the idea of having children myself; what mattered to me was shaping minds and souls — I would be a teacher, I decided." She was to keep this promise. Instead of "shaping" flesh-and-blood bodies, she would devote her whole life to the "shaping" of minds. In order to do so, she would choose to emulate her father instead of her mother; this time the mind/body dichotomy is explicit. De Beauvoir writes that for her father, "I was neither a body nor a soul, but a mind. Our relationship took place in a limpid sphere where no conflict could occur.... He had unreservedly given over to my mother the task of looking after my organic life and supervising my moral instruction." Of course, this was a classic division of labour — just what one would expect in an upper middle class French family at the beginning of the 20th century. De Beauvoir's rejection of all things maternal, however, was to have an effect on her theoretical work.

Though it is not good practise to go rummaging around in an author's private life in order to inflict "psychoanalytic" interpretations on her novels, it is more justifiable to make connections between the two when the author herself has published thousands of pages of autobiography, as well as openly autobiographical novels. In Beauvoir's, case, the connections are sometimes rather startling. She says, for instance, that when her father learned she had begun to menstruate, she was "overcome with shame. I'd always thought the female community took great care to conceal its secret flaw from men. In my father's presence I believed I was pure mind; I was horrified to think that he now suddenly saw me as an organism. I felt permanently dethroned."

In de Beauvoir's novels, this perception of menstruation as a "flaw" gives rise to passages such as the following one in *The Mandarins*: "When I told her she would be having her periods and what this meant, she listened to me with a distraught look on her face, then smashed her favourite vase on the floor. After her first uncleanness, her anger was so great that eighteen months went by before she bled again."

And in *The Second Sex*, de Beauvoir refers to menstrual blood as "the flow of red which plunged the young girl into horror." But is menstruation horrifying for *all* young girls, or only some of them? Is horror a "natural" reaction to this natural phenomenon, or is it, rather, the result of the taboo placed upon it, and the unfortunate ways in which it has been presented to young girls — and their mothers, and their fathers?

Let us take another example. The section of *The Second Sex* entitled "The Mother," begins with half a page about contraception, followed by fifteen pages about abortion. Of course these are crucial issues, and they were were even more so in 1949, when abortion was illegal and contraception woefully inadequate; still, the fact of starting off a chapter on motherhood with the *rejection* of motherhood reflects perhaps a bit too accurately the personal choices of the author. As for pregnancy, Simone de Beauvoir describes it in almost entirely negative terms. "Those who endure the ordeal of pregnancy most easily," she says, "are, on the one hand, matrons wholly given over to their 'laying' function, and, on the other hand, virile women who are not obsessed with the adventures of their body...: Madame de Staël handled her pregnancies as briskly as her conversations." Here again we see the familiar equations at work: woman = body, man = mind. Isn't de Beauvoir implying that de Staël was a "woman" because she knew how to handle pregnancies, and "virile" because she knew how to handle conversations?

Immediately after having decided never to become a mother herself, Simone de Beauvoir imagines what her future life will be like: "I would plan my days down to the smallest detail, leaving nothing up to chance; combining occupations and distractions with ingenious exactitude, I would get the most out of every second and not waste a single one of them." Might there be a connection between this paragraph and the preceding one? Between the rejection of motherhood and the merciless control of time? Between the denial of "Difference" and the sense of urgency which characterized Simone de Beauvoir's style — not only her literary style but her lifestyle?

Being "with it," up to date, aware of everything that goes on, everywhere, at all times. Opting for "Modern Times"* — the *present*, current events — once and for all. Ardently following political and cultural developments, all sorts of movements and ideological currents; you are in these currents, now and not one minute later. Living your life as intensely as possible, transcribing it in your diary, writing incredibly detailed letters to Sartre on a daily basis whenever you are apart. Missing nothing. Grabbing time as it passes and flattening it out on the page, endlessly marking it out with words, words and more words — Sartre: "I've always considered abundance to be a virtue" — discussing everything together, concealing nothing, being "transparent" to one another, knowing and saying everything, about themselves, each other and the world. The self and the world might

---

*The title *Les Temps Modernes*, the journal founded by Sartre in 1945, was borrowed from Charlie Chaplin's film.

change, of course — but language will deal with these changes and be their mirror image. Never stopping. Taking work with you wherever you go; making your work and your life coincide as closely as possible; turning your life into art and your art into life; leading an exemplary existence at every second and from every point of view — not because you are "better" than the others but because you are more demanding, more efficient, devoid of self-indulgence and self-pity — *moral,* too, but according to a moralism whose criteria are regularly redefined, in the free choice of the individual facing the world. Most importantly: doing things, keeping busy, keeping active, an activist, none of whose actions are ever gratuitous — everything must count; everything must be countable and calculable. And given that life is work, it logically follows that laziness is death — everything you do has to be "edifying" in one way or another; every activity has to have a double justification — it must be carried out not only for its own sake but because it is good for you, teaches you something, makes you a better person. Turning your back on everything shadowy and inchoate; zooming in on light and truth, living in the spotlight and being yourself a spotlight — a beacon swinging through the darkness of past and future for the benefit of your contemporaries. Being omnipresent. Living in a perpetual present. *Modern Times.* "Sartre lived in order to write; he had been mandated to bear witness on all things and analyze them in the light of necessity; my own job was to lend my consciousness to the multiple splendours of life, and I had to write so as to wrench them away from time and nothingness."

In *The Woman Destroyed*, a woman decides after twenty years of marriage to accept her husband's love affair in the hopes that he will grow tired of it. Aghast, she watches helplessly as her life collapses in front of her eyes. And she says, "My biggest mistake was not having realized that time passes. It had been passing, and I was frozen in the attitude of the ideal wife of an ideal husband.... (Perhaps my father's death had something to do with this. Something broke in me then. That was when I stopped time.)"

On the back cover of this novel, Simone de Beauvoir calls her heroine "the stupefied victim of the life she chose for herself — a marital dependence that leaves her stripped of everything." The author is not as different from her character, however, as this declaration would have us believe. In her autobiography, Beauvoir often admits that she identified with the weakest of her female characters — those who were the most devastated by their husbands' infidelities and the most obsessed with aging; some of Sartre's attempts, in his letters, to reassure her about his love affairs are reproduced almost verbatim by the unfaithful husbands of the *The Woman Destroyed* and *The Mandarins*. And in *The Force of Circumstance*, the volume of her autobiography covering the years 1945 to 1963, de Beauvoir (born in 1907) writes that "the most important, the most irreparable thing that has happened to me since 1944 is that… I have aged… The threads that connect me to the Earth are being gradually eroded, they are snapping and will go on snapping…The too-brief hours are leading me to the grave at top speed…. Looking back incredulously at the credulous adolescent [I once was], I realize with stupefaction to what extent I have been cheated."

De Beauvoir has often been reproached for having ended this book on such a bleak note; certainly a wish to "descend from the pedestal" may have been one of her reasons for doing so. What I want to emphasize is not the negativity of this passage, but the fact that in the long run, even for those who adamantly embrace the present, time does pass. Did de Beauvoir's father's death play the same role in her life as in that of "the woman destroyed"? We cannot know the answer to that question — but this very impossibility is significant: whereas she devoted an entire book to the disintegration of her mother's body (*A Very Easy Death*), her father's demise is summed up in a single paragraph of *The Prime of Life*. It is as if her father, having remained pure spirit to the end, had simply evaporated.

Nonetheless, time passes. De Beauvoir grew old (she published a book on aging); Sartre died (she published *Adieux: A Farewell to Sartre*); and at last she herself died…. Now only we are left to carry on her mad, courageous, passionate and pathetic endeavour to understand who she was.

If I'm so fascinated by the control of time and the rejection of motherhood in Simone de Beauvoir's work, it's because for a very long time these were my own obsessions. I didn't want to have children either — I defended this choice so long and so adamantly that I shall always consider it worthy of respect. It is obvious that unmarried people — particularly unmarried women — have greater freedom than married ones. Objectively, quantitatively, they have more time at their disposal for working, travelling and learning than mothers do. But I came to see that although there was "more" of it, time still tended to pass, and that I disliked its way of doing so. No matter how desperately I tried to measure it, distribute it, and get the most out of it, I could never manage to bring it to heel and make it *stop*. It kept slipping through my fingers.

And when, after a decade or so of living as an independent-active-unmarried-adult woman, I ultimately chose to share my life with a child (and also with a man, but that's another story), it was, among other reasons, because I wanted to change my relationship to time… force myself to accept a certain "waste" of time… learn everything I could about laziness, repetition, and "empty" time. Perhaps more than any other experience of human life, having a child confronts you with both necessity *and* contingency. When you wipe a baby's nose, it's not because that's the thing you care the most passionately about doing at that particular instant, it's because that's what you have to do. Same goes for buying its diapers. Mashing its carrots. Getting up in the middle of the night. Walking more slowly down the sidewalk. There is no way of "making up for" this lost time, or "capitalizing" on it by turning it into an edifying tale. It is not saveable, not tellable, not recuperable. That's just the way it is. And that's the way it is again. And yet again. Pure life. A relationship to another person who is simply *there*, and for whom you are responsable. You help it stay alive, that's all; there's no profit to be made from it. This means that your life can no longer be forced to coincide with your work — it overflows into everything, disrupts limits, crosses borders, turns you into someone else. De Beauvoir was quite right in saying that parenthood is not a "chosen relationship with a chosen person." The child is *there*; it is *that* child and not another, and you are required to fulfill its needs. This is *necessary*. The pleasure the child gives you, on the other hand, is perfectly *gratuitous*. It is not the result of a "proper choice" — the proper choice of a bottle of wine, a walk in the woods, a book, a friend. You've done nothing whatsoever to "earn" it. A smile, a cuddle, a whispered secret — these things are not only "gratuitous," they are priceless.

The parent-child relationship, though certainly not a relationship between "equals" who "choose" one another, hinges neither on altruism nor on alienation. It is an aspect of humanity which has traditionally been valued by women rather than men, and there is no reason in the world to devalue it. In an interview with Jean-Paul Sartre in 1974 for the magazine *L'Arc*, Simone de Beauvoir wonders whether "the oppressed status of women may have led them to develop not only certain defects but also certain qualities, different from those of men." We have no way of knowing what "qualities" de Beauvoir might have had it mind, but it is highly significant that in Sartre's opinion, their hypothetical superiority could only lie in "a better knowledge of the self" — a project to which both of Sartre and de Beauvoir had devoted countless years and books.

The truth of the matter is that because of the roles allotted them (wife, mother, prostitute, muse or secretary), women have developed gifts in just the opposite direction — *a better knowledge of the other*! True, to Sartre's mind, if I may quote his most famous line bass-ackwards, "other people are hell." (And whenever he and de Beauvoir talk about each other, they do so in terms that abolish all differences between them: "Sartre was my other self," "We are as one, my good Castor," and so on and so forth.) I am by no means implying that having a child is the only way a human being can learn about generosity or have a genuine relationship to with another person. Yet I cannot help regretting that de Beauvoir's prodigious intellectual performance should have *structurally* excluded this experience — an experience which has been of incommensurable importance to the vast majority of women from time immemorial.

Several recent books — Tillie Olsen's *Silences*, for instance — seem to embrace de Beauvoir's outlook, implying that nothing can ever be more important than a work of art. Of Rilke, for instance, who refused to take a job to support his wife and child, or to live with them, or to attend his daughter's wedding, or even to receive his daughter for a two-hour visit during her honeymoon, Olsen says that his attitude was "extreme — but justified. He protected his creative powers."

Today, women, too, have the right to exercise those creative powers — but they also have the duty to recognize and revalue the ones which the have always exercised. If we ever hope to abolish this absurd arithmetic of numbered sexes, the "second sex" must treat the "first" not only as its master but as its pupil.

(1983)

Two Stars, Polarized
*Sylvia Plath and Ted Hughes**

Three quotes.

1. "Someday when I am stumbling up to cook eggs and feed milk to the baby and prepare dinner for my husband's friends, I shall pick up Bergson, or Kafka, or Joyce, and languish for the minds that are outleaping and outskipping mine." (Plath's *Journal* March 6, 1956, before her marriage.)

2. "Here is a day in the life of the writing Hugheses... I get up, take the two litres of milk left daily on our doorstep in a can and heat it for my café-con-leche and Ted's brandy-milk... Ted and I write... from 8:30 till 12. Then I make lunch... Then two more hours of writing from 4 to 6, when I make supper." (Letter from Sylvia to her mother Aurelia Plath, written during her honeymoon on 25 July 1956).

---

*This piece was written in 1986, long before Ted Hughes published his extraordinary collection of poems in honour of Sylvia Plath, *The Birthday Letters* (1998), and *The Unexpurgated Journals of Sylvia Plath* (2000), and of course before Hughes's own death in 2001. In the meantime much squabbling has gone on; much blame has been distributed; several books and even a film have been devoted to the couple's tragedy; I can only hope that my own approach to the subject will shed fresh light on it.

3. "Well, I think our domestic life is practically indistinguishable from that of all the people who live around us; the only main difference is that Ted doesn't go out to work at nine and come home at five; he *retires* about nine, to his *room*, and works, but I certainly have a life just like all the other housewives and mothers in our district — shopping, dishes, and taking care of the baby [*she laughs*] and so forth. I think very few people have an idea I do anything at all except household chores and so on." (Interview with Sylvia Plath on the BBC, after five years of marriage.)

Two poets who live together continue to be two bodies.

❊ ❊ ❊

"Sometimes, lying awake at night," I recently confessed to a white-haired friend whose wisdom I have long admired, "I think about the fact that when Sylvia Plath was my age, she'd been dead for three years." "Yes," said my friend, "but you've learned an important thing she *never* learned." Seeing me frown in perplexity, she added, "How not to kill yourself."

The fact that Sylvia Plath committed suicide at age thirty-three is no doubt one of the reasons for which she is better known in France than her husband Ted Hughes. (This does not imply, as a Parisian journalist stupidly suggested after having seen the play based on *Letters Home*, that the poet's suicide was basically a narcissistic gesture, motivated by her wish for literary immortality.) In the

English-speaking world, numerous literary critics have bemoaned the fact that Plath's work is so often interpreted solely in the light of her (admittedly dramatic) life. My own intention, however, is NOT to interpret her work; it is precisely to study the *relationship between* life and work in this writing couple which was perhaps, along with Morante and Moravia, far more than Aragon and Triolet or Sartre and de Beauvoir, one of the most evenly-talented literary couples of the 20th century.

More is known about Plath's life than about Hughes's, and one of the reasons for this is that, from adolescence almost up to the day of her death, Plath kept a diary. She grew up in a middle-class family on the North coast of Massachusetts. She received early recognition for her brilliance, valued her intellect and associated it with her father. It may be worth mentioning that the latter — a renowned biologist by the name of Otto Plath — had been Aurelia's professor before he married her. Sylvia went through what can surely be called, despite all Freud's disclaimers, an Electra complex. A fertile breeding-ground for hysterical, anorexic, and artistic tendencies in women, the Electra complex, unlike the Oedipus complex, has little or nothing to do with incestuous desire. In both the Oedipus and the Electra complex, the mother is Body and the father is Mind; Word; Law; God. The young girl therefore has no wish for physical but rather for intellectual union with her father; she aspires to join with him in the supercilious repudiation of all things female, especially the female body.

In the BBC radio interview already quoted (one of a

series entitled *Poets in Partnership*), Sylvia describes a spiritual crisis she underwent in her youth: "At nine," she says, "I was rather disillusioned; I stopped believing in elves and Santa Claus and all these little beneficent powers, and became more realistic and depressed." As the BBC interviewer may not have known, but as most readers of Plath do know, what she lost at the age of nine was not only her belief in male makers of magic, it was also her father. Death — actual, physical death — served to make Professor Otto Plath even more powerful, abstract and ideal in the eyes of his daughter than he had been up until then.

Plath had an extremely, perhaps excessively close relationship with her mother Aurelia; she says that she felt threatened by their closeness. Throughout her adolescence, despite Aurelia's constant encouragement of her creativity, despite the sacrifices she made so that her daughter could attend the best colleges, Sylvia saw her intellectual strivings as a way of escaping from her mother's world — the world of physicality, propriety and good housekeeping to which she also, desperately, wanted to belong. The split is evident in the systematic difference of tone and style between her letters home, which are almost uniformly cheerful and filled with tokens of her intention to become a "total woman," and her poems and diaries, rife with anxious speculations about her capacity to reconcile artistic creativity with love.

At university, Sylvia displayed not only outstanding intelligence but a powerful wish for independence; she did not find the prevailing ideal of marriage appealing. "It would mean," she wrote in her journal, "getting up at seven o'clock and making him bacon and eggs, toast and coffee, hanging around in my nightgown and curlers after he left for work, washing the dirty plates and making the bed, and then when he got home after a fascinating, stimulating day, he'd expect to find a big meal all ready, and I'd spend the evening washing more dirty plates until I fell into bed completely exhausted."

"I am not only jealous," she went on a few months later (September 1951), "I am vain and proud."

"*Never* will there be a circle, signifying me and my operations, confined solely to home, other womenfolk, and community service, enclosed in the larger worldly circle of my mate, who brings home from his periphery of contact with the world the tales only of vicarious experience to me. No, rather, there will be two overlapping circles, with a strong riveted center of common ground, but *both* with separate arcs jutting out in the world... Two stars, polarized.... In moments of communication that is complete, almost...fusing into one. But fusion is an undesirable impossibility — and quite nondurable. So there will be no illusion of that" (May 1952).

This, then, was Plath's life project at the age of twenty — love and independence. This was her voice when she was feeling optimistic — strong, sure of her gifts and her rights. But Plath had another, darker voice — a voice of depression and self-deprecation, an irresistible urge to destroy herself. November 1952: "I am afraid. I am not solid, but hollow. I feel behind my eyes a numb, paralyzed cavern, a pit of hell, a mimicking nothingness. I never thought. I never wrote. I never suffered. I want to kill myself, to escape from responsibility, to crawl back abjectly into the womb." As we shall see, the equivalency between death and the return to the womb, constantly reiterated in Plath's diaries of this period, was later to play an important role in the sense of kinship between her and Ted Hughes.

In 1953 — she was now 21 — between two semesters at university, Sylvia's application for a summer course in creative writing was turned down. Rejected by the professor, a man she held in high esteem, condemned to spend the summer at home with mommy, she collapsed. "At home, I will not have the little man in my head, mocking me: is this worth it, worth it, worth it? ... Stop thinking selfishly of razors and self-wounds and going out and ending it all." (July 1953); "God, god, god: Where are you? I want you, need you; the belief in you and love and mankind. You must not seek escape like this. You must think" (July 14, 1953). Following these words, the journal broke off for two years. Sylvia made her first suicide attempt — serious enough to all but succeed; it would leave a permanent scar on her face.

That same summer, the United States had condemned the Rosenbergs to death by electrocution. When Sylvia was given electric shock treatment (with insufficient anesthaesia) following her suicide attempt, she may have felt that she was being punished for a crime as heinous as theirs: having betrayed not atomic secrets, but the "feminine mystique" which was then the American ideal of womanhood. Be this as it may, she would never be the same again. When the journal picked up again, her tone was much humbler and less "feminist" than before the trauma — as if, following her close brush with death, Plath was punishing herself for having been too ambitious. Now, for instance, she was prepared to see her new boyfriend Richard Sassoon as a "blazing angel" or a god ("In the beginning was Sasson"; November 22, 1955), and she asked him, "Why is it that I find out so slowly what women are for?" (January 22, 1956). According to Nancy Hunter Steiner, her friend and room-mate at the time: "Sylvia had decided that her husband would be a very tall man"; "she talked, half-jokingly, of producing a race of superchildren, as superlatively tall as they were intelligent. The children, according to her predictions, would all be boys." Fantasizing Ted Hughes before actually meeting him, Plath now seemed to be looking quite consciously for a husband who would be as enormous as her dead father had become.

On February 19, 1956, now pursuing graduate studies in Cambridge, England, Plath wrote in her diary: "And I cry so to be held by a man; some man, who is a father." One week later, she wrote, "My God, I'd love to cook and make a house, and surge force into a man's dreams, and write, if he could talk and walk and work and passionately want to do his career."

That very night, she met Ted Hughes.

Born and raised on the moors of West Yorkshire, Hughes was an ardent lover of nature and animals. After having studied English, archaeology and anthropology at Cambridge, he had renounced Western rationalism and immersed himself in the study of mysticism: the Tarot, the Indian Vedas, astrology, hypnosis, automatic writing.... Moreover, he was already well known as a writer in Cambridge, and Plath admired his poetry. She went to a poetry get-together with the express intention of meeting him — and it was love at first sight. "Oh," she wrote in her journal a week later, "to give myself crashing, fighting, to you... He said my name, Sylvia, and banged a black grinning look into my eyes, and I would like to try just this once, my force against his." She described him to her mother as "the only man I've met yet here who'd be strong enough to be equal with" (March 3, 1956).

At first she was utterly euphoric: "Dear Mother, I shall tell you now about something most miraculous and thundering and terrifying.... It is this man, this poet, this Ted Hughes. I have never known anything like it. For the first time in my life, I can use *all* my knowing and laughing and force and writing to the hilt all the time, everything, and you should see him, hear him! He has a health and a hugeness.... The more he writes poems, the more he writes poems... Daily I am full of poems; my joy whirls in tongues of words" (April 19, 1956).

There are words, and then there is daily life. Both poets write, but only the poetess does the cooking. In her letters to Aurelia, Sylvia seems to find this quite natural. "I cook steaks, trout on my gas ring, and we eat well. We drink sherry in the garden and read poems; we quote on and on: he says a line of Thomas or Shakespeare and says: 'Finish!'" (April 21, 1956). "If you have a chance, could you send me over my *Joy of Cooking*? It's the one book I really miss !" (April 26, 1956). The poems Plath was writing at the very same time as these letters, however, give a very different image of Hughes's ferocious appetite. "Pursuit," for instance:

In the wake of this fierce cat,
Kindled like torches for his joy,
Charred and ravened women lie,
Become his starving body's bait.

I hurl my heart to halt his pace,
To quench his thirst I squander blood;
He eats, and still his need seeks food,
Compels a total sacrifice.

The striking thing about this encounter and the poetry to which it gave rise was that Plath and Hughes seemed to be fascinated by the same images (birds of prey, wild animals) and by the same violence; but the violence took on a different meaning in the woman's work than in the man's. Hughes talks about two rival wolves, for instance, whereas Plath sees herself as a lamb confronted with a wolf. Yet in her letters to her mother after their marriage in June 1956, she continued to insist on the fact that they were not only close but virtually identical: "Ted is the only man I've ever met whom I'd rather be with than alone; it's like living with the male counterpart of myself…. We finished typing a manuscript of about 30 of his best poems and sent them off…." (July 14, 1956); "I could never get to be such a good person without his help" (August 2, 1956); I can't for a minute think of him as someone 'other' than the male counterpart of myself, always just that many steps ahead of me intellectually and creatively so that I feel very feminine and admiring" (September 11, 1956).

Ah. So the adjective "male," when annexed to "counterpart," implies superiority? Just so. The twins are identical, only one of them has more identity than the other. Aurelia Plath footnotes one of Sylvia's letters with the recollection of her daughter's contentment when, in junior high school, she came in second to a boy in a spelling bee. "It is always nice to have a boy be first!" (February 24, 1957). Similarly, Sylvia was now ecstatic to be able to wear high heels and still feel small standing next to Ted.

"I can appreciate the legend of Eve coming from Adam's rib as I never did before — the damn story's true! That's where I belong... Away from Ted, I feel as if I were living with one eyelash of myself" (October 8, 1956). Hughes, too, was interested in the legend of Adam and Eve — but whereas Plath expressed it in terms of a heavenly ideal, he invariably derided it, sometimes (as in "Theology") in frightening terms:

No, the serpent did not
Seduce Eve to the apple.
All that's simply
Corruption of the facts.
Adam ate the apple.
Eve ate Adam.
The serpent ate Eve.
This is the dark intestine....

However, before going on to speculate about the advantages Hughes might have drawn from this strangely asymmetrical twinship, I would like to suggest one of the reasons for the asymmetry. It has to do with a significant etymological constellation, that which connects authorship to authority through the rootword *auctor*. In the modern Western world, and particularly in the two hundred years since the Enlightenment, the Sacred has undergone a displacement from religion to literature. The belief in God, pure spirit and creator of the material universe — "the author of all things" — has gradually been transformed into a belief in the superhuman rights and powers of the Artist. Both of our protagonists adhered to this sacralisation of the Word ("the Word was God"), but Plath — while genuinely wishing to become an *author* — was less comfortable with her wishes and less convinced of her *authority* than Ted Hughes. One of the reasons for this is that the Creator, in Western historical tradition, has always been male, and females have always been construed as the created par excellence. Countless myths — from Pandora to Pygmalion, from the past Eve of the Bible to the future one of Villiers de l'Isle-Adam — reinforce this perception of woman as a work of art produced by man. That these myths at least partially reflect men's denial of, and competition with, women's procreative capacities has not prevented women themselves from believing in them.

Given the fact that Sylvia Plath saw her husband as both her twin and a god, what could her own role next to him be, if it were not to be the traditional ones of muse, model or "mothering mind?" At all costs, she had to avoid "falling" from the spiritual heights to which her father's hopes and her husband's example had summoned her, and plummeting back into the role of malleable matter — or, rather, *mater*, the second rootword crucial to this story, as it links the material to the maternal.

❈ ❈ ❈

"You once referred to [the mainstream English poetic tradition] as a 'terrible, suffocating, maternal octopus,'" said scholar Ekbert Faas in an interview with Ted Hughes. "What I meant by the octopus," replied the latter, "was the terrific magnetic power of the tradition to grip poets and hold them." Hughes did not say what he meant by maternal, but I think the association is clear: the octopus is the squid is the sticky, engulfing, mothering, smothering threat that *mater* represents to mind.

Perhaps more than anything else, what the two poets had in common at the outset of their marriage was just this powerful ambivalence with respect to *mater*. In a woman, this ambivalence (part and parcel of the Electra complex) invariably entails dissociation — hence the "bright" and "dark" voices of Sylvia Plath. In both her life and work there is a constant tension between her optimistic, efficient, loving, good-little-girl "personality" and the terrifying monsters lurking just beneath the surface. As Ted Hughes would later put it, "The opposition between a touchy, fastidious defense system and an imminent volcano is, in one way or another, a constitutive element of all her poems of the first years."

As his own work did not suffer from this dissociation, he wrote well — as prolifically, Plath said, "as shooting stars in August;" his poems were like "controlled explosions of dynamite" (May 18, 1956). When Hughes's first collection — *The Hawk in the Rain* — received a prize, she wrote in her diary, "I'd rather have it this way, if either of us was successful: that's why I could marry him, knowing he was a better poet than I and that I would never have to restrain my little gift, but could push it and work it to the utmost, and still feel him ahead" (August 9, 1957).

Violently opposed to the values of the society in which he lived, Hughes attributed the blame for all modern ills to the Protestant Reform and its attendant ideology: "The subtly apotheosised misogyny of Reformed Christianity," he wrote in a passage quoted by Ekbert Faas, "is proportionate to the fanatic rejection of Nature, and the result has been to exile man from Mother Nature — from both inner and outer nature.... Since Christianity hardened into Protestantism, we can follow her [Nature's] underground heretical life, leagued with everything occult, spiritualistic, devilish, overemotional, bestial, mystical, feminine, crazy, revolutionary and poetic."

Though it purports to be anti-misogynistic, and though all its elements have positive connotations for Ted Hughes, this list of adjectives in which femininity is associated with bestiality and madness can scarcely be construed as a feminist credo. That the poetic has female overtones by no means implies that women are privileged authors of poetry. "She cannot come all the way," says Hughes in "Crow's Undersong"…

She comes to the fringe of voice…
She comes singing she cannot manage an instrument…
She comes dumb she cannot manage words…
She has come amorous it is all she has come for
If there had been no hope she would not have come
And there would have been no crying in the city
(There would have been no city)

Who is "she?" Mother? Nature? Woman? All of the above. Herself impotent to create culture, she is the only foundation upon which the edifice of culture can be erected. Man must act upon this matrix to turn it into art; thus, the *poem* is female, not the poet.

Now, Sylvia Plath was determined to become that contradiction in terms, a woman poet. Unlike Simone de Beauvoir, for instance, who took pride in having "a man's brain, a woman's heart" *(Memoirs of a Dutiful Daughter)*, she wanted to take pride in having a woman's brain. "I shall be one of the few women poets in the world," she wrote on May 26, 1956 in one of her ever-optimistic letters to Aurelia, "who is a fully rejoicing woman, not a bitter or frustrated or warped man-imitator." Yet another letter on the same subject reminds us that woman is a thing created, rather than herself a sovereign creator: "[Ted] sees into my poems and will work with me to make a woman poet like the world will gape at…; he sees into my character and will tolerate no failings away from my best right self" (April 19, 1956). In other words, Ted is a poet; Sylvia needs to be trained and helped to become a woman poet. From the start, it is Ted who decides what her "best right self" is, and encourages her to bring it out in her poems.

The poems themselves, however, comment on this situation in a dissonant (or dissident?) minor key. "Soliloquy of the Solipsist," for instance, describes it sarcastically from the male *auctor*'s point of view:

I
Know you appear
Vivid at my side,
Denying you sprang out of my head
Claiming you feel
Love fiery enough to prove flesh real,
Though it's quite clear
All your beauty, all your wit, is a gift, my dear,
From me.

Even if Hughes did go so far as to claim that all Plath's wit and beauty were a gift from him, a poem written at the same time as "Soliloquy of the Solipsist," "Fallgrief's Girlfriends," indicates that he might have felt them to be superfluous:

Any woman born," he said, "having
What any woman born cannot but have,
Has as much of the world as is worth more
Than wit or lucky looks can make worth more.

By the end of the poem, we learn that Fallgrief "has found a woman with such wit and looks / He can brag of her in every company." Is this, perhaps, why is name is Fallgrief? Has he fallen to grief because his woman is not content to have "what any woman born cannot but have" — a womb?

"We plan on seven children," Sylvia Plath wrote to her mother, "after each of us has had a book and travelled some" (May 18, 1956). Both her letters home and her diary between 1956 and 1958 speak of motherhood as something which must be put off until her identity as a writer is established — a reasonable attitude, and one which is probably shared by the majority of women writers today. What about Ted Hughes? In a letter to friends during divorce proceedings several years later (quoted in Faas's introduction to *Ted Hughes: The Unaccomodated Universe*), Plath was to reveal that he had not wanted children. And given the fear and rage his work expresses towards *mater*, this is hardly surprising. In poem after poem, Hughes's male protagonists are portrayed as being dragged down into the mud by frantic women hanging onto their necks ("Lumb," in *Gaudete*) or attempting to murder their mothers and winding up killing themselves into the bargain ("Crow and Mama"), or attempting to escape from their mothers and finding themselves back in the womb ("Song for a Phallus", in *Crow*). "Crow's Account of Saint George" describes a man threatened by three hideous monsters in succession. In a frenzy of terror and disgust, he manages to kill them all; at the end of the poem, covered in gore, he "Drops the sword and runs dumb-faced from the house / Where his wife and children lie in their blood."

Given the fact that the destitution of the mother goddess is something Hughes explicitly and repeatedly deplores, one might object that these images are merely illustrations of the crime committed by patriarchal ideology. "Christianity," Hughes asserts, "deposes Mother Nature and begets, on her prostrate body, Science, which proceeds to destroy Nature" (Faas, 109). Yet this metaphor is strongly reminiscent of the myth of Medusa, from whose prostrate body rises Pegasus, the winged horse of poetic imagination. Hughes drew his inspiration, in other words, from the very crimes he denounced; his poetry obsessively re-enacts the murder it claims to vituperate.

Far from upsetting her, this attitude was highly amenable to Sylvia Plath during the first few years of their life together. She followed Ted enthusiastically into the realm of the occult, dabbling in astrology, Ouija boards, magic and fortune-tellers, repeating to her mother how glad she was to type his poems, cook his meals, and push her "little gift" to the utmost. In 1958, however, a difficult year during which both poets were working as teachers in America, Plath began to complain of feeling "apart from [her]self, split, a shadow" (*Journal*, 20 February 1958). As she had not yet realized the nature of this split, she produced a symptom to express it: eczema. In May, she wrote: "I feel like scratching my own skin off" (May 14, 1958). Two months later, without making the connection, she wrote: "My danger, partly, I think, is becoming too dependent on Ted. He is didactic, fanatic...Between us there are no barriers — it is rather as if neither of us — or especially myself — had any skin, or one skin between us and we kept bumping into and abrading each other" (July 7, 1958).

The eczema expressed Sylvia's difficulty in preserving some sort of limit which would prevent her identity from flowing totally into Ted's. In other words, for her, twinship still did not entail fusion. She decided to stop showing her poems to Ted: "I must be myself — make myself — and not let myself be made by him" (July 7, 1958).

Hughes's own attitude towards marital oneness was complex but not contradictory. The poem "Lovesong" describes the efforts of a man and a woman to achieve physical and emotional union, biting and gnawing and sucking at each other until they have exchanged arms, legs, brains and faces. *Intellectual* oneness, on the other hand, contributed a great deal to Hughes's ability to write. In the "Poets in Partnership" interview, he spoke of a "telepathic union" between himself and Sylvia, and claimed that they possessed a "single shared mind." This, he went on, enabled him to use not only his own past experiences but also hers as material for his poetry. Asked whether that was how *she* would have put it, Sylvia evasively replied that, being more "practical" about it and "not quite so abstract," she had become interested in her father's bees and the image of beekeeping thanks to Ted's passion for animals — which, indeed, is not at all the same thing. In fact, whenever the interviewer suggested there might be stylistic similarities between the two poets, Sylvia begged to differ, insisting that they'd both been writing for ten years before they ever heard of each other, and would probably have been alike — if indeed they *were* alike — even if they'd never met.

This is a far cry from the "male counterpart" vocabulary she'd been using five years earlier. What had happened in the meantime? What made her want to affirm her autonomy and difference with respect to Ted, rather than wallowing in the "feminine and admiring" cult of him? The answer to this question, I submit, can be summed up in a single word: motherhood. What I should like to suggest is that in becoming a mother, Sylvia Plath broke the pact of twinship that had bonded her to Ted Hughes, revealing the spuriousness of its symmetry, and that her subsequent jilting and suicide were at least partly the results of this rupture.

❊ ❊ ❊

"He is a genius. I his wife," Plath wrote in her journal on 2 September 1958. And a few days later, on September 14: "I picked a hard way which has to be all self-mapped out and must *not* nag [omission]... (anything Ted doesn't like: this is nagging); he of course, can nag me about light meals, straight-necks, writing exercises, from his superior seat."

Yes. Ted Hughes was now giving *writing exercises* to Sylvia Plath. Not only that, but he was hypnotizing her. All sorts of methods were being employed to help his wife pry open the barriors of consciousness and get at what Hughes called her "true voice," buried in the murky depths of her unconscious. He would write after his wife's death that Sylvia's psychic gifts gained her "access to depths formerly reserved to the primitive ecstatic priests, shamans and Holy men...." But, he added, she "had none of the usual guards and remote controls to protect herself from her own reality."

Sylvia knew very well that she lacked the necessary "guards and remote controls." She was often terrified and depressed. In Boston in the winter of 1958, unbeknownst to either Ted or her mother (whom she spoke to on the phone every day), she started seeing Ruth Bennett again — the therapist with whom she'd been in counselling after her suicide attempt five years earlier. Psychotherapy helped her bring to light the hatred of *mater* she shared with her husband.

"A stink of women," she wrote after the first session. "Lysol, cologne, rose water and glycerine, cocoa butter on the nipples so they won't crack, lipstick red on all three mouths" (December 12, 1958). Ruth Bennett gave Sylvia something she described as "better than shock treatment" — the permission to hate her mother. (Aurelia's condonement of the EST therapy may have played a role in Sylvia's Electra complex, for images of electricity recur whenever she speaks of her mother with resentment and anger.) "It makes me feel good as hell to express my hostility for my mother," she wrote on the same day — "frees me from the panic bird on my heart and my typewriter." This exhilarating new-found hostility no doubt brought

Sylvia even closer than usual to Ted, but it wasn't as easy to manage for her as it was for him. It's never as easy for women as for men to kill the Angel in the House, or the panic bird on their typewriters, given that women are liable to become mothers themselves and that their violence often boomerangs.

One of the crucial "main questions" raised in Plath's first therapy session was the following: "Ideas of maleness: conservation of creative power (sex and writing). Why do I freeze in fear my mind and writing: say, look: no head, what can you expect of a girl with no head?" Male *auctors* do, often, conserve their creative powers by cutting off women's heads, casting them in the role of pure body — the id, the unconscious, savagery, nature, and so forth.

However resentful she may have been of her mother's paralyzing benevolence and affection, Sylvia Plath had positive feelings about motherhood as such. In June 1959, when told she was not ovulating, she was devastated to think she might be sterile. She became pregnant a month later, however, and her procreative power, far from being antinomical with her creative power, enhanced it. In the process of becoming the very thing she ostensibly "hated," she allowed her ambivalence to bloom. "Poem for a Birthday," written during her pregnancy, marked the turning-point in Sylvia's attitude towards the "Dark Mother," and the point of no return in her relationship with Ted:

*The month of flowering's finished. The fruit's in,
Eaten or rotten. I am all mouth ...*

*Mother, you are the one mouth
I would be tongue to.
Mother of otherness. Eat me.*

*Mother, keep out of my barnyard,
I am becoming another.*

She and Ted returned to England for the birth of their child. Ted was present at the delivery; indeed he hypnotized Sylvia to help it go more easily. But from that point onward, the objective inequality between the poets increased, and the myth of twinship grew more difficult to sustain. As usual, Plath's letters to Aurelia tried to make her life sound idyllic: "It's impossible for [Ted] to work in this little place with me cleaning and caring for the baby, and when he is out, I have the living room to myself and can get my work done.... I find my first concern is that Ted has peace and quiet" (May 11, 1960). "I am just crawling out from under the mountain of baby notifications, thank-you letters and answers to Ted's voluminous correspondence..." (May 21, 1960). "I am very excited that children seem to be an impetus to my writing, and it is only the lack of space that stands in my way" (December 17, 1960).

Ted was later to confirm the positive effect of motherhood on Plath's work: "With the birth of her first child she received herself, and was able to turn to her advantage all the forces of a highly disciplined, highly intellectual style of education which had, up to this point, worked mainly against her, but without which she could hardly have gone so coolly into the regions she now entered. The birth of her second child, in January of 1962, completed the preparation."

The problem was that the "regions she now entered" were the very ones which had always terrified Hughes himself. Between the births of their two children, Plath had a miscarriage and used this experience as material for a magnificent elegy to motherhood, *Three Women*. Here, for the first time, she described her formerly idolized "angels" — her lover and her dead father — as "cold":

*Am I a pulse
That wanes and wanes, facing the cold angel?
Is this my lover then? This death, this death?
As a child I loved a lichen-bitten name.
Is this the one sin then, this old dead love of death?*

Plath's love of death, she seems to be saying, is dead; she will no longer collaborate with Hughes in literary matricide; she is overcoming her Electra complex at long last. Many poems from Hughes's *Crow* collection seem to respond directly to the themes of *Three Women*: men are flat, cardboard figures who invent bulldozers and abstractions to protect themselves from the "time bombs" ticking between women's legs. In "Fragment of an Ancient Tablet," Hughes underlines and reinforces the split between women's seductive and reproductive powers:

Above – her brow, the notable casket of gems.
Below – the belly with its blood-knot.
Above – many a painful frown.
Below – the ticking bomb of the future...
Above – a word and a sigh.
Below – gouts of blood and babies...

The *Crow* poems were written mostly after Plath's death. But in February 1962, one month after Sylvia gave birth to their second child, Ted wrote "The Wound," a radio play based on a dream in which the dissection of a live woman is conducted under the auspices of an international scientific assembly. The woman's body turns out to contain, not "gouts of blood and babies," but gold teeth, plastic gums, glass eyes, steel skull-plates, jawbone rivets and rubber arteries. In Hughes's dream world just as in Villiers de l'Isle-Adam's *Eve future*, woman recovers her rightful status as an artificial creature, a man-made object.

Plath's *Three Women* was accepted by the BBC at the same time as *The Wound* was broadcast — nothing could be more indicative of the rift in the poets' partnership. In her letters home, Sylvia's tone now reached a peak of hysterical happiness: "I have such lovely children and such a lovely home now, I only long to share them with loving relatives" (April 16, 1962). The "lovely home" was in Devon: the Hugheses had left their London apartment to set up housekeeping in the country. But Ted was making regular trips to London to see another woman, and Sylvia found herself alone with two babies, the garden, the house and her need to write. She worked frantically at *The Bell Jar*, a novel about her breakdown of nine years earlier. Not wanting her mother to read it, she signed the book with a pseudonym: Victoria Lucas.

The victory of light.... She still wanted desperately to believe in such a victory. Day after day, she assured her mother that everything was just fine. "This is the richest and happiest time of my life," she wrote on June 17, 1962. "The babies are so beautiful." Only a matter of months later, she initiated divorce proceedings.

"I simply cannot go on living the degraded and agonized life I have been living... I have too much at stake and am too rich a person to live as a martyr" (August 27, 1962). Another letter explained that "America is out for me.... If I start running now, I will never stop. I shall hear of Ted all my life, of his success, his genius.... I must make a life all my own as fast as I can" (October 9, 1962).

Just as at the time of her first suicide attempt ten years earlier, Plath has been rejected by a man and left high and dry (or rather low and wet) in the world of motherhood. "The flesh has dropped from my bones. But I am a fighter," says the same letter to Aurelia. "Everything is breaking." And it was now, as everything broke, that she wrote the most beautiful poetry of her life. She rose every morning at five o'clock, before the children woke up, and worked on the poems which would become *Ariel* — poems without the slightest trace of the facility, structural rigidity or preciousness of her earlier work. Everyone agrees that *Ariel* is her best collection.

Apparently, as long as the poems delight us, it matters little that they are symptoms of a fatal illness. For years already, Plath's most successful work had been about depression and death. Now she had stopped eating and sleeping, she was writing in a state of fury, mistreating her body, seeing it dead, dismembered, electrocuted. Art justifies everything and makes everything forgivable. Plath herself was convinced of this: "The one thing I retain," she wrote to her brother Warren on October 12, 1962, "is love and admiration of [Ted's] writing. I know he is a genius, and for a genius there are no bonds and no bounds.... It is hurtful to be ditched... but thank God I have my own work." This, at least, was what she said in her *Letters Home*. What she said in her journal we cannot know, because the last two notebooks — those covering the period from Ted's departure to Sylvia's death — no longer exist. One of them was lost, and Hughes burned the other one to spare their children suffering later on. He published *Ariel*, however, affirming that in these poems Plath had finally removed all her "masks."

"The truly miraculous thing about Sylvia Plath," he said in 1956, "is that for two years, whereas she was almost totally caught up in children and housework, she underwent a poetic transformation which, for its suddenness and totality, is virtually without a known equivalent.... All the different voices of her talent came together, and for six months [that is, from August 1962, when he abandoned her, to February 1963], until a day or two before her death, she wrote with the full power and the full music of her extraordinary nature. It is not easy to comment on poetry like *Ariel*. There is not much poetry like it. It is her. Everything she did was exactly like this, and this was exactly like her — only permanent."

❄ ❄ ❄

Were we to follow Hughes's reasoning, according to which the poetic is the feminine is the insane, we could indeed interpret Plath's suicide as a "return to the womb" — a final, paroxystic poem, the ultimate regression to *mater*. If we listen to Plath herself, however — who, from *Three Women* to "Daddy," denounces the "cold angels" and their obsession with power and death, connecting her "black brute" of a father and his "Meinkampf look" with the "vampire" husband who had "drunk her blood for seven years" — then it is also possible to interpret her decision to die with her head in an oven as a means of ascribing guilt to the man who had turned her into the absolute victim — into, she said, "a Jew." Most of the poems in *Ariel* can be read as suicide notes (this is why it is jejune to protest against "biographizing" tendencies in writing about Plath's work). Before gassing herself, Plath had bled herself to death — and said so:

The blood jet is poetry,
There is no stopping it
You hand me two children, two roses.

A mere few days after this poem, the "blood jet" finally stops.

Hughes wrote the inscription on Plath's tombstone, "Even amidst fierce flames / The golden lotus can be planted." For three years after her death, he would publish no major poetic cycle — only disparate poems such as "Heptonstal," about the village in Yorkshire where she was buried. Moreover, he would undertake the enormous task of publishing Plath's poetry, prefacing all the collections and meticulously establishing the chronology of her work. This was a reparative act of kindness — and also, perhaps, a way of assuaging guilt feelings. Some years later, however, in a poem entitled "Fleeing from Eternity," Hughes would return to the "blood jet" and cast a glaring light on the connection between the female body and the male mind:

Then, lying among the bones on the cemetery earth,
He saw a woman singing out of her belly.
He gave her eyes and a mouth, in exchange for the song.
She wept blood, she cried pain.
The pain and the blood were life. But the man laughed —
The song was worth it.
The woman felt cheated.

(1986)

A Tongue Called Mother

It is often said — by men, but yes, by women, too (we rarely beg to differ on this matter) — that language is maternal. And why is that? Because our mothers flooded us with liquid sonorities as they rocked us in their arms? Because they were the first to acquaint us with the rhythms and the scansions of our tongue — and then gradually with its meanings as well, through fairy tales and fables and their morals? It is also said — by men, and sometimes, yes, by women — that the father represents Reason. But basically everyone agrees on what constitutes the basis of our speech: our mother's voice, our mother's tongue, simultaneously licking our wounds and tickling our ears and instructing us, so that the word *tongue* itself has become an inextricable mixture of body and mind, concrete and abstract, the wet pink mass of tastebuds and the invisible Idea.

Men say this, and so do women, and these phrases have been dancing in our heads for a long time. Jacques Lacan with his neologism destined to become famous: *lalangue*. "The so-called — and not for nothing so-called — mother tongue." Julia Kristeva with her *chora*, the presymbolic space to which poets may so advantageously regress, the "receptacle" which she obsessively describes as analogous to the mother's body. And Barthes with his endlessly cited phrase: "Writers play with their mother's body." All these old phrases are virtual truisms in the discourse of modern literary theory. But some of us have started following them up with an interrogation: "So then how do women...?"

How do women what? Well, er...how do women manage to write? Where do they go? How do they (re)turn to their mothers, how do they play with and/or destroy their mothers' bodies? What sorts of flights and dives and glides do they make, in and through the mother tongue? Does their tongue mother them in the same way as it mothers men? Does their writing always contain, as Hélène Cixous once claimed it did, in a glorious exhortative text called "The Medusa's Laughter," a bit of "good mother's milk," so that they inevitably write "in white ink?"

And how does one go about reading white on white?

Where do people go in order to to be able to write?

In "family romances," those childhood fantasies first described by Freud, then masterfully analyzed by Otto Rank and Marthe Robert among others, children reinvent their origins. The essential goal of this activity is to turn a creation of the body into a creation of the mind. According to Marthe Robert, there are two basic story lines: "The Foundling" and "The Bastard." The supernatural birth of heroes (ego ideals) is a universal trait not only of fantasy but of myth. Yet there again, in almost every psycho-literary study, the heroes are assumed to be male. What happens to heroines? Do little girls make up the *same* stories, the *same* beautiful lies, as little boys? Do they imagine themselves springing fully armed, Athena-like, from the heads of their Zeusified fathers? Or conferred as a gift upon their mothers, like Thumbelina, thanks to the intervention of a witch? Is Violette Leduc's *La Bâtarde* in the *same* predicament, does she suffer from the *same* anxiety about her origins and her place in society, as the famous bastards of Shakespeare or Dostoevky? I tend to doubt it.

Children inevitably perceive the relationship between their parents — even if it is the most ordinary, stable, mediocre, predictable and boring marriage in the world — as an alliance of omnipotent, superhuman beings. If actual tragedy occurs, if serious conflict makes itself felt, then things become grandiose, and the bottomless, dizzying abyss of mythology can open up before the children's eyes. Marital quarrels take on the dimensions of a combat between Titans, the war waged by the Centaurs on the Amazons, the threats of Hera and Zeus resounding through the heavens. Deaths resulting from accident or illness are turned into Clytemnestra's murder of Agamemnon, Jocasta's suicide....

Since the beginnings of the Western novel, but especially since the Enlightenment (which promoted individualism to the rank of an absolute value), it is artists themselves who have become heroes. The similarities are striking: a random sample of writers' biographies will show that, when young, almost all of them — like Oedipus, Hamlet or Antigone — suffered some devastating tragedy, loss, or accident. Their father died. Their mother died. Both parents died. Or divorced. Or abandoned them.

In other words, the family romance of these individuals is highly novelistic from the outset. It lends itself wonderfully to speculation, fantasy, revision and repression — in a word, to the art of writing. The myth is born. The hero-writer can draw endlessly on his childhood (just as Homer drew endlessly on the body of Greek mythology), rewriting his story by means of countless transpositions, projections, displacements and symbols.

"The hero," writes Marthe Robert, "is someone who wishes to owe his existence to no one; born outside the laws of nature, without copulation, he is self-engendered, the son of God...or...the son of his works." In any case, *the son.* In the book she devotes to this subject *(Roman des origines, origines du roman),* one hundred percent of Marthe Robert's examples, whether authors or characters, are male. The same is true of Shoshana Felman's *Madness and Literature,* which deals with essentially the same themes. These two theoreticians seek to understand the different ways in which Flaubert and Balzac, Kafka and Zola, handled their Oedipal complexes in and through their writing, without ever wondering whether the parameters of the problem might not be different for writers of the same sex as themselves — and as their mothers.

In an article published a few years ago in the *New York Times,* Cynthia Ozick nostalgically evoked the unshakeable faith "Modernist" writers had in their muses. In the midst of all the political turmoil, she said in substance, thre was one thing you could count on, namely "the artists' pledge to the self. Joyce, Mann, Eliot, Proust, Conrad...they *knew*. And what they knew was that — though things fall apart — the artist is whole, consummate. At bottom, in the deepest brain, rested the supreme serenity and masterly confidence of the soverign maker." Ozick excluded Virginia Woolf from her list of "self-annointed" Modernist writers because, she said, "her diaries show her trembling."

Women tremble. Even the best of them. Authority, sovereignty, the conviction that one is a prophet, a child of God or of one's own works (or even God Himself, *author* of all things) — these things are generally harder to come by for women than for men, perhaps because women know their bodies to be capable of creating other bodies — know, therefore, that mind springs from body and not the other way around....

So they tremble.

In *Aurora Leigh*, Elizabeth Barrett Browning describes the intellectual and sentimental education of a woman who aspires to be a writer. Towards the middle of the book, the heroine is shown meditating upon her work. She trembles. And she says:

> *I am sad.*
> *I wonder if Pygmalion had these doubts*
> *And, feeling the hard marble first relent,*
> *Grow supple to the straining of his arms,*
> *And tingle through its cold to his burning lip,*

Supposed his senses mocked, supposed the toil
Of stretching past the known and seen to reach
The archetypal Beauty out of sight,
Had made his heart beat fast enough for two,
And so with his own life dazed and blinded him!
Not so; Pygmalion loved — and whoso loves
Believes the impossible.
But I am sad:
I cannot thoroughly love a work of mine,
Since none seems worthy of my thought and hope
More highly mated. He has shot them down,
My Phoebus Apollo, soul within my soul,
Who judges, by the attempted, what's attained,
And with the silver arrow from his height
Has struck down all my works before my face
While I said nothing. Is there aught to say?
I called the artist but a greatened man.
He may be childless also, like a man.

The irony, of course, is that — unlike Simone de Beauvoir, for instance, who renounced motherhood and the uncertainties to which it can give rise in the mind of a woman artist — Barrett Browning managed to transform these very uncertainties into beautiful verse. The fact remains that, like de Beauvoir, she believed all her life that it was impossible to reconcile the two sorts of fertility: motherhood and the artistic imagination. Like most women artists, she simply could not convince herself that she was "the daughter of God" or "the daughter of her works."

In my opinion, a concept at least as useful as the Oedipal complex for understanding the family romances of certain writers would be the "Jesus complex." It consists, not in wishing to kill one's father and sleep with one's mother, but in having a deified father (dead or distant, absent-abstract, idea/ideal) and a pure and perfect mother (who may or may not be accompanied by a bland and boring father surrogate, the sort of nonentity stepfather Joseph was for Jesus).

This complex produces writers like Charles Baudelaire, Albert Cohen, Elias Canetti, Jean-Paul Sartre, Roland Barthes. As adolescents, they were able to take their fathers' place in their mothers' lives and perceive themselves as a cross between an immaculate woman's body and the Holy Ghost. The father's absence allowed the son to avoid having to face up to the "primitive scene" (the traumatizing image of the erotic mother), thus allowing him to see himself as the result of a virgin birth. He usually rejected the idea of getting married and having children of his own — manifesting, on the one hand, an undying love for his mother, and, on the other, a contempt mingled with horror for other women — on whose shoulders fell the responsibility for all things physical, from mud to eroticism and beyond.

The Jesus complex is but one type of soil propitious to the growth of young male geniuses, one family romance attractive to — and common among — our modern-day writer heroes.

Can similar tales spun be around our modern-day writer heroines? What would they be? How does a woman go about *author*izing — that is, becoming herself an author? What family fables does she invent to justify her taking up the pen?

Her father may be dead or absent and idealized like those of the little boys just mentioned. The girl will then identify strongly with the paternal mind and devalue the material/maternal. Such is the case of Karen Blixen, Flannery O'Connor, Sylvia Plath and others. Her mother may be dead or totally submissive; living with her father, the daughter will start to write, but at the cost of agoraphobia, neurasthenia, hysteria or excruciating guilt. Such is the case of Emily Brontë, Emily Dickinson, Virginia Woolf, Elizabeth Barrett Browning and others.

Why is this? The mother's role is connate with presence: real, physical presence. Because our mother is so close to us, because she is so very much *there*, we can and must proclaim our distance from her — or even, symbolically, murder her. In legitimate defence, Woolf said, one has the right (and even the duty) to kill "the Angel in the House." However (as Woolf herself was to discover again and again), it is frightening and depressing to murder someone who resembles oneself.

"It is very likely," says Julia Kristeva in an interview on women and art, "that, for a woman, the...gesture of putting to death which underlies all artistic creation, all transformation of form and language, presupposes a confrontation with the maternal image, that archaic and genetic guarantee of one's identity. However, because a women artist is of the same sex as her mother, this confrontation can be more violent, more difficult to control." According to Kristeva, the "limit examples" of this confrontation are, on the one hand, homosexuality (one thinks of Marguerite Yourcenar, Djuna Barnes, Gertrude Stein, Jane Bowles, Renée Vivien, Nathalie Barney) and, on the other hand, suicide (Virginia Woolf, Sylvia Plath, Charlotte Perkins Gilman, Anne Sexton, Unica Zürn, Marina Tsvetaeva...). Homosexuality and suicide are, indeed, two ways in which a woman can handle the dialectic between self and other — either to love her other/self or to kill it. They are not the only ways, however. Alternate solutions are offered by reclusion and/or exile, and it so happens that an inordinately large number of women writers have chosen one or the other of these two solutions.

Burying oneself alive. Wandering over hill and dale. Departing, then returning home to renew one's strength. Repudiating, laying claim to or denying one's origins, one's *origin* in a woman's body — are these the same acts for a woman as for a man? How could they be? When Alice James wrote in bed, was she doing the same thing as Marcel Proust when he wrote in bed? I doubt it. I also doubt that a *wanderlust* novelist like Isabelle Eberhardt has much in common with a *wanderlust* novelist like Ernest Hemingway.

You can lock yourself up in the "room of one's own," whether the house containing that room belongs to your father (Brontë, Dickinson), your husband (C.P. Gilman), or your brother (Alice James). There, you can explore your own brain like a foreign country, meticulously examining every nook and cranny of your imagination, heating your soul "to the white heat" (as Dickinson put it), sometimes in an exalted, quasi-mystical starvation of the body.

Or else, on the contrary, you can renounce the family roof once and for all, turn your back on the sights and smells of childhood, reinvent yourself by putting down fresh roots in alien soil. You can make the familiar and the familial as strange and exotic as possible, either by writing in the mother tongue while surrounded by a foreign idiom (Djuna Barnes, Gertrude Stein, Marguerite Yourcenar), or by changing languages. "It is as if women needed to affirm a different language," says Kristeva in the same interview, "in order to defy their mothers who are a threat to them in their rivalry for identity."

Being a Bulgarian who lives in France and writes in French, Kristeva knows what she's talking about. I also know what she's talking about, being an English Canadian who lives in France, and I generally say so in the same different language as she does. Are Kristeva and I in the *same* position — the *same* linguistic displacement — as Kafka, Conrad or Beckett? I doubt it.

A tongue called mother: might we venture the hypothesis that, whereas men try to turn their mothers into language, women do everything in their power to turn their language into a mother? "As you can hear," says Kristeva in a different text, "I am speaking a language of exile. A language of exile stifles a scream, *it is a language that doesn't scream*" (emphasis mine). "Mama," she writes, in yet another text. "Almost nothing visual — a shadow that plunges into blackness, absorbs me or vanishes in a few flashes of light. Almost no voice, in its placid presence."

It would seem that most of us, in order to dare lay claim to our own voices, still need to deprive our mothers of theirs.

In one way or another, you have to "split." Take to your heels. *Détruire, dit-elle*, as Marguerite Duras puts it. Build a *Sea Wall (Barrage contre le Pacifique)*. In my case this has meant absurdly repeating over and over again, "No, no — you didn't leave *me, I'm* leaving *you*!" (For how can you reject a mother who has rejected you? How can you define yourself by opposition to someone who has vanished?) Thus I abandoned my language and continent with grandiloquent and superfluous declarations of independence...so much hot air, of course.

Where is the room that one can call "one's own?" Where is the woman who manages to find it in her mother's house — who manages, in other words, to create right next to the source of her own creation? Colette — yes, after Sido's death, she was able to return to her mother's garden and cultivate its beauty. Colette, yes, because she had formerly been *La Vagabonde*. And Flannery O'Connor — a unique and fascinating case — who wrote in her mother's house because she was dying of her father's illness, a blood disease to which, in the title of her best-known novel, she gave the name of wisdom. Next to her mother, Flannery wrote against her mother. In the short story entitled "An Enduring Chill," the hero goes so far as to write his mother a letter (comparing it explicitly to Kafka's "Letter to His Father"). "I came [to New York]," he writes her, "to escape the enslaving atmosphere of home — to find freedom, to set my imagination free — take it out of its cage like a falcon and send it "spinning in the increasing turn" (Yeats) — and what did I discover? — that it was unable to fly. It was a bird that you had tamed, and it remained there in its cage, irascible and refusing to come out! ... *I have no imagination. I have no talent. I have nothing other than the desire for these things! Oh, why didn't you kill that, too? Woman, why have you pinioned me?*"

A woman writer attributes these words to a man. Yet O'Connor, like her hero John Asbury (as-buried?), after having set her hopes on becoming a writer in New York, had been condemned by her illness to return to her mother's dairy farm in the South. "Woman, why have you pinioned me?" For Barrett Browning, an English poetess living in Italy, it was Phoebus Apollo — that "soul within [her] soul" — who shot down her poetic efforts with his poison arrows. For Sylvia Plath, an American poetess living in England, it was now her mother, now a male superego named Johnny Panic, who sat on her typewriter and prevented her from believing in her work. Someone, always, it would seem, tries to break the wings of young women's literary aspirations and keep them from taking flight.

Yet they *do* fly — sometimes soaring far above the clouds, sometimes plummeting headlong to the earth —

but because of hopes and errors different from those of Daedalus and Icarus, because of delusions of grandeur different from that of Phoebus Apollo.

And they *do* travel, far and wide, descending into hell for reasons different from those of Ulysses; reascending (at least occasionally) to reunite with their mothers in joyful celebrations of fertility.

And they *do* write — constructing their art, in ways different from Orpheus, upon that contradiction in terms, that myth *par excellence*, that dream of lost oneness, that golden age which is as illusory as it is necessary: *the mother tongue.*

(1988)

Novels and Navels

Once upon a time, there was a little boy and he had a whole bunch of adventures. Obviously his mother was dead. Or else, like Pinocchio, he didn't have a mother at all. Once upon a time there was a little boy and a little girl and they had a whole bunch of adventures. Obviously their mother was dead and their stepmother was trying to kill them. Once upon a time there was a little girl and she had a whole bunch of adventures. Her mother wasn't dead; as a matter of fact her mother loved her and also loved her own mother, who was the little girl's grandmother, and she warned the little girl to stay away from adventures but the little girl didn't listen to her and she got into some very deep trouble and some say she never got out of it again and others say she had to be helped out of it by a man. Same for a whole bunch of other little girls whose mothers were dead and who would have been murdered by their stepmothers, stepsisters and jealous fairy godmothers had not a man stepped in in the nick of time.

However, this is supposed to be not a story-telling session but an article. A piece, not of fiction but of non-fiction. So let us jump outside the story to the moral which always comes immediately after it. The moral of the story is, clearly, that mothers and adventure, *ça fait deux*, as the French would put it. They simply do not go together. If you want to have an adventure, which necessarily entails risking your neck, you must at all costs get away from your mother — who, invariably, predictably, boringly, wants to save your neck. (Adventure is described by Sara Ruddick in her book *Maternal Thinking* as "a quintessentially mother-free notion.") Now, what are stories about, if not adventure, risk and death? This has meant that an awful lot of women novelists have been writing from the position of the "disobedient daughter." And this position is a problematic and even dangerous one, not so much because the wolf will eat you up as because, with the passage of time, even disobedient daughters tend to turn into moralizing mothers, and then they've got one hell of a schizoid situation on their hands. Half of their mind is still running off into the exciting woods of the imagination, while the other half is desperately trying to make the world sound sensible, solid and stable to their kids.

The questions I want to raise, then, concern maternal ethics and the writing of fiction and non-fiction. (As a friend recently put it, parents wonder how much they can give, whereas artists wonder how much they can take.)

The "neutral" point of view on the subject of ethics — that is, the one most commonly espoused by white male literary critics in the Western world — can be summarized as follows. Ethics are good for philosophical, theological, political and pedagogical discourse; they are poison for literature. This point of view was first promulgated in the middle of the 19th century (clearly this date is no accident, for it was about that time that God died and authors began aspiring to take His place) by such scandalous geniuses as Baudelaire and Flaubert. Flaubert is an interesting case in point because he developed the idea, among other places, in a lengthy correspondence with George Sand, who was vehemently opposed to it and who happened to be a daughter and a mother. Sand was perhaps the last of the great novelists to believe whole-heartedly in the moral responsibility of artists — that is, in the idea that they should endeavor to convey value through the content of their books, the elaboration of stories with easily discernable morals, characters who embodied good and evil, and so forth. The only way Flaubert was interested in conveying value was through the *form* of his books: "good," for him, was the quest for perfection, harmony, precision, concision and balance, whereas "evil" was leaving things as they were, stagnating in petty-bourgeois mediocrity.

This same quest — for formal perfection — is what makes apparently nihilistic writers (Kafka, Beckett, Genet) "moral." It is the art-making gesture *per se* that proves one's belief in the loftiness of mankind, and seeks to stir one's readers by taking them into "absolutes" they had never dreamed existed: absolute paranoia, absolute derision, absolute amorality, absolute snickering, absolute arbitrariness, and so forth. Modernity is perhaps the only period in human history in which the reading public has regularly turned to its spiritual mentors for a message of despair. This went on and on and got worse and worse until, in the late 1930's and early 40's, Simone Weil (again a woman, though not a mother), revolted by the foolish goings-on of the Surrealists and Dadaists, and considering them partially responsible for Western Europe's moral decline, declared that writers could not have it both ways:

they could not simultaneously insist on playing the role of spiritual guides, *directeurs de conscience* for the reading public, and demand total impunity and freedom in the name of art for art's sake.

Today as in the time of George Sand, women seem to have a harder time endorsing the latter notion than men. Certainly writers like Kathy Acker or Emily Prager could be cited as counter-examples, but they are what I call "disobedient daughter" writers — less because neither of them is a mother than because the corpses of mothers strew the pages of their bawdy, bloody, funky prose. If women seem on the whole to have less enthusiasm (and/or talent?) than men do for purely formal literary experimentation, utterly divorced from ethical concerns, I would guess that it is because, as mothers or potential mothers, they have been entrusted with the morality of the species. Not that they make the laws, of course (and indeed, as the incredibly tiny number of women philosophers suggests, they are rarely perceived by themselves or others as credible spiritual mentors, either) — no; their morality is supposed (and assumed) to be innate, natural and everyday, like their maternal instinct and indeed indissociable from it. Mothers are supposed (and assumed) to be, if not gentle, at least protective, nurturing of life. Morever, they are expected to transmit clear ideas about right and wrong to the children whose life they nurture.

Real fiction — good fiction — must exercise our moral muscle, and if it tells us too clearly what is right and what is wrong, our moral muscle gets lazy and flabby. If you're a philosopher, like Simone Weil or Sara Ruddick, you are clearly doing your duty when you say, in sitting down at your desk: I shall write the following book in order to achieve this or that good. If you're an artist, the same utterance is likely to be fatal to the book in question. Suspension of judgement, a serious defect in non-fiction, is virtually a *sine qua non* of great fiction — including, indeed, children's fiction. *Monsieur Seguin's Goat*, for instance, whose ostensible moral is that little goats who aspire to freedom will be savagely murdered by slavering wolves, nonetheless unforgettably portrays the joys of freedom, and suggests that it is honourable to fight to the finish to defend it. Still, as a mother, I must admit that I find it harder to read this story to my children than the revoltingly edulcorated versions of *Little Red Riding-Hood*.

This leads me to the heart of the problem. Here it is: apparently, writing non-fiction is more compatible with motherhood (because both are avowedly and as it were intrinsically ethical activities) than writing fiction. Let me emphasize that I am not talking about how to reconcile, in the space of one working-day, the activities of changing diapers and inventing characters, thickening the sauce of one's *boeuf bourguignon* and thickening the plot of one's novel. These are mere logistics, though it has admittedly taken several thousand years of economic evolution and political struggle for a few women to be able to call them "mere." I am talking about ethics.

Mothers tend to want everything to be beautiful for their children. They more or less force themselves to adopt an optimistic world-view in order to protect them, comfort them, and foster hope. Novelists may or may not have the same temptation — to put across a message of hope — but if they paint a world in which human existence is hunky-dory, their readers' response will be not hope but boredom. To write a meaningful story, one must be prepared to accept meaninglessness; face ugliness; describe horror; comprehend betrayal and loss.

Again, mothers are necessarily moral creatures: even if they make their decisions not according to any rigid set of precepts, but according to a complex mix of factors (the child's age and personality, the outside circumstances surrounding its acts, and so forth), it is absolutely incumbent upon them to distinguish right from wrong. Novelists must suspend their moral judgement (again, at least in advance) and be prepared for anything: they are often surprised by what appears on their pages, and what would never have dared to appear had the authoritative voice of knowledge been speaking.

Mothers are virtually required to be cheerful. In Sara Ruddick's words, "To be cheerful means to respect chance, limit and imperfection and still act as if it is possible to keep children safe. Cheerfulness is a matter-of-fact willingness to accept having given birth, to start and start over again, to welcome a future despite conditions of one's self, one's children, one's society, and nature that may be reasons for despair." A novelist may need — in fiction — to be violent, or lascivious, or crazy, or bitterly pessimistic; all of these are terrible qualities in a mother.

Mothers *qua* mothers must be "other-oriented"; they

embody connectedness and attachment. Novelists *qua* novelists must be selfish; they demand for themselves disconnectedness and detachment. This does not mean that people who write novels don't need other people, or that women who have children don't need time to themselves. Of course no mother is only a mother, no writer only a writer. But is it possible to be generous half the time and selfish the other half; moral half the time and amoral the other half?

Ultimately, as I went back and forth between these two apparently split and irreconcilable halves of my personality, I realized that what it boiled down to was this. *Mothers must not kill their children.* Sara Ruddick again: "Preserving the lives of children is the central constitutive, invariant aim of maternal practice; the commitment to that aim is the constitutive maternal act." Everyone agrees that if you kill your own kids, you have failed as a mother. Novelists, on the other hand, must be prepared to kill their characters. In each of my three first novels, I murdered a woman and accused her of doing it herself: once by drowning, once by electrocution and once by hanging. (In my more recent work I have managed to restrain this unfortunate tic.)

Mother. Novelist. Mother. Novelist. Suddenly a lightning flash brought these two apparently antithetical identities together. I recalled the unlikely, even grotesque connection between the famous novelist Marguerite Duras and the infamous mother Christine Villemin. Villemin had been accused of killing her five-year-old son, and all the scandal sheets were following the story with their usual viciousness, revealing as many intimate and incriminating details as possible. Over and over again, Villemin protested that she was innocent, that she had loved her son more than anything in the world; the evidence against her was nonetheless considered sufficient to warrant her being arrested and imprisoned while awaiting trial. She was pregnant at the time with another child. She went on a hunger strike. All of France was thrilled to have interesting reading for its summer vacation that year. A serial novel, as it were. And then the novelist Marguerite Duras stepped in and put an end to it. In an article published by the left-wing newspaper *Libération*, she said, in essence: I can believe that Christine Villemin killed her son, and I can understand that Christine Villemin killed her son, and I can not only forgive but exalt Christine Villemin's murder of her son. She can only have murdered him in the same way that I write — that is, without knowing what she was doing. Her gesture can only have been sublime (*Sublime, forcément sublime* was the title of the article). Beyond good and evil. Beyond the petty calculations of human justice.

Duras turned *The Death of Little Gregory* into a novel by Marguerite Duras. She invented a beginning and a middle and an end for it and made it more credible to the French public than Villemin herself had been able to do. Indeed, Villemin became one of the characters. Many people protested, of course: "How dare Marguerite Duras intervene publicly in a case that hasn't even come before the courts? How dare she influence the jury and judges by pronouncing Villemin guilty whereas she may be innocent?" Nonetheless, Duras succeeded in convincing her readers that the story had come to an end. Truth never quite got as interesting as fiction again, and the journalists turned away from Christine Villemin in search of fresher bait.

So a mother who is willing to kill her own child is pretty much the same thing as a novelist — is that the conclusion I want you to draw from this enlightening true story? It almost is, as a matter of fact. However problematic I find Duras's intervention in this particular case, I'm convinced that she is a great writer partly because motherhood did not lead her into what Sara Ruddick calls the "degenerative form" of cheerfulness, "cheery denial." "Mothers are tempted to deny their own perceptions of harsher realities because they so wish the world were safer for their children." As a child in Indochina and a young woman in France during the War, Marguerite Duras witnessed so much death, both directly and indirectly, that she was made forever incapable of denying the "harsher realities." That is what allowed her to become a novelist.

You can't invent good stories if you don't accept the idea of death. By their very nature, stories evolve through time and bespeak their characters' mortality. In the beautiful words of Ursula Le Guin, "narrative is a stratagem of mortality. It is a means, a way of living. It does not seek immortality; it does not seek to triumph over or escape from time.... It asserts, affirms, participates in directional time, time experienced, time as meaningful. If the human mind had a temporal spectrum, the nirvana of the physicist or the mystic would be way over in the ultraviolet, and at the opposite end, in the infrared, would be *Wuthering Heights*."

Historically, mothers have been represented on exceedingly few occasions as intelligent or artistically creative, for the simple reason that giving birth is considered to be incompatible with giving death. Make up your mind: do you want to be a novelist or a navelist? Navel means "middle." Though in fact each human being is utterly unique, a new beginning, the severed umbilical cord is evidence of a process which connects this being's present with its past. Novel means "new." Though in fact all novels owe their existence to literary ancestors, they invariably attempt to appear original, created *ex nihilo*. They are like so many Athenas springing fully armed from their fathers' heads and proclaiming: "I am a motherless child, and therefore immortal." All novels say, "Look Ma, no navel."

I happen to be a "Ma." So I shall look. And I shall ask you to look with me, a little more closely, into this question of killing parents and killing children. "Killing" in both senses: as an adjective and as a gerund. The parents of authors. The children of authors (their characters, who may in turn be parents — or authors). Dead parents. Dead characters. Dead children. Authors killing their parents, their children, their characters, and giving birth to new ones. Children killing their parents, the "authors of their days." And so forth.

Where, in literary tradition, are the brainy mothers? Leaving aside Mother Goose, I can think of only two examples. The first is Scheherazade, whose literary brio is fed by the image of the death that awaits her morning after morning, postponed only by the suspense she manages to create night after night. Scheherazade invents first a tale, and then a tale-within-the-tale, and then a tale-within-the-tale-within-the-tale, an ever-renewed brilliance of imagination serving to defer decapitation by her cruel, yet insatiably curious, husband. Finally, after a thousand and one of these nerve-wracking nights, having also — we are not told how — conceived, gestated and given birth to three children while thus holding forth, she obtains a permanent suspension of her...sentence.

The second example — from the Greek rather than the Arabian tradition — is that of Medea. Her name means "she who thinks." It can also be translated as "cunning."

Medea is very important. She is remembered largely because of the play Euripides wrote about her, in which she murders her two children. According to several other versions of the myth, she had not two but several children — some by Jason, some by other men — and she murdered, not them, but a considerable number of other people, first in her effort to assist Jason and later in her effort to punish him. What counts, however, is what is remembered.

Medea is a powerful sorceress, an earth-goddess with a serpent chariot. Her mother is Hecate, the patron goddess of witches, and Circe the magician is her aunt. She is also an unconditional and uncompromising lover. She abandons her father and homeland, murders her half-brother, uses her spells and wiles to help Jason find the Golden Fleece, and willingly accepts the loneliness of exile — all because she is in love. But Jason breaks his promise: for him, politics come first. And Medea puts her children to death, not out of spite or jealousy, but *for their own sakes*, because she refuses to see them subjected to the inexorable laws of the city. She knows that if Jason remarries their children will be persecuted, enslaved and dispossessed. She prefers that they die. She did not bring them into the world on those terms. She will not condone their survival on any terms. She kills them in order to prove that she is a human mother, a civilized, intelligent, cunning mother, and not merely a creature of maternal, animal, natural instincts.

Only mothers who are capable of comprehending Medea's gesture — facing death, including the death of their own children — can invent great stories. A case in point is Mary Shelley, whose life was steeped in death from the moment it began. Her own mother, Mary Wollstonecraft, died of puerperal fever ten days after giving birth to her. Her first child by Percy Bysse Shelley, a premature and feeble daughter, died at the age of ten days, when Mary herself was only seventeen and a half. The following year (1816) she gave birth to a son; shortly afterwards, just as she began writing *Frankenstein*, her half-sister was found dead from an overdose of sleeping-draughts. A few months later, when the novel was half completed, Shelley's wife Harriet, who was pregnant, drowned herself. (Mary's two other children were to die in the years immediately following publication of the book, and Shelley himself was to drown a mere four years later; this explains the author's otherwise strange statement, in her introduction to the 1831 edition, that *Frankenstein* was "the offspring of happy days, when death and grief were but words which found no true echo in my heart.") The tale of the book's conception is well-known: Mary and Percy Bysse Shelley were spending the summer in Switzerland with Byron and his doctor; the group decided to compete to see who could make up the best ghost-story. Mary went first, and the men were so flabbergasted by the result that nobody really went second.

Within Mary's story, a certain Robert Walton is writing to his sister Margaret. He's on his way to the North Pole and, in the midst of the ice floes, has come across the wandering scientist Victor Frankenstein and saved him from drowning. Within Walton's story, then, Frankenstein tells his story. His own mother is dead; that goes without saying. His story evokes another motherless (and very probably navel-less) "child" — the monster he manufactured. How does a man go about giving birth? He studies corpses. "To examine the causes of life, we must first have recourse to death", he explains to Walton. And the child thus conceived will, in turn, send others to their deaths...

Within Frankenstein's story, the monster tells *his* story. (Mary Shelley is as great a virtuoso of the *mise en abyme* as Scheherazade.) He is miserably lonely, and jealous of human ties: "No father had watched my infant days," he says, "no mother had blessed me with smiles and caresses." After killing little William, whom he knows to be Victor's brother, he sees their mother's portrait and recalls painfully that he is "forever deprived of the delights that such beautiful creatures [can] bestow." Hated and feared by all he meets, he begs Frankenstein to at least create a female companion for him, of the same species as he and with the same defects — he swears he will depart with her to South America and never bother anyone again. Frankenstein agrees, only to destroy the second monster just as it is on the verge of completion. His first brainchild laments, "Shall each man find a wife for his bosom, and each beast have his mate, and I be alone?" He venges himself by murdering his maker's best friend, then his bride; Frankenstein expires in Walton's arms, exhausted by endless years of tracking his hideous progeny through the wilderness. The monster himself, who has no name, but to whom posterity has correctly attributed the name of his "father," is devastated at the loss. He commits suicide... by drowning.

At every level of this multi-layered tale, the storytellers are male, with the exception of Mary Shelley herself. That "exception" seemed to her contemporaries downright unbelievable, and she was repeatedly required to defend herself against the accusation of having signed a story written by her husband. It is not really so surprising, however, that a woman who had lost to death the bodies with whom she'd been the most intimately entwined — a mother, a daughter — the process of gestation and delivery should have seemed inextricably linked to horror and decay. Mary Shelley was fully capable of giving birth to characters — William, Justine, Henry Clerval, Elizabeth — only to put them to death a few dozen pages later; but she was not capable of conceiving a female storyteller. This, apparently, would have been an even greater transgression for an author of her sex. What stories, indeed, could a woman have to tell? Did women go on expeditions to the North Pole? Did they have access to scientific laboratories? We may suppose that had Frankenstein given life to his monster's mate, she, too, would have been a demure and devout "listener."

But this, of course, was 19th-century, pre-modern literature. A great deal has changed since then.... Let us turn to two contemporary novels, one by an extremely gifted man and the other by an extremely gifted woman, and examine their metaphors of giving birth and death to children and to stories.

The first is *See Under: Love.* The author is a young Israeli named David Grossman. Death is all around him. Death is the air he breathed as a child. His novel is about a young Israeli writer, Schleimeleh, whose parents, like Grossman's own, are survivors of the Holocaust. In the first section of the book, Schleimeleh is a little boy growing up in Israel and trying to invent stories which are convincing enough to overcome the "Nazi beast." In the second section, Schleimeleh has grown up, he has a wife Ruth and a mistress Ayala, and he is attempting to reconsitute the last, lost manuscript of the Polish writer Bruno Schulz. In the third section, Schleimeleh has retired to a "white room" and is writing the story of his grandfather Anshel Wasserman, also known as Wasserman-Scheherazade, who in his youth had been the author of a famous series of children's adventure tales, *The Children of the Heart.*

In Schleimeleh's story, Wasserman is back at the death camp. He's been there for years, working in the shit-houses; everyone who matters to him has been either gassed or shot to death, but he himself is miraculously, tragically, incapable of dying. By chance, the director of the camp, a man named Neigel, whose job it is to organize mass murder from morning to night and who takes pride in his work, turns out to be a fan of Wasserman-Scheherazade's. They make a deal: Wasserman will live in Neigel's quarters and make up a new episode of *The Children of the Heart* just for him; in exchange, Neigel will attempt to kill him at the end of each installment.

This is where we must go into a little detail. There is a sort of God-to-Adam touching between Wasserman and his grandson-writer Schleimeleh: "Suddenly there was moisture on my fingertips, and I understood that I was drawing the story out of nothingness, the sensations and words and flattened images, embryonic creatures, still wet, blinking in the light with remnants of the nourishing placenta of memory, trying to stand up on their wobbly legs, and tottering like day-old deer, till they were strong enough to stand before me with a measure of confidence, these creatures of Grandfather Anshel's spirit, the ones whose stories I had read and searched for and sensed so ardently."

Shortly after this, he says, "we gave birth to others as well" — that is, Anshel gives Schleimeleh permission to add characters to their creation from his own life. Very cautiously, almost against his better judgment, the author-grandson attempts to discover what "humanity" his two characters might share. Thus, as the days go by, Wasserman and Neigel gradually come to discuss parts of their personal experience. (Neigel is a monster, of course. Yet Grossman never suggests, as did Mary Shelley, that his monstruosity results from lack of love: we are told nothing of his childhood; of his youth we learn only that he was a virgin until marriage.) Both Wasserman and Neigel have "ethical" wives. Sarah Wasserman, who used to illustrate her husband's books, has of course been exterminated. As for Christina Neigel, she violently condemns both the Nazi regime and her husband's involvement in it. In fact, she was on the verge of leaving Neigel when he started secretly copying Wasserman's story in his letters to her as though he himself were writing it. Christina is thrilled, for she is convinced that a man who invents such a beautiful story cannot be evil at heart. (And she is right: far more disturbing than "the land of Goethe and Heine" having produced Nazis would have been *Nazis writing like Goethe and Heine*. This, fortunately for our already-spinning minds, is inconceivable.)

In this new episode of *The Children of the Heart*, all the heroes are elderly Jews in the Warsaw ghetto. They live at the zoo, hiding and helping each other as best they can... As agreed, Neigel shoots the storyteller through the head at the end of each installment. But to no avail: "In me," says Wasserman, "between the ears, flew the familiar buzz." One day, however, "when the shot rang out, an exceptional message was engraved in my heart: unto my tale a child shall be born." The following evening, the story revolves around Fried, a doctor whose wife Paula died before she was able to "give him a son." For several years already, Fried has noticed that a "greenish fungus" springs up about his navel on the anniversary of her death. This year, it seems a little worse than usual.... Lo and behold, upon his very doorstep, a little boy-baby is discovered. This is the moment of maximal *rapport* among Wasserman, Neigel, and Schleimeleh who is telling their tale. All three of them bask in the joy of discovering the tiny child: ah yes, the soft fontanelle at the front of its skull, and how on earth will Fried manage to find milk for it? Ah, and as it turns out, both the young Nazi and the old Jew have secretly tasted a drop of the thin warm sweet liquid that seeps from a mother's breast....

A short while later, "[a] fearful premonition made [Fried] peek at the baby's tummy: there were no signs of clotted blood on the navel. In fact, there were no signs of tearing or cutting on the navel: in fact, there was no navel."

Aha. Unto the tale a child shall be born, but not of woman born. Jesus Christ, according to a zillion paintings and sculptures, at least had a navel! Grossman strongly hints that this miraculous child can only be the Messiah. But a child without a navel, I shall humbly submit here, can only be a novel. Fried names him Kazik, the name which he and Paula had chosen for the son they never had, and discovers a second, far more serious anomaly: the child is growing at the rate of three months every four or five minutes. Its entire life span will be twenty-four hours, approximately the time it takes to read a long book like this one by David Grossman. Within this time, its "father" will have to teach it everything he knows about humanity.

Every novel is a foundling. Every novel, in the short time allotted it to live, must be inculcated with the totality of human experience — joy and suffering, hope and despair, good and evil. Kazik, who commits suicide one and a half hours before he can die of old age, is at once the innermost kernel of *See Under: Love* (being the spiritual son of Fried who is the spiritual son of Wasserman who is the spiritual son of Schleimeleh who is the spiritual son of Grossman), and also the over-arching metaphor for the Novel as such.

There ain't many women in there, as you may have noticed. At each level, the heroes have wives, mistresses, mothers, daughters or sisters, described as strong, sometimes beautiful, always ethical human beings. None of them are involved in anything even remotely resembling an adventure or the telling of an adventure (even Scheherazade is now a man!); the insistent imagery is that of spiritual fecundation and delivery among males.

My final case in point is Toni Morrison. It is probably no coincidence that in *Beloved*, the novel she published in 1987, Morrison invented an amazingly Medea-like character named Sethe. Here is the central scene of the book, the event around which all the other events, before and after it, branch out like fault-lines from the epicenter of an earthquake: "Inside [the shed], two boys bled in the sawdust and dirt at the feet of a nigger woman holding a blood-soaked child to her chest with one hand and an infant by the heels in the other." Of her four children, to whom she gave birth on condition that they could hope for freedom, and who are now threatened with being taken back into slavery, Sethe only actually manages to kill one. And the name of that one is "Beloved."

Like David Grossman, Toni Morrison took childhood lessons in death. Her people were not gassed and cremated but deported and enslaved, tortured and maimed, beaten and raped, lynched and worked to death. Like Grossman, she grew up listening to the tales of survivors.

In *Song of Solomon*, Toni Morrison invents a character without a navel.

This time, the character is a woman. Death is everywhere around her. Her mother, like Mary Shelley's, died giving birth to her. The midwife present at her delivery, whose name (like that of Medea's aunt) is Circe, describes the event to her brother: "Borned herself. I had very little to do with it. I thought they were both dead, the mother and the child. When she popped out you could have knocked me over. I hadn't heard a heartbeat anywhere. She just came on out. Your daddy loved her."

Her surname is Dead. (A government official had once asked her father: "Who are your parents?" "They's dead," he had answered. And the name was registered forever.) Her Christian name, about as unChristian as you can get, is Pilate. Her father chose it by putting his finger down at random in the Bible. It was the only word he ever wrote down on a piece of paper.

When Pilate was four, her father was shot to death before her very eyes. His ghost appears to her often, however, giving her advice in moments of crisis. Though she has no navel, she has a self-inflicted wound — a hole she gouged through her ear after her father's death, to carry the little brass box containing the scrap of paper with her name on it. This is the wound that festers and must be healed: it connects her to her dead father, whereas no wound connects her to her dead mother.

We are given no explanation for Pilate's lack of a navel. We are simply told that "once the new baby's lifeline was cut, the cord stump shrivelled, fell off, and left no trace of having ever existed." This quirk of her anatomy is perceived by everyone she meets as not only singular but potentially dangerous. She is "believed to have the power to step out of her skin, to set a bush afire from fifty yards, and turn a man into a ripe rutabaga — all on account of the fact that she had no navel." Men fear her and she grows up in isolation. Her own brother describes her as "fluky"; "odd, murky, and, worst of all, unkempt"; a "raggedy bootlegger" and a "snake." But Pilate is also a natural healer. She knows how to do things with voodoo dolls. And when her sister-in-law wants another baby, she gives her an aphrodisiac in the form of a "nasty greenish-gray powder" — the same colour as the fungus around

Fried's navel in *See Under: Love*. And, just as the greenish fungus mysteriously foreshadows the arrival of Kazik, here the greenish-gray powder is responsible for the birth of "Milkman" Dead, Pilate's nephew and Morrison's central character in *Song of Solomon*. Greenish-gray, we recall, is also the colour of the corpses with which Frankenstein tinkered to produce his "progeny."

In short, Pilate is a sorceress, exactly like Medea. And she is a stunning character because Morrison makes it clear that her capacity to love, her generosity, forthrightness, integrity, courage and cunnning, all result from her familiarity with death. "Since death held no terrors for her (she spoke often to the dead), she knew there was nothing to fear." And despite the fact that she herself has no mother, and that her mentor is her father, what she learns from the latter, the message his ghost repeats without cease — "Sing, Sing" — turns out in fact to be her mother's name. And thus she wanders, and has adventures, and a baby daughter Reba whom she loves more than anything in the world, and then a baby granddaughter Hagar whom she dotes upon — and Morrison shows us that it is as a mother, with the ethics of a mother, that Pilate Dead would be prepared to kill. When she discovers that a man has been beating her daughter, she grabs him from behind, jabs a sharp knife-point into his chest and explains her predicament to him: "I'd hate to pull this knife out and have you try some other time to act mean to my little girl.... Still, I'd hate to push it in more and have your mama feel like I do now." The man hastily assures her that he will never bother Reba again.

Yes, for a mother who can think that clearly about death, it is possible to be a sorceress — that is, a great writer. If Grossman's navelless son is the emblem of the novel, Morrison's navelless daughter is perhaps the emblem of the novelist mother: "living proof," so to speak, that certain entities hitherto thought to be logical monstrosities can and actually do exist!

(1989)

Letter to Simone Weil, with Passages of Time

Is it possible for a woman's body to produce Western philosophy and is there not something in the philosophical project per se which is incompatible with femaleness which is to say irrefutable *embodiment*? I recall an evening devoted to the exiled Egyptian poet Edmond Jabès in a Paris bookstore, with interminable and very boring abstract interventions by several men and finally one by a woman — no less interminable and not an iota less abstract, only her listeners were distracted from it by the fact that she was dressed in a very tight skirt and a low-necked blouse in which necklaces were jingling around between her startlingly-visible breasts; the blouse itself was so tight that the only thing one could possibly concentrate on as one listened to her was the question, not of the ontology of the human face, or the specific contribution of Judaic monotheism to Jabès's work, but whether or not the three or four buttons desperately holding, apparently by a single thread each, the jiggling bouncing breasts behind the stretched material of the blouse were going to pop. And what everyone realised at that moment was that a physical sexual body was making an abstract philosophical intervention; and what I was perhaps alone to realise was that this had been the case since the beginning of the evening but we hadn't noticed it. The young and middle-aged men sitting or standing casually in the bookstore wearing suits or blue jeans had allowed us to listen and hear and think and reason as though they did not have glands and penises and anuses and digestive tracts and the rest; the woman had spectacularly disturbed this mode of reasoning.

Now Simone Weil was obviously a woman and obviously a philosopher but she, too, clearly felt that the two were incompatible; this is what set me to reading her and the more I read her the more I sensed there must be a connection between her philosophy (indeed, the very style in which she wrote) and the way she treated her body. Since I myself am not a philosopher but a writer, what I then produced was not a professional critique of her theories, but rather a woman-to-woman letter.

❊ ❊ ❊

Dear Simone,
Yes of course I realize you're dead — that is, that your flesh has ceased to exist. But since your words continue to resonate across the century (and, indeed, have been resonating louder and louder for the past few years), I'll take the liberty of addressing you a few words in turn. If you find my tone familiar, it's because I feel close to you for a number of reasons, including our age: yours was arrested once and for all at 34, a figure I've just recently gone beyond.

Didn't you yourself write, "The only people we can love are the dead, that is, souls insofar as, by destiny, they belong to the other world" — authorizing me, however much I disagree with that idea, at least to speak to you? I who still belong to this world, and believe it to be the only one there is; I whose soul is still encumbered by a body, and exactly as perishable as it is — I love you, Simone, *despite* the fact that you're dead, and not *because* of it.

Almost half a century after your death, I'm not the only one who loves you — far from it. But I have the feeling people almost always love you for the wrong reasons. One of the reasons for which people frequently claim to love you is that, unlike most intellectuals, you practiced what you preached.

But that isn't true. Here, for instance, are some words you wrote — magnificent words: "No one believes that a man is innocent if, having food in abundance and finding a person three-quarters starved to death on his doorstep, he goes his way and gives him nothing." But you yourself were three-quarters starved to death, Simone, and you went your way and gave yourself nothing.

Or again. You say that the basic physical needs "are relatively easy to enumerate. They involve protection against violence; shelter; clothing; warmth; hygiene and adequate care in case of illness." All of these things, too, you refused yourself. You sought out every violence the world could possibly exercise against your body: hunger, cold, extenuating fatigue, danger, illness.

People love you in large part because of the suffering your body elicited and embraced. (Almost invariably, this leads them to conclude that you were not beautiful, since for them it's inconceivable you could have been beautiful in body and in soul. I think you're beautiful, Simone. Really. Very.) They adore the image of Simone the saint, Simone the martyr, Simone spurred on by a "relentless exigency for truth," a "profound indignation" and nothing else. They declare this image to be sacred and untouchable. They warn against looking into the forces that compelled you to immolate your body on the altar of your mind. They peremptorily declare that such was your vocation. If they talk like this, it's because they need a sacrificial lamb — an intellectual who had the "courage"(so sorely lacking in the rest of us poor hypocrites) to make first-hand acquaintance with the misery of the poor, instead of merely theorizing about it.

But that isn't true, Simone. Firstly because your misery did *not* lessen the amount of misery in the world; it increased it. Secondly, and more importantly, because your suffering had *nothing to do* with that of the poor. "Undistinguishable in everyone's eyes, including my own, from the anonymous masses, the misery of others penetrated my flesh and my soul," you wrote in a letter to Joe Bousquet. No: just because you were *looking for it* and they weren't. The common workers whom you so longed to resemble knew that your hunger, for instance, was the opposite of theirs, because it refused to be appeased (they had a snack during coffee-break; you didn't). In the same way, your work was the opposite of their work because it eschewed repose (by adding night-hours of reading and writing to the day-hours of factory work; or by intentionally exacerbating your migraine headaches). Workers acknowledge and accept the needs of their bodies (not, of course, because they are innately "closer to the natural rhythms of life," but because they have no choice in the matter); you denied and combatted these needs.

Thus, the suffering you desired was *your own* suffering; you wanted it — all — for yourself. You decided to join your fate to it as if it were a husband: "Espousing poverty," you wrote, "that is the loveliest image." And this husband, freely chosen by you, abused you day after day. Month after month he penetrated your body and panted on top of you; year after year you smelled his fetid breath and perspiration. He raped and violated you... until, at long last, death did you part.

Passage of Time I

Meanwhile, on a dimly-lit dance-floor in New Orleans, a small orchestra is playing the blues; couples are dancing together, they're exhausted and the syncopated rhythms respark their energy, they're aching and the filtered light is like a balm for their wounds, they're afraid of the future and the music is there — a present.

In her little dressing room backstage, Billie Holliday slowly slips her arms into her gloves, which go all the way up to her armpits to hide the countless needle tracks. She looks at herself in the mirror — just for an instant, but a pitiless instant —, then lights a cigarette and motions for the curtain to be raised. Unmoved by the applause, she walks straight over to the mike and grabs hold of it as though she needed it to keep her balance. She knows that her voice is nearly broken already, but she's just learned a new song and she needs to sing it. The voice comes out, bitter, frightening, suspended between life and death just like the fruit the song is about — the strange fruit, blood on the leaves, blood at the root, that dangles from Southern trees.

So I'm going to ask the question which, to respect the "miracle" of your oeuvre, one is not supposed to ask: *why did you make that choice*, Simone? You're not around to answer that question — or to defend yourself when other people use it as a pretext for expounding their own, preconceived theories. A case in point: the two women psychoanalysts who, just recently, attributed the obstinacy with which you destroyed your body to a weaning trauma — proving only (once again) that in the enquiries conducted by these detectives of the human soul, the guilty party is always and exclusively the mother. Thus, even after having described your mother Selma as an intelligent, open-minded, musically-gifted woman who had taken great pains to foster in you the "uprightness of a boy" rather than the "graces of a girl," these theoreticians find it reasonable to conflate your case with that of the typical anorexic, victim of a mother love which, "concerned exclusively with the well-being of her body, never responded to her need to be."

I approach you not as a psychoanalyst, Simone, but as a friend. And to answer the crucial question of "why," I'd like to try to take not only your words but your silences into account.

Yes: you talked about the oppression of workers, peasant farmers, and Blacks. Belonging to none of these groups by birth, you turned yourself into a riveter at the Renault factory, then a farm-hand in the Southern vineyards; had you stayed long enough in the United States, one of your friends remarked, you would undoubtedly have become a Negress.

There are two oppressed groups you *never* talked about: Jews and women; the ones to which you belonged. The ones in which, to borrow a term upon which you built a beautiful and complex theory, you were *rooted*. The injustices done to the Jewish people — particularly spectacular at the time when you were thinking and writing — scarcely deserved passing mention from your pen. And you could grow indignant about the fact that for a man who was unemployed, the voting ballot had "no meaning," without pointing out that neither unemployed nor employed women even had so much as the *right* to vote.

I share with you not Jewishness but womanhood, and this is what I most want to talk with you about. Yes, "with" you; for as a matter of fact — in the interstices of your arguments which always purport to deal with "more important" subjects — you did say a few things about what it was like to be a woman.

For example, in your "Poem to a Young Rich Girl," you predict that one day this coquette will find that she is nothing but "dead flesh, turned to stone by hunger," and, elsewhere, you describe yourself as a "sterile stone on which seed cannot sprout." Wasn't one of the goals of your chronic hunger strike just that — to preserve your "stone" state so that no seed could ever sprout in you? Didn't you find the endless chain of generations revolting — and isn't that what you meant when you wrote, "I didn't see my birth, but I certainly hope to see my death?"

And if conception was inconceivable for you, wasn't it because physical desire was, its very essence, "outrage?" "A man can love his daughter with desiring love, identical to sexual love," you say, and the example you provide is Balzac's Pere Goriot. In the same way, you add, a warrior can love victory — and you go on to point out the "analogy between the taking of a city and rape, [the] resemblance between murder and rape." Of the soul, you say, "It is the human being when considered as having an intrinsic value. To love the soul of a woman is to refrain from thinking of her in terms of one's own pleasure, etc. Love no longer knows how to contemplate, it wants to possess." And you deplore our legal system which "metes out a far harsher punishment for ten petty larcenies than for one rape."

So here is what I wonder, Simone.... I wonder whether perhaps an event might have taken place — not in your early childhood (as the psychoanalysts invariably postulate), but during your adolescence — which made your woman's body permanently uninhabitable to you. It may have been in 1922-1923 — the year during which, at age thirteen, you sank into a deep depression and came close to getting lost in your "inner darkness." You yourself later said this "bottomless despair" was due to the fact that you could "hope to have no access to the transcendent realm where only authentically great men enter and wherein truth lies. I preferred to die rather than live without it." Tormented by your aspiration to the realm of mind, you began to mistreat your body — wearing sandals in the middle of winter, indifferent to the frostbite that purpled your hands and legs....

Passage of Time II

Meanwhile, China and Japan are at war. Kyoko, who lives in the suburbs of Tokyo, is already a widow at age 25. Her in-laws have come to live with her and her two children, so that five people now share a one-room apartment.

Behind a makeshift screen, her seven-year-old son is practicing the violin. He's been working on the same piece for the past three weeks, it's by Mozart, Kyoko knows it by heart, its beauty has almost evaporated for her. But today, for the first time, he succeeds in playing it from beginning to end without a single mistake. "Bravo!" cries Kyoko, clapping her hands in delight. Her son blushes with pleasure. Mozart has suddenly gotten all his colours back. The baby starts to cry, it needs to be changed. As she does every day, Kyoko takes a washcloth and wipes the excrement from the thighs and buttocks of the little girl. The baby's eyes follow its mother's movements. Its eyes are black, black and sparkling. Kyoko kisses its stomach, tickling it by blowing air through her lips at the same time.

The tiny girl bursts out laughing. The grandparents turn their heads toward her, a smile playing on their lips.

You were going on fifteen when you first formulated your ideal of the "unknown friend." This friend was to appear to you on many occasions, often in the form of a "brother." As time went on, you detached yourself increasingly from actual, living friends in order to cultivate these intangible relationships. And a sister's love for her brother would always seem to you the highest form of love attainable in this life: the only women you praised unreservedly were those who had loved their brothers enough to give up their own lives. Antigone, of course. Electra (whose sister, Iphigenia, had been put to death by their father — but of this you say nothing...). The young heroine of the Grimm Brothers fairy-tale, who refrains from smiling and speaking for six years, weaving six shirts out of nettles to save the lives of her six brothers who have been turned into swans. Accused of witchcraft, she is already tied to the stake to be burned when her brothers arrive — and, just in the nick of time, they set each other free. What fascinated you about this story, you said, was the "theme of slandered innocence forbidden to defend itself."

Joan of Arc, who was similarly "slandered" and whose death penalty was *not* suspended, is another one of your heroines. Like you, she dressed as a man in order to defend a glorious (and virtually hopeless) cause; like you, she was constantly accused of being starry-eyed and overexalted, if not insane.

Do you know what strikes me, Simone, concerning your passions for real and legendary people? Though you are remembered especially for your love of humanity, you loved neither men nor women.

The women you admire are always virile young virgins, wholly dedicated to a man or an idea. Never lovers or wives; in particular, never mothers. There is one exception, which not only confirms but underscores the rule. The very year of your adolescent depression, you wrote a poem in praise of Madame Bessarabo — a woman who, after having murdered her husband and stuffed his body into a suitcase, packed him off to another city by train. Your poem was entitled "Sainte Bessarabo." It begins, "You of the great heart, you of the beautiful crime"; and it ends, "Virgins will come on their wedding-day/ to lay flowers on your grave." Why did you see this woman as being the patron saint of virgins? Was it because she'd been raped by her husband, and because all virgins must undergo the same treatment on their wedding night?

As for men, my dear Simone... The men you liked best were those who, though they hadn't been murdered and stuffed into suitcases, were mutilated, impotent, tortured, dying or dead. Suffering brothers — yes, like the six swans — who depended on the suprahuman patience of their sisters for their salvation. Polynice, who needed his sister Antigone to bury his body with the respect that it deserved. Or Prometheus... bound. Or Christ... crucified. Among the living, most of your male friends had taken the vow of chastity; one of the few who hadn't was the poet Joe Bousquet — but he lived in a wheelchair, paralysed from the waist down by a war injury. In the final year of your life, your most fervent dream was to rush to the side of wounded and dying soldiers: in 1942, you told Charles de Gaulle about your idea of parachuting a group of nurses (naturally including yourself) into the firing-line, for the purpose of providing solace and medical treatment to the Allied troops in the thick of the battle, "wherever the carnage is the most brutal."

Passage of Time III

Meanwhile, stunned and incredulous crowds are piling up in the concentration camps. Their bodies are covered with filth and sores. Fear is a constant nausea in their stomachs, and the air brings tension rather than oxygen to their lungs.

It is the beginning of summer. It is evening — after the hours of their labour which is more than labour; before the hour of their meal which is less than a meal. In one of the barracks, a small group of men talk earnestly together in low voices. Others are sitting apart, apathetic and motionless, dazed by the endless waiting without hope. But now — suddenly — the door flies open and an elderly Jew with his head shaven rushes into the room. "Come and see — all of you! — Come! Come!" he cries. "There's the most beautiful sunset!" And all of them rise and go outside, for they know that nothing in the world is more urgent than a sunset.

So let me ask you — ever so gently, Simone. Am I right to surmise that something happened to you one day? And that, in your innermost being, you thereupon resolved that nothing would ever happen to you again... that you would never again receive the imprint of another human being...that between you and other people, there would never again be the least *exchange*?

Am I right to surmise that, having once been constrained, you decided to wish only and always for constraint? That having once been treated as a thing ("Force," you write, "is anything which turns a person into a thing"...), you decided to treat your own body as much like a thing as possible? Pure, inert, inanimate matter? Since your will had been helpless to *prevent* pain, you would make your will *coincide* with pain. You considered suicide, but it was a solution of which you disapproved — adding, however, in one of your notebooks. "N.B.: Eusebus has nothing but unreserved and superlative praise for Christian women who kill themselves to avoid rape."

Am I right to surmise that from that moment onward, you willed — with the immense ardour of which you were capable — *for there to be no more moments*? You sought to escape time by every means possible; there is no doubt about that. Yet you yourself had written, after your experience in the factories, "Manual labour. Time entering the body.... Through labour man becomes matter just as Christ does through the Eucharist.... Joys parallel to the pain. Physical joys. Eating, resting. Sunday leisure-time." Everyone had the right to these joys and pleasures... everyone but you.

Just as you no longer wanted to have a body capable of

setting something into motion, you resolved that your mind should formulate nothing but eternal truths. Never again, in love or in knowledge, did you want to be subjected to another person's influence. The idea of your body or ideas interacting with the body or ideas of someone else was intolerable to you.

Good was one and indivisible, and you would reveal it to the world whether the world wanted to hear it or not. The only people you would ever actually *listen* to would be those who were willing to describe their misery (from them, you wanted as many lurid details as possible) — but despite your apparent willingness to descend to the "level" of the sufferers, you demonstrated your superiority over them at every instant, deepening the gap between you rather than bridging it — precisely because you couldn't bear the idea of interaction. Thus, you listened to the poor and spoke to the rich. In both cases, you remained untouchable.

You were able to love only what was distant, motionless, ideal, "classical." In music: Monteverdi, Bach, Mozart, and especially Gregorian chants, because "when you sing the same thing for several hours a day and every day, that which falls even slightly short of supreme excellence becomes unbearable and is eliminated." In philosophy: Plato, of course, with his ideal forms located "above" fluctuating reality. In literature: Proust — because the past, in his books, is "time with the colour of eternity." As for the stage: "immobile theater," you said, "is the only really lovely kind."

But it couldn't be helped — time went on nonetheless.

And as time went on, you hated your body (which, unless I am mistaken, had elicited *the impossible*), more and more. Even the imperceptible, involuntary movements it made in order to remain alive came to seem shameful and outrageous to you. "When I am somewhere," you wrote, "I sully the silence of sky and earth by my breathing and the beating of my heart." Yet you yourself had enthusiastically quoted a 4,000-year-old inscription which ascribes the following words to God: "I created the four winds in order that every man might breathe like his brother." Elsewhere, you had formulated the hypothesis that "everything which is cyclical and ceaseless in man — blood circulation, respiration, all the known and unknown exchanges — corresponds, on the level of mortal individuals, to the rotation of fixed stars.... Rhythms and alternations of exertion and recuperation. Take part — can also take part — in the harmony." Everyone had the right to breathe, to exert themselves to and recuperate... everyone but you.

Far from being motionless (if we leave aside your hours of prayer), you were, according to all the witnesses of your life, amazingly — no, disturbingly — active. Paying no attention to meals, you chain-smoked so as to be able to get more work done, keep on going, never get drowsy, never let down your guard. In spite of this, you constantly accused yourself of "laziness" and "cowardliness" — and this permitted you to despise yourself even more. In a word, you felt that you *should* have been pure Thought. Only thought is at once active and motionless, efficient and invisible, needless and weightless. Such, indeed, are the qualities of "grace" — whereas the body, even if one doesn't feed it, pig-headedly goes on subjecting us to the laws of "gravity."

So you prayed to God to grant you the following: "That I be incapable of making any bodily movement — or even the shadow of a movement — in correspondence with any of my wishes, like a totally paralyzed person. That I be incapable of receiving the least sensation." Here, too, you claimed to be asking for this so that God might "devour" the being thus extracted from you, transform it into "Christ substance" and feed it to "the poor, whose bodies and souls lack every sort of sustenance." As if God needed to masticate and digest certain of his creatures in order to feed the others! No: once again, "the poor" were a pretext. *You wanted the paralysis for yourself.*

In the end, you aspired to death — death as perfection, because it transforms one into a finite, immutable whole: "To be just," you wrote, "one must be naked and dead. Without imagination." In this glacial conception of justice, everything that lives is *ipso facto* falsehood, illusion, deceptive appearance. "Imagination" is the worst enemy of all, for it hypnotizes us with the glitter of unreal things: things from the future (non-existent by definition); things from the present (teeming, chaotic and impossible to grasp)... but also, Simone, things from the past which, refusing to freeze into Proustian eternity, keep coming back to haunt us in sudden moving pictures — flashes of intimate film — fragments of nightmare so hideous that one must avoid sleep so as never to have to confront them?

Passage of Time IV

Meanwhile, in New York City, a Puerto Rican man with greying temples is making supper for his lover. She works as a cashier in the supermarket where he sells fish. It's a Saturday evening, around eleven o'clock, they don't have to get up to go to work the next morning. The apartment is tiny and badly heated, but its windows give onto a fabulous view of the Bronx — including Yankee Stadium — and they have just finished making love. A lot of love and pain have rolled over their bodies in the course of their lives, leaving them tender and older and astonished.

The man, wielding a large knife with precise, rapid movements, chops the cheap, starchy vegetables into thin slices before putting them in the frying-pan. The woman has brought her chair over to be close to him but she remains seated; her varicose veins are hurting. She slips a hand beneath the man's shirt to caress his round stomach and hairless chest. He laughs and says, "It's just about ready, all I've got to make now is the hot sauce."

This meal is a sheer wonder. The nearby rumble of city traffic is a part of it; so is the earlier mingling of their saliva.

Finally, Simone, after years of crying in the wilderness, you received the revelation of the presence of Jesus — the only "presence" you ever really allowed near you. It came to you as you read the poem "Love" by George Herbert (an English poet dead these 300 years).... The last verse reads as follows: "Sit down, says Love, and taste my meat." Jesus offered you his meat, Simone. He said, "Take, eat, this is my body...."

Even then, you refused to believe that *love does not necessarily destroy its object*. You believed that Jesus was not diminished by communion, but you refused to believe that human communion, too, can be a miracle — multiplying its own resources, just as the bread and fish were multiplied for those who believed in Christ.

In the final analysis, Simone, the theme of virginity and the theme of food, both of which recur obsessively in your writings, are one and the same thing. "We want to consume all the other objects of desire. Beauty is that which we desire without wanting to consume it." Why? Because you were beautiful, and someone had been unable to renounce "consuming" you? "Distance is the soul of beauty." In spurning food, what you were rejecting was your body. You wanted not to *have* it, so as not to ever have to *give* it. A gift which — had you been able to make it — would have left you not the poorer but the richer; a gift which, the more generous and overflowing it is, the more it has to give. This gift, the most incalculable, inexhaustible gift of all (and thus the one which most closely resembles "divine" love); this gift, which neither lowers human beings to the level of the beast nor raises them to the level of God but rather celebrates that inextricable mixture of animality and divinity which is humanity (since in love-making physical movements can become utterly imbued with spirituality); this joy of discovering the soul in every particle of the body — yes, Simone, in *every particle*; this miraculous possibility (not a certainty but a possibility, and a miraculous one) of meeting another person, reaching another person in a communion beyond words which is simultaneously scream, prayer and song; this mutual sacrifice in which the abandon of each enhances the existence of both…this was the capacity that was obliterated in you, probably by the use of "force."

"To sully is to modify, to touch. Beauty is that which we cannot wish to change. To take power over is to sully. To possess is to sully. To love purely is to consent to distance; to adore the distance between oneself and what one loves." No. No human being is beauty, Simone. But love can make us beautiful. And when that happens, being touched does modify us — yes: we are transformed, magically improved, by the other person's desire.

Passage of Time V

The earth turns and turns, half of it is always in shadow, and under cover of the darkness bodies seek each other out, find each other or miss each other. The bodies are of all ages and all colours; they are men and women together or men together or women together; noble or ignoble; mortal, anxious, groping in the dark, searching, weeping, many are exhausted, many are hungry, others are humiliated or confused, all of them are seeking, in anger, hope, disgust, or joy, fingering each other, mauling each other, embracing each other, falling asleep, the earth turns and turns, indifferent to our poor caresses, whether exalted or obscene.

Yet you recognized that *Christ was body*; that He was the entry of divinity into time, into the fragile miracle of reality. He referred to himself as "the Lamb" and "the vine," acknowledging the necessity of eating and drinking — like Dionysus, like Vishnu and certain others...like Sham, the only one of Noah's sons who was not ashamed to contemplate "the drunkenness and nudity" of his father.... You even suggested that, thanks to this premonition of the Incarnation, Sham "might well have lost the shame which is the lot of the sons of Adam!" So you knew that, just *because* of their vulnerability, human bodies are worthy of respect. All human bodies...except your own.

You found it increasingly difficult to go on, given the truth which had been stamped into your flesh, and which was not only unspeakable but unthinkable. This is why, in the end, you endorsed a couple of lies — the quintessential religious lies — namely, that a child can be born without there having been sexual contact, and that a body which has ceased to live can resuscitate. In other words, that birth is not birth; nor death, death.

You who had insisted so fervently and for so long on the importance of *living in reality* (as of age four, when your friends at kindergarten asked you, "What about you? Were you born in a cabbage or a rose?" you had answered, "I was born in my mother's stomach"); you who had always been contemptuous of the dreams, false consolations, and fabulations people invented to make their existence bearable — this time, you complacently agreed to pull the wool over your eyes. Like so many others, you decided to believe it was possible to be a mother and a virgin at the same time. You wrote, "Under many different names, all of them equivalent to Isis, the Greeks were familiar with a female being who was maternal, virgin, ever intact...." Oh, Simone.

It's just not true. Your mother wasn't a virgin, and neither was mine. No mother has ever been "intact." A mother is "tact" by definition: she is someone who *has been touched*. She is a body with which another body, and even *two* other bodies, have commingled.

If men have so often split our eroticism off from our fertility, it's because they've been terrified of entering into contact with our female bodies. Less terrified when they were virginal (like yours at adolescence) — before, that is, by virtue of their relentlessly regular rhythms and irreversible stages, they had become the living proof of human mortality. If so many men have needed to turn love-making into an act of victory, revenge or vandalism it is because of the fear inspired in them by women's hour-glass bodies. Oh my poor, poor Simone. You believed the worst and most destructive lie of all, the very lie that was at the origin of your devastation — that *it is possible for time not to pass*, for people to escape its effects, for mothers to be virgins.

The truth is that we are mortal beings who, through copulation, produce other mortal beings; and who, through dreams and ideas, invent new worlds: creation and procreation are the only forms of our immortality.

You found it unbearable to remain on this earth longer than Jesus had: it was at age 33 that you stopped eating almost entirely. Thus, just as you had hoped, you were able to witness — emaciated and weak but lucid, hyperconscious and concentrated, almost pure mind at last — your own death.

Of Christ's life, too, we are shown the end rather than the beginning. No macabre detail of His Passion is spared us: the thorns, the blood, the sweat, the exhaustion, the nails, the last-second doubt, the spear thrust between the ribs.

Passage of Time VI

Here, then. Mary has never felt a contraction before, but as of the first pains she knows it is beginning, and so it will have to happen here, tonight, in this stable in Bethlehem.

Night has already fallen; the sky is very black and the stars are uncannily distinct. She presses Joseph's hand to her breast and stares into his eyes. Like his, her skin is swarthy and her hair black and curly, both of them are Palestinian Jews, they are fleeing death and they are terrified, they stare into each other's eyes, they had not intended for their baby to be born in a stable but that is what is going to happen. Now Mary closes her eyes, attentive only to the pinching in her entrails, a thing that seizes and squeezes her, harder and harder, then gradually lets her go. She bites her lips to keep from crying out, the stable has been lent to them for the night and the owners mustn't be disturbed... Suddenly she gasps — in a rush, her waters have broken, whooshing down her legs to form a puddle on the earthen floor.

Joseph prepares a place for her to lie down in the straw, he spreads out one of the stuffs they've brought with them on their voyage, he kisses his wife's moist forehead and smooths back her sweat-soaked hair. The pains are following each other faster now, stronger and stronger. Mary is totally absorbed by the vise that seems to be gripping her very being, twisting it almost to snapping-point. She can no longer contemplate the stars, but during her moments of reprieve the coolness of the night reassures her and calms her thumping heart. Then it starts up again, even worse than before... Joseph's heart is thumping, too; his lips are trembling with emotion; he already feels a surge of love for this child who is struggling to come into the world. Now, when the pain submerges her, Mary grabs her husband's arm and digs her nails into his skin. Her face is ugly, her features are distorted and trickles of sweat flow into her hair and down her neck. She can feel the child's movements, the uncontrollable pitching of her womb, then the pain moving away...A soft night breeze comes and wafts across her denuded chest...She smiles at Joseph, takes a deep breath, draws in the smell of donkey and cow, mud and dung, the pain returns. She screams. She will be broken. She will burst, crack, fly apart, be fissured and quartered and destroyed. Joseph sees the top of the child's skull, covered with blood and mucous. He weeps, his tears wet his beard, his nose is running, he says, "I can see it — our child — I can already see its head!" Mary says, "Oh! Can you really?" "Yes, I can already see it, it's almost here!" Mary disappears again, sucked under by the pain. She pushes with all her might, spreading her lips in a hideous grin of effort, the veins in her forehead swell up as if they would explode, and suddenly, she emits a different sort of cry. Enormous. A cry utterly drenched in pleasure in muscles in marrow in blood in nerves in tissues in mucous membranes in juices of joy — the hot flesh abruptly leaving her to be received into Joseph's shaking hands — the pain is gone, she lifts her head to glimpse the new face of love.

Love incarnate, Simone.
Love, Nancy

(1989)

Note: I read this "Letter to Simone Weil" at the University of Columbia in New York in October of 1989. Unbeknownst to me, Simone Weil's niece Sylvie was in the audience. The next time she saw her father, the great mathematician, André Weil, she told him of my hypothesis. Stunned, the latter confirmed that his sister had indeed experienced a traumatic erotic event in adolescence.

Erotic Literature
in Post-War France

They were people of great energy and ardour, people in the prime of life, people without illusions but not without ideals. They were certain of their destinies as writers, and of the elevated place assigned to literature in the destiny of mankind. The women were strong, brilliant and independent, although they did not yet have the right to vote; the men were leaders, invested with divine missions, or so they believed, by virtue of the fact that God was dead. They belonged to rival not to say inimical schools of thought, represented every sort of literary allegiance from surrealism to existentialism, held political convictions that ran the gamut (sometimes within a single person) from the far left to the far right. The war broke out, in 1939, in the very midst of their intellectual hopes and strivings, but — despite the shock or because of it — they talked and wrote more prolifically than ever; some of them also became involved in direct political action. They knew each other more or less personally. Their paths would cross from time to time, and when that happened they often quarrelled: they were brothers and sisters in a family under duress, living in a house haunted by the German monster and subjected to curfew. Through fear and darkness they continued to advance, cogitate, express their alternately divergent and convergent opinions on the issues of the day: fascism, communism, revolution, resistance, sacrifice, and the role of their artistic gifts with respect to the above. They joined the National Committee of Writers. They had names. Real names like Paulhan, de Beauvoir, Sartre, Blanchot, Duras, Bataille, Vailland, and pseudonyms like Réage and Angélique. They made choices and decisions that were difficult to make, and occasionally took risks as well. Some of them turned their offices or apartments into clandestine meeting places where political discussions were held, declarations made, subversive struggles planned against the enemy. Others withdrew, presumably to delve more deeply into their philosophical speculations. All of them saw their destinies transformed before their very eyes, taking on strange shapes they could never have foreseen. How could they have imagined that their talents would be subjected to such extenuating ordeals?

The ordeals went on and on. Four years. Then five. During this time they read and reacted to the newspapers, revising their convictions as they went along in an effort to deal with the incredible facts that kept assailing them. Even when people close to them were persecuted, arrested and deported to the East, they did not give in to panic. They may have despaired in private for the space of a few minutes or a few days, wept in rage or terror at the enormity of what they were being required to understand. But despair and terror never appeared in their public words and gestures: these remained firm, courageous and resolute. Vichy censorship gave its stamp of approval to all their creative and reflective works, authorizing their publication year after black year. None of them were Jewish.

At last it was over. There was a small detonation, and then two large ones: in Berlin, Hitler pointed a gun to his head and pulled the trigger; in Japan, the cities of Hiroshima and Nagasaki rose to the sky. It was over.

There was not a minute of silence, not the slightest hole in the fabric of life, events continued to follow on one another's heels, the hubbub of human existence went on uninterrupted.

These people had assigned themselves the task of deciphering the hubbub, and they were determined to carry out this task to the best of their abilities. They continued to read the newspapers. They went to the Lutétia Hotel or the Austerlitz train station to see the camp survivors with their own eyes (Robert Antelme, Duras's husband, was among them). Little by little, they began to grasp the true extent of the horror. What they learned, at the same time as the rest of the world, had never before been learned by human beings. It was unlearnable, imaginable, incompatible with life and history as they had hitherto been conceived.

These people had bodies which had walked in the streets of Paris, eaten more or less their fill, made love when they felt like it, suffered runny noses and sore throats more often than usual. In the meantime, in a neighbouring country, more than six million bodies like their own had been tortured and killed in a totally unprecedented manner.

They stared at the photos of the mass graves, watched the documentaries on the liberation of the camps. They listened to, read about, and tried to understand these things. Their vocabulary was suddenly forced to expand to include the impossible: cattle-cars, platforms, barking dogs, selections, chimneys, ovens, Zyklon B, children ripped from their mothers, mountains of eye-glasses and shoes and hair, lampshades made of human skin, medical experiments, gold teeth, sticks where legs should be, caverns where eyes should be, shaven heads, striped pyjamas, numbers tatooed on forearms, careful bookkeeping, "Muslims," lice, diarrhoea, screamed orders, endless roll-calls in the dark, skeletons standing barefoot in the snow, inextricable masses of dead limbs and rolling heads being pushed along by mechanical shovels, wreaths of foul-smelling black smoke, burned flesh and more burned flesh and more burned flesh, an unfurling of pure, unmitigated Thanatos. This had happened while they were alive, and they were still alive and this had happened. All of their political and literary sophistication had been helpless to prevent it. Worse, those whose hope still drank at the fountain of the Soviet Union discovered, shortly after the war, that the glorious homeland of the Revolution bore several unpleasant resemblances to Nazi Germany.

They did not fall silent — on the contrary. Some of them founded journals and began to write plays for the theatre others turned out polemical pamphlets, still others found fresh impetus for their careers as novelists. The meetings and debates also continued — now in the open. Yet beneath it all, another sort of activity was going on, a frenetic digestion and transformation, a formidable reworking of guilt feelings which would take on specific forms for each of these diverse writers, but whose contents would, in the following decade, once the digestion was completed, converge in astonishing ways. They would converge around a theme far less disquieting than Thanatos but also intimately connected to it (as most French intellectuals had been aware since long before Freud — since Baudelaire at least, if not since Lautréamont, de Laclos or de Sade) — the theme of Eros. This much was new, however: the women, who in 1944 had at last obtained the right to vote, would explore and exploit this theme with as much inventiveness and daring as the men, because it was every bit as vital for them to understand — or, more accurately, to *translate* — what had gone on in the years of darkness. The new, inhuman world had to be given a human language. The unknown had to be converted into the known. Everyone — the writers, their readers, humanity in general — longed to be reassured: evil was a known quantity. Cruelty had always existed. It was frightening, but it was also pleasurable.

The French literary scene of the 1950's, by the intensity of its efforts at reframing and scale reduction, was not unlike a photographic laboratory. (In Duras's work, the theme of framing is explicit and occurs repeatedly in both contexts, holocaustal and erotic: "Aurelia Steiner my mother stares in front of her at the large white rectangle of the camp courtyard"; "And now, the rectangle of the open door is occupied by the body of the man who is about to strike.") In effect, it was as if the mass murders committed by a totalitarian regime could only be grasped if they were apprehended through the paradigm of rape or sexual torture; conceptualised in terms of transgression, ecstasy and love-unto-death; explained away by the irrepressible immorality of the libido. Auschwitz would become recognizable, and therefore cognizable, if it was compared to the macabre fantasies of de Sade (Pasolini would explicitly renew the same attempt two decades later, in *Salò, or the 120 Days of Sodom*). The Shoa would thus gradually take on the appearance of a Black Sabbath ceremony.

Whereas totalitarianism had erased the borderline between public and private life, *érotisme noir* ("black eroticism," as this tradition is called) would not only redraw but underscore it. People's heads were filled with images of barbed wire and miradors, secret walled enclosures within which unspeakable suffering was inflicted on human bodies; it sufficed to transpose these images into an erotic context for the "unspeakable" to become arousing. "The action of the play unfolds," writes Jean Paulhan in his 1945 preface to *La Nouvelle Justine*, "in some wild and virtually inaccessible castle — some monastery lost in the heart of a forest." The reference is no longer to the forests of Poland or Siberia, where man himself had gotten lost — no, the reader is back on familiar ground: the violence which rages in the mini-cities of the libertines is only sexual, in other words private, in other words basically enjoyable and all right. "Here," Paulhan goes on, "it is no excuse to say: don't punish me, I was ignorant of the law. Here one is forewarned of nothing and punished for everything." This is exactly the *Hier ist kein Warum* logic that had held sway in the death camps — however, terrifying in the political world, it becomes titillating in the erotic one.

Above all, then, it was urgent to rehabilitate de Sade. True, this project had already been undertaken in the twenties, after it had been conclusively demonstrated (theoretically by Freud and practically by the Great War) that modern civilisation, with its dreams of rationality and scientific progress, was not going to get the better of the death instinct — but now it became virtually a moral imperative. As of 1948, *Les Temps modernes* published Maurice Blanchot's "Lautréamont and de Sade," an eloquent and laudatory analysis of the Sadian "demand for sovereignty" which was to appear in book form the following year. 1949 also marked the publication of Simone de Beauvoir's feminist blockbuster, *The Second Sex* — but it was not long before its author was asking the rhetorical question *Should de Sade be Burned?* and answering in the negative, on the basis of arguments which would have stuck in the throats of many other champions of women's rights. Far from being burned, de Sade was now enjoying unprecedented attention: his censors and supporters were fighting it out in public; Georges Bataille and Jean Paulhan were defending him in court and writing erudite prefaces for his intrepid publisher.

True, in the works of de Sade as in Nazi Germany, evil was methodical and organized; but in de Sade it was motivated by passions with which everyone could identify; moreover, it was wielded against individuals, not crowds. When its victims died, it was not because they had been slowly starved or stacked inside unheated barracks or forced to perform hard labour or shoved pell-mell into gas chambers. "By these crude hecatombs," de Beauvoir accurately noted, "politics too obviously demonstrates that it considers men to be a mere collection of objects; de Sade, on the other hand, needs to be surrounded by a universe peopled with singular existences." It therefore mattered little to this feminist that, in the life as in the works of the *divin marquis*, the victims were overwhelmingly female; what now needed to be demonstrated was that "guilt is primarily the result of accusation," and that the true guilty party was none other than society. "It was [society] that" — by forcing him to revolt against its injustice and hypocrisy — "made de Sade a criminal."

Sartre was thinking along similar lines during these same years (and, as usual with this couple, it is difficult to know who was borrowing whose ideas) — his *Saint Genet, Comedian and Martyr* first appeared in 1952. Whereas this phase in Sartre's life was also that of his greatest indulgence towards the Communist Party, Jean Genet was anything but a downtrodden proletarian struggling for social justice and equality; the homosexual-thief-poet-thug-playwright-ex-con-genius fascinated the committed intellectual not *in spite* of his antisocial attitudes but *because* of them. When Genet declared, "I decided to become what crime had turned me into," he beautifully embodied existentialism's all-time ideal: that of giving birth to oneself. Sartre's enthusiasm resulted in over 600 pages of superbly crafted paragraphs in praise of the dregs of society; the ex-*Normalien* was so enchanted to be philosophizing about abnormality that he sometimes got carried away and started producing clunkers: "When Genet decides to want the Worst, he knows that the Worst has lost... and that there would have been no more Evil, from time immemorial, were it not for the existence, in each generation, of a few obstinate individuals who desperately go on cheating at a game which their opponent has already won." One wonders what would have constituted proof, to Jean-Paul Sartre (who at this very time was debating whether or not, and deciding not, to make a fuss about the Soviet concentration camps), that evil existed above and beyond the perverse games of "a few obstinate individuals."

The idea that guilt derives primarily from accusation would have sounded pretty frivolous to the Nuremburg jurors who had handed down their sentences a scant few years before the publication of these lines. But it was crucial to replace the incomprehensible images of Nazi criminality — its bloodchilling banality, bureaucratic rigidity and petty-bourgeois conformity — with the violently individualistic and heroic versions of criminality as embodied by de Sade or Genet, who had the advantage of being not only infinitely more romantic, but also French.

Jean Paulhan, for his part, apparently forgetting the distinction he had so painstakingly established in *The Flowers of Tarbe* between literature and reality (pleading in favour of a radical autonomy of the former with respect to the latter), invoked in defense of *La Nouvelle Justine* a still more hair-raising text.... but one which happened to be an historical document: Father Bartholomé de Las

Casas's *Very Brief Relation*.... "The upshot of which," Paulhan concludes triumphantly, "is that the victims are counted not by the dozen [as in *Justine*] but by the million. Twenty million, to be precise, according to the author." We can safely assume Paulhan was not seeking to convince his readers that Las Casas was even nastier than de Sade. Was he perhaps suggesting that imaginary atrocities are always surpassed by actual ones? If so, he had a recent example close at hand — why bother looking to 16th-century Mexico for his twenty million dead?

At the end of her essay on de Sade, de Beauvoir devotes a lengthy passage to the ambiguous relationship between torturer and victim (a theme which Genet had also exploited in a passage Sartre quotes with gusto: "I am the wound and the knife / the victim and the torturer"; Bataille was to whistle the same tune a little later). According to this exercise in dialectics, a variation of Hegel's famous master-slave analysis, "torturer and victim recognize one another — with surprise, esteem, and even admiration — as equals"; "they truly form a couple." Liliana Cavani, in *Night Porter*, would attempt to resuscitate these troubling harmonies in the framework of a concentration camp, and the result would be grating to say the least. No matter how many narratives of camp survivors one reads, examples of this mutual attraction between victim and perpetrator are strikingly few. The objectification of human beings in the camps was literal and total; the victims — numbered, bald, naked, fleshless, filthy, lice-infested, ill and exhausted — were, to themselves often as much as to their tormentors, objects of horror and disgust rather than desire. Skeletons do not get hard-ons, as Robert Antelme points out in his account of the year he spent in two German camps, *The Human Species*: "The laughability of these genitals. One is still male. My underwear has disappeared and my trousers are torn; the wind comes in and raises the skin of my thighs." So much for sensuality.

In fact, of course, all apparent similarities between concentration camps and the Sadian universe are fallacious. Scatology is a major feature of both worlds, for example — shit is ubiquitous in almost all survivor accounts (cf. Robert Antelme, Primo Lévi, Charlotte Delbo), but it is in no way "redeemed" by perversion; the abjection it causes is pure and undiluted. On the contrary, scenes of coprophilia in *Salò, or 120 Days of Sodom* serve to *humanise* shit: where taboos and their transgression exist, humanity still exists. Here again, Sartre's memory is amazingly short: "Shit flows profusely in the works of Genet," he writes, "because it represents absolute Evil: for Evil and Shit both presuppose the insolent healthiness of a well-functioning stomach." Duras, who had to closely witness the lamentable diarrheas of one camp survivor, could never have written such a piece of nonsense.

In sum, whereas the Nazis — as part of a vastly ambitious political undertaking — systematically debased human beings, not in order to capture some mirror-image of their own passivity but in order to break them, *érotisme noir* invariably draws a profit (in the form of sexual or at least literary pleasure) from the victims' debasement.

This is a decisive difference. Yet the idea according to

which there is no transgression without pleasure and the other way around (an idea implicitly present in literature since its beginnings and explicitly conceptualized in France since the 19th century) was so deeply implanted in the French mind that *some* means had to be found for making pleasure appear in the wake of the Nazi inferno. The repulsive, inadmissible image of an entire population being coldly exterminated in death factories had to be replaced by a more satisfying (if still sulfurous) image — that of a woman joyfully consenting to being hurt, humiliated, or put to death by the man she loves.

It was almost as if, Christ's message of love having failed, postwar France needed a new saviour — one who preached a different sort of love. The Good News appeared on cue, brought by a female messiah whose very name was the opposite of X, the cross of Christ. She was called O. Her story was written by a woman, the companion of Jean Paulhan — and also, like him, a former member of the Resistance. The two of them had collaborated (so to speak) in the struggle against the fascists; now they collaborated in writing the new Gospel. *The Story of O* was published in 1954, with a preface by Jean Paulhan entitled "Happiness in Slavery" (in English: "The Love of the Lash").

Here again, Paulhan went as far away as possible to look for his analogies: to prove that women yearned for sexual enslavement, for instance, he did not suggest that occupied France had adored the virile violence of the Germans — a suggestion which would have been considered indecent; rather, he invoked a case remote enough to be quaint, almost amusing — that of a handful of "negroes" from Barbados who, in the 19th century, purportedly revolted against their liberation because they were "in love with their master." No one, apparently, found this preface outrageous — either for its legitimation of slavery itself or for the conclusions it casually jumped to concerning male-female relations. *The Story of O* contained a message that the world badly wanted to hear in 1954: that evil was not really evil; that pain was inseparable from pleasure and thus acceptable; that the suffering and mutilation of a woman in love could, like Christ's Passion, offer a form of redemption and absolve us of our sins. Indeed, one didn't even need to feel guilty about this saviour's death because she herself had begged for it: the true "new Justine" was invented not by de Sade, but by Pauline Réage.

Whereas the literary decor of O's martyrdom, with its castles, capes and chains, was outdated not to say medieval, Réage included a few references to recent history in the novel, as if to vaccinate her readers: "Wouldn't a day of death and ashes eventually come, a day among days, when madness would be proved right, when the gas chamber would not reopen? Ah! may the miracle last forever, may the state of grace continue, may René never leave me!" This is the only truly obscene passage in *The Story of O*: less than ten years after Auschwitz, a "gas chamber" is nothing but a locked room in an eros-center, inside which a voluptuous fashion photographer anxiously awaits the return of her "living God" who has been held up by a business meeting.

Of course, novelists are free to write what they want, and no taboos should hamper their imagination within the space of their work. It nonetheless remains true that this space is defined in relation (and in opposition) to something one can only call the real world. To take an element of the real world that is as massive and negative as the gas chambers, and use it nonchalently in an erotic novel, is not only incongruous but shocking. Either the word "gas chamber" means something or it does not; if it does, its meaning is so highly specific as to render its use as a vague poetic metaphor offensive.

On the other hand, that O's lover should be referred to as a "living God" is no accident: it was just because their other God, the old one, was dead but incompletely buried, that so many French writers set out to locate "the sacred" — absolute meaning which is also supreme meaninglessness, meaning beyond meaning — in the realm of sexuality. This transfer was admirably illustrated by the itinerary of Georges Bataille, former seminarian turned theoretician of the sacred in all its forms. Bataille had published numerous books during the Occupation (*Inner Experience, The Guilty One, The Archangelic, On Nietzsche*), while continuing to work on *The Accursed Share*, which would appear in 1949. As for his erotic novels, several of which had been written before the war and signed pseudonymously (occasionally prefaced by the philosopher... Georges Bataille), these were increasingly successful in the fifties. Finally, in 1957, Bataille felt that he could publish *Blue of Noon* (written in 1935) under his own name; almost simultaneously, two theoretical works appeared which were to consolidate his fame: *Literature and Evil* and, especially, *Eroticism: Death and Sensuality*. The latter work undertakes to explore human history in search of "limit experiences" — those paroxystic encounters, long familiar to mystics of all persuasions, which combine pain and pleasure, death and bliss. Bataille disusses the phenomenon of war, but alludes *not once* to the war which has just laid waste to Europe — perhaps because, by its dismaying absence of erotic *frissons*, it would have contradicted not to say defeated his main argument. Like Paulhan, Bataille prefers exotic and "primitive" horrors: citing anthropological sources, he describes evil deeds committed by warriors in Accra, Dahomey and the Fiji Islands (all of whom happen to have a skin colour reflecting the metaphorical darkness of the human soul), but breathes not a word about, for example, the treatment inflicted on Jews by ordinary Frenchwomen at the Pithiviers transit camp in 1943. His examples are intended to convey the frightening presence of damnation within us ("the accursed share"), while at the same time highlighting its undeniable libidinal advantages. And if Bataille can blithely compare a woman in the hands of her lover to a sacrificial victim in the hands of a priest, it is because by 1957 this comparison was so banal as to seem self-evident. Pauline Réage calmly reiterates it in the course of an interview with Régine Deforges (*O Told Me*): "What O says to her lover without saying it is what all believers ceaselessly repeat: *in manus tuas, Domine*.... What we want is to be killed. What else does the believer want but to lose himself in

God? To be killed by the person one loves seems to me the height of rapture."

An identical sort of "rapture" was to appear in Marguerite Duras's writings during this same period (whereas it had been absent from her novels of the Forties). Duras's ecstasy had the same sacred overtones as that of Réage, but was based on a more direct acquaintance with the unspeakable: the novelist herself, and to a far greater extent her husband Robert Antelme, had experienced the worst of the war. Their son, born in 1942, had died because of food restrictions during the Occupation. Both of them had joined the Resistance in 1943 and the Communist Party the year afterwards; but in June 1944 Antelme had been arrested and deported to Germany by the Gestapo, and Duras had remained without news of him for a whole year. The journal she kept in the spring of 1945 (published forty years later as part of *La Douleur*) unforgettably describes the anguish of women awaiting the return of men whose lives are in danger. "We are glued to God, hanging onto something like God," she says at one point. And, elsewhere: "I wish I could give him my life." When her husband returns at last, weighing less than eighty pounds, she nurses him back to health, watching over him day and night, gradually teaching him to eat again, anxiously examining his excreta, experiencing a terrifying sort of intimacy with his skeletal body. Once Antelme has recovered, however, she withdraws from him (having fallen in love with their best friend Dionys Mascolo, with whom she would have a son in

1947) — but her sacrificial wish was to be fulfilled in her novels, where women would repeatedly offer themselves up in holocaust to men. In the first and most chilling version of *The Man Seated in the Corridor*, published in 1958, instead of Nazis striking and insulting innocent prisoners, a man strikes and insults an amorous woman. Instead of lice-infested prisoners forcing themselves to chew small chunks of bread as slowly as possible, the woman takes the man's "crime" into her mouth, "devours it in spirit," "feeds on it, gluts herself with it in spirit." Duras systematically sublimates the experience of abjection — which Antelme had endured in a political context — into love-suffused pain.

The reason for this can perhaps be found in another section of *La Douleur*, a narrative entitled "Albert of the Capitals," which Duras calls a "sacred text." It tells of how "Thérèse" (Duras herself) took part in a torture session organized by her Resistance group. The scene is described in almost intolerable detail, including everything from the colour of the elderly "Collabo's" testicles to the precise tonality of his reiterated screams. Duras apparently emerged from this experience convinced of the usefulness of extreme violence in eliciting truth from a body (and whereas here it was she, a woman whose husband had been denounced, who supervised the beating of a man, in her erotic texts, it is invariably the man who watches the woman die.) Moreover, the ostensible reason for which Thérèse and her friends torture "the squealer" is to force him to tell them the colour of his Gestapo ID card — this colour finally turns out to be green. Coincidentally or not, all the women in Duras's novels who agree to be beaten, humiliated or raped by men, have green eyes — as if the colour of vitality and innocence were forever doomed to connote mortal guilt.

In *La Douleur*, Duras uses the word "shape" to describe Antelme upon his return from the concentration camps. ("The doctor came in. He went over to the shape and the shape smiled up at him....") A few years later, the same word turns up in *The Man Seated in the Corridor*, but this time it refers to a woman's body: "The man rolls the shape down the stone pathway with his foot. The face is against the ground." In both cases, the author is exploring the scandal of reducing a thinking being to the state of pure body. Indeed, these bodies are neither alive nor dead; they float on the borderline between *corps* and corpse.... "And then he understood: the shape wasn't dead yet... and we had called him, the doctor, to try and bring it back to life." "I see nothing of her but immobility. I have no idea, I know nothing, I don't know whether she is asleep." The first version of *The Man Seated in the Corridor* ended less ambiguously, with flies eating the arm of the woman on the ground. But in a sense, the murder wasn't a murder at all, since the heroine of this book — who appeared on the French literary scene just four years after O — had, like O, begged to die at the hands of her lover.

The following year, in the opening pages of *Moderato cantabile*, a woman is murdered by her lover, also at her request.

The year after that, the heroine of *Hiroshima mon amour* tells her Japanese lover, over and over, "You kill me. You make me feel good." The opening images of the film, Duras specifies (in what is probably *her* most obscene sentence), should show "mutilated bodies — at the level of the head and hips — moving — in the throes of either love or death — and covered successively with the dews and ashes of atomic death — and with the sweat of accomplished love."

It was imperative, in France in the 1950s, that nuclear bombs and gas chambers be turned into love stories; that atomic ashes be confused with erotic sweat; that death no longer be blind, massive and anonymous but longed-for and joyfully welcomed by a woman in love. In this way, the horror could be replayed — but without the annihilation of will and desire — and, thanks to this rewriting, progressively tamed and exorcised. *Erotisme noir* allowed a number of French writers (and their readers) to take part in a limited version of the limitless atrocities to which they had been witness.

In the opening pages of *The Human Species*, Antelme takes care to stress how difficult it was for camp prisoners, on their return, to cover the distance "between the language at our disposal and the experience which... we were still pursuing in our bodies." All of them felt that they were "henceforth the victims of a sort of infinite, untransmittable knowledge." One wonders (indeed, this question deserves to be studied in depth, and separately) whether this sense of a world beyond language experienced by the Nazis' victims did not, in France, turn into a new motivating force in literature: the unspeakable (or the blank, or the resonating silence) was to become the veritable hallmark of such authors as Blanchot, Sarraute, Beckett, Duras and others. Theodore Adorno famously suggested that, following the Nazi abominations, literature itself could only be an obscenity. The survivors had seen those abominations at close hand: some of them remained forever silent about what they had seen. Others — such as Antelme — strove to put it into words almost immediately after their return. For still others, like Jean Améry, decades were to elapse before they found a language adequate to the task — and when they found it, it was sometimes strangely reminiscent of that used by the novelists. The latter, profoundly affected by the horror without having experienced it directly, projected their own "unspeakable" into that darkness. Paulhan himself pointed out this tendency: "I see so many writers, these days," he wrote, "consciously rejecting artifice and literary play in favour of some unspeakable event which is continually implied to have been totally erotic and terrifying." Again, however, he saw this as resulting from the influence of de Sade — "I wonder if, in such an extreme form of terror, we should not recognize less an invention than a memory, less an ideal than a reminiscence — in a word, if our modern literature... is not... very precisely determined by de Sade."

World War I, too, had been a bloodbath, a butchery, an unprecedented massacre; it, too, had left France traumatized, and inspired many sobering reflections on the themes of Evil, male bonding, and the heightened sense of life that often occurs in the face of death. World War II, however, far from confirming these already-ancient (and already disturbing) truths, pulverized them. It demonstrated that transgression and sacrifice could occur without eliciting any pleasure at all, either in the perpetrator or the victim. It proved that Evil could unfold in all its appalling variety — violence, torture, humiliation, mass murder — without producing the least compensating spark of sensuality. This war was not, by any stretch of the imagination, a "sacrifice." It was therefore not a "holocaust." It was not a "potlatch." It was not a "feast," a "carnival," or a "spree." All the concepts which (however shakily and insufficiently) had helped the French intelligentsia to understand primitive warfare — and even classical warfare — and, stretching it somewhat, even World War I — withered and died in the light of the cynical phrases at the gateway to modern Hell. These phrases were not "Abandon hope, all ye who enter here," but *Arbeit macht frei* (over the entrance to Auschwitz) and "Baby is born" (in the telegram announcing Hiroshima's annihilation to President Truman).

After that, understandably, French literature started finding metaphors offensive. It aspired to rid itself of its "flowers" and come to grips with reality at all costs. It was not in 1945 — I hasten to repeat myself — that France invented the dialectics of eroticism and death, or pleasure and transgression, or sacredness and sacrifice. But it was then that these themes were brought to the forefront; it was then that they took on the solemnity and awesomeness of religious dogma.

Much has been written, and made, of the "wind of freedom" which ostensibly swept across the French literary world at the war's end. A spate of novels in which sexuality played a central role were published at this time, and all of them — from Réage's *Story of O* to Miller's *Tropics* and Nabokov's *Lolita* — have generally been lumped together as indicative of this libération. Though these books often had the same publishers — and the same "morally outraged" persecutors — the resemblance between them was only superficial. Each society, each political and religious system engenders its own erotic fantasies: and while *érotisme noir* has its adepts in other countries (Susan Sontag was one of its first proponents in the United States), it nonetheless remains a quintessentially French specialty. Like police thrillers (interestingly called *Série noire*), it came into vogue *post bellum ergo propter bellum*: because at the end of that war, France — vanquished and victorious, humiliated and triumphant — needed to sing the praises of ambiguity.

It is undeniable that everyday, age-old atrocities like rape and prostitution on the one hand, war and murder on the other, confront us with something like an absolute: a seemingly irreducible Evil, the "accursed share" of the human race (this, indeed, is why these phenomena have always existed and will continue to exist, despite every sane person's horror of them). Yet it is not the *same* absolute in both cases — unless, that is, we dismiss the entire social dimension of humanity as irrelevant. *Erotisme noir*, which already tells us precious little about the truth of sexual assault and abuse, is obviously even *less* effective as a political weapon, or as an explanation of the political catastrophes of the 20th century. It does, however, seem to have served admirably — and this is what is most troubling about it — as a "repos du guerrier" for those French intellectuals who had remained on the sidelines of the conflict.

Perhaps, having fought a "phony war," they needed a phony rest?

(1991)

THREE MEN AND A CRADLE
Kundera, Bobin, Handke

"Fecundity, whether it be of a physical or a spiritual nature, is 'one': for the work of the mind proceeds from the work of flesh and shares its essence... In a single creative thought live a thousand forgotten nights of love which give it its grandeur and sublimity." Thus spoke a poet who fled far from wife and child so as to be ever-receptive to his inspiring "angels" — the great Rilke. His praise of carnal fecundity and carnal embrace, though it may seem paradoxical in his case, is sufficiently rare in the history of male thought on the subject of creation to deserve to serve as a frontispiece.

That male writers are sons, and take a passionate interest in the fate of sons, is anything but new — since Jesus Christ at least, most of the heroes Western civilisation has invented for itself have been sons; among famous literary sons one could mention, off the top of one's head, those immortalised by Kafka, Bruno Schulz, Dostoyevski, Philip Roth.... But writers who think of themselves as fathers, and show an interest in fathers' fates, are a relatively recent phenomenon — after all, hasn't "literary paternity" always referred to the creation of spiritual works?

French thought, at least since the Second World War, is quite generally pervaded with what one might call, pardon the neologism, genophobia: the rejection of child-bearing.

This stance has characterized both the theory and the practise of most French *maîtres à penser*, from Sartre and de Beauvoir to Barthes, Foucault and Althusser. It is obvious that non-procreation facilitates, on the one hand, fantasies of eternal youth, and, on the other, perpetual rebellions agains "the Father."

The disparagement of children differs from all other forms of ostracism and prejudice, for a reason that is at once banal and highly singular: whereas, with a negligible number of exceptions, Whites have never been Black, nor Gentiles Jewish, nor men women, every adult has of necessity been a child. Castigating, hating or making fun of child-bearing implies revolting against the fact that one was oneself, at some point in the past, an unintelligent, bawling, babbling and slobbering creature incapable of writing, reasoning, walking or even wiping one's own ass — in a word, that one was *born*.

Thus, first hypothesis: genophobic people are enraged at having been born. Second hypothesis, which follows naturally from the first: they are enraged at having to die. Third hypothesis, quite easily verifiable: they do not enjoy living (this is not a crime, of course; a defensible case can be made for it!).

Sartre, in *Words*: "Death was my obsession because I had no wish to live. That is why it filled me with such terror." Or, as Kundera's character Jakub in *The Farewell Party* puts it, "Fathering a child would be like proclaiming to the world: I was born, I tasted life, and I found it so good that I deem it worthy of being multiplied."

In the final analysis, what genophobic people dislike

about child-bearing is that it points up the terrifying *humanity* of the human condition — its finite, vulnerable, mortal nature, and one might also add: its animal and material nature, the confrontation with the material world which it entails. This is not unrelated, as we shall have numerous other occasions to observe, to the depreciation of the body in the Judeo-Christian tradition.

This, too, is defensible.

As an idea. But not as art.

For art is matter, not ideas. Artists are usually aware of this; theoreticians of art are continually forgetting it.

Flannery O'Connor, though herself childless and a Catholic, expressed it beautifully in "The Nature and Aim of Fiction": "The beginning of human knowledge is through the senses; and the fiction writer begins where human perception begins. He appeals through the senses, and you cannot appeal to the senses with abstractions.... Fiction is about everything human and we are made out of dust, and if you scorn getting yourself dusty, then you shouldn't try to write fiction. It is not a grand enough job for you."

My intention, here, is by no means to set the birthrate soaring. Charlotte Brontë, Gustave Flaubert, George Eliot, Franz Kafka, Samuel Beckett, Virginia Woolf, to name only a few childless writers, were nonetheless constantly at grips with everything filthy, unpredictable and ephemeral in human existence. What I would like to do, very simply, is look at some examples of the ways in which literary paternity has been affected, in our day and age, by the advent of new ideas about fatherhood.

Let us examine three writers, all of them (as yet non-dead) white European males who enjoy a certain notoriety in France, and whose writings often revolve around cradles. We shall attempt to see just what each of their cradles contains, and why.

Kundera: The Empty Cradle

Like Jean-Paul Sartre, many of whose themes and theses he espouses (whether consciously or not), the Czech writer Milan Kundera is a direct inheritor of the Christian theologians. Almost all the "positive" heroes of his novels see the body as lowly and the mind as elevated, and describe embodiment *per se* as a curse for which woman are to blame. Pregnancy, delivery and nursing are repulsive phenomena, unbecoming to thinking beings; eroticism is problematic unless one manages to abstract oneself from the bodies which jerk about, perspire and turn red; when fecundation takes place sexuality becomes an abomination; the result is an amorphous, aphasic thing that spends its days gurgling and flailing about in a hideous parody of man.

In this perspective, Enemy Number One is determinism (which Sartre called the *En-Soi* or "immanence"). Thus, all forms of necessary, unavoidable connection to other human beings are seen as intolerable, in particular the connection to the mother. "No bondage is more oppressive," says Jakub in *The Farewell Party*. "It cripples the child forever, and a maturing son causes his mother the cruellest of all love's pains." But even the simple fact of physically resembling someone else, being related to them, deriving one's name and features from them, is described by Kundera as a sort of scandal. We all remember Sartre's Roquentin, nauseously contemplating his own face in the Bouville bistrot mirror; similarly, in *Immortality*, Agnes finds it absurd that individuals should have to identify with their patronyms and physiognomies. She has the obsessive fantasy of a man arriving on Earth from another planet, a planet whose inhabitants would simply not have faces: "Where I live," this man tells her, "each person is his own product. Each of us invents himself entirely." It is easy to see that the planet in question is none other than Existentialist Heaven.

Just as the church father Tertullian, in the second century of our era, advised men who were tempted to embrace a woman to remember that this would imply clasping a "bag of excrements" in their arms, Jakub, in *The Farewell Party* (echoing Mathieu in Sartre's *Age of Reason*), declares, "I am disgusted by the idea of a beloved breast turning into a milkbag." In all of Kundera's novels, physical existence is basically construed as a bad stretch on the road that leads from nothingness to immortality. Here again, Sartre said it first (and far more humorously) in *Words*: "Viewed from the height of my tomb, my birth appeared to me as a necessary evil.... [I]n order to be reborn, I had to write; in order to write, I needed a brain, eyes, arms. When the work was done, those organs would be automatically reabsorbed. Around 1955, a larva would burst open, twenty-five folio butterflies would emerge from it, flapping all their pages, and go and alight on a shelf of the National Library."

For these writers preoccupied with immortality, again as for the church fathers, women bear the responsibility for bodiliness (it was Eve, as we all know, who introduced death into the human destiny): they're the ones who give birth and they're the ones who seduce; through their "mucus membranes," they hold diabolical sway over men from birth to death. "That mucus smeared him, marked him. Throughout Jakub's life," writes Kundera, "it exerted its secret power over him, summoning him at will and ruling over the various mysterious mechanisms of his body. He'd always felt a distaste for this humiliation, and he resisted it to the extent that he never gave his soul to women, he safeguarded his freedom and solitude, and restricted the 'reign of mucus' to certain limited hours of his life" (*The Farewell Party*).

Do not women, too, have souls? The question, as is well known, was debated for centuries by the hierarchy of the Catholic Church. Do not women, too, aspire to freedom and solitude? In Kundera's novels, the answer is sometimes yes, provided that they are not mothers. "There is no possible compromise between a woman who believes in her uniqueness and her sisters enveloped in the shroud of common femaleness." In *The Farewell Party*, Ruzena, who believes she is pregnant by the trumpet player Klima, refuses to have an abortion (just like Marcelle in *The Age of Reason*, pregnant by the philosopher Mathieu) — thus renouncing all hope of ever inhabiting the exalted kingdom of the mind. "Her whole soul ... was drawn inward, into the depths of her body, and she became determined never to part from the person who was peacefully germinating inside her." True, Agnes — the positive heroine of *Immortality* — is a mother, but this is simply the exception that proves the rule; her most ardent desire is to abandon her husband and daughter and be reunited with her dead father (in the rarefied atmosphere of the Alps, in case we needed things spelled out for us).

As de Beauvoir so inimitably put it in *The Second Sex*, "a man coincides with his body." "A woman," on the other hand, "is her body, but her body is something other than herself." Kundera could not agree more. He attributes to Agnes the conviction that men age differently than women: "Her father's body was gradually turning into its own shadow, it was dematerialising — leaving behind it, here below, nothing but a casually embodied soul. Conversely, the more useless female bodies become, the more bodily they become: heavy and voluminous, they look like ancient factories condemned to be torn down, in which the woman's self is forced to stay on to the end as doorkeeper." Apparently, neither Agnes nor her author have ever run across dessicated old women or voluminous old men.

The children who appear on Kundera's pages belong to a number of different categories, but they invariably represent evil, and a highly specific form of evil at that — the lack of intelligence, memory, a past, in a word, the lack of language (this, indeed, is the literal meaning of *infans*). For this reason, children in Kundera's novels are systematically deprived of the faculty of speech.

- There are *hypothetical* children: "When I imagine myself bending over a crib with an idiotic smile like millions of other dizzy daddies, it makes me shudder," declares Jakub. (Note the "idiotic smile," which is the seal of abjection in Kundera's fictional world.)
- There are *fantasized* children, such as the snickering, sneering swarm of adolescents who torture Tamina in *The Book of Laughter and Forgetting*, ultimately allowing her to drown beneath their sadistically attentive gaze... or the ethereal blond angel who leads Bartlef away in *The Farewell Party*.
- There are *imagined-real* children, like the two-year old toddler in *The Farewell Party*, who does nothing but "babble" and "gurgle unintelligible words," as his young father looks at him in besotted bliss.
- Finally, there are *symbolic* children, filled with laughter and forgetting, the emblem of contemporary civilisation in all its inanity. When former Czech president Husak declares, for instance, "My children, you are the future," it is not, Kundera tells us, "because they will one day be adults, but because humanity is getting more childish all the time" (*The Book of Laughter and Forgetting*).

The unbearable lightness of being (which is the key to all of Kundera's novels, not only the one thus titled) derives from the fact that we live in the present, and that it is impossible to walk with any degree of confidence on a temporal ground that is constantly being pulled out from under one's feet. The consumer society tends increasingly to glorify the present, sluffing off the weight of the past (history, books) as cumbersome and superfluous. "Children, too," Kundera points out sarcastically, "are without a past — whence their mystery, the magical innocence of their smile." In other words, children symbolize everything Kundera considers to be wrong with this lowly world, namely that it is lowly and that it is the world, which is to say impure, arbitrary, rotting.... In books, on the other hand, Goethe and Hemingway (*Immortality*) or Goethe, Petrarch and Lermontov (*Laughter and Forgetting*) can converse together endlessly, delivered at last of the burden of flesh... and women... and children.

Bobin: The Idealized Cradle

At the opposite end of the spectrum from Kundera, the French poet Christian Bobin enjoys life; he writes in positive terms not only of books (Kundera would agree with him on that point), but also of things and people, clarity and simplicity, the passing moment and the bird on the wing. Generally speaking, it can be said that whereas the Czech novelist's tone of voice is ironic, the French poet's is tremorous; he might have written exactly the same words as Kundera — "the magical innocence of their smile" — but he would not have put sarcastic quotation marks around the phrase.

In many ways, Bobin can be compared (and I know this comparison would please him) to Rilke: in order to sing the praises of life, he leads a solitary existence in the country, cut off from human beings and doings. Still, there are limits; there are many things about humanity he does not condone. As much as Kundera, he has a saintly horror of all things "modern" — the mass media, the suburbs, the rat race, white-collar jobs, big cities, factories, men between the ages of twenty-five and forty-five, and so forth. What he really loves, apart from a handful of sacred authors ranging from Beckett to Mallarmé (and rarely including women), are the following: nature, women, old people, mad people, lovers, and, especially, children. And, among children, especially one child — Hélène.

"Hélène is an extremely intelligent person," he explains in *The Marvel and the Obscure*. "It so happens that this person is also a child." This, certainly, is a sentence which could never have been penned by Kundera. "When I met her she was only a few months old.... Her parents, friends of mine, suggested that I look after her for a few hours every now and then. And those few hours at once became an eternity — a light, laughing, loving eternity."

It can be seen that Bobin, unlike Kundera, values and cherishes "lightness": in his opinion, it is only when we realize that we are light — that is, alive, dying, dancing on the tightrope of time — that we can be struck by the sense of beauty. "Were a child to ask me what beauty is — and it could only be a child, for only at that age does one desire the flash of illumination, and worry about what is essential — I would answer the following...: beauty is the sum of all those things that pass through us and ignore us, suddenly intensifying *the lightness of life*." (*The Eighth Day of the Week*, emphasis mine.)

Yet Bobin resembles Kundera in that he rejects out of hand all forms of necessary connections to other people, in particular couples and families. "A bond is something that binds you," he writes in *The Marvel and the Obscure.* "Here, with the child, I had a bond that delivered me of all my other bonds." Children, it would seem, are naturally autonomous beings, with no attachments and no genetic determinations of any kind. It would be absurd to look for any form of resemblance between them and their parents: "Such resemblances are the poorest ones of all. The good destiny, the clear road for childhood is, rather, to be like life — that is to say, like nothing and no one at all.... Life is more spacious, thank heavens, than these dark familial forests."

In an ideal world, to follow Bobin's reasoning, the "dark familial forests" would be chopped down: men, women and children would wander endlessly through fields and orchards, stopping just long enough to munch an apple, read a poem out loud or embrace one another, then resuming their solitary peregrinations. Couples are to Bobin what pregnant women are to Kundera — namely, the renunciation of all things fine and beautiful in human existence. "Married life is, to my mind, the most peaceful image of death. Both people agree that nothing will ever happen again — nothing, or at least as few things as possible."

Thus, women can bear children, fine — but children should, like Jesus Christ, renounce their terrestrial parents as soon as possible and strike off to forge their own destinies.

A bond is something that binds you — here again, we recognize the existentialist refrain, with its familiar themes of solipsism and voluntarism, to say nothing of elitism — a profound contempt for the fate of common mortals. "Instead of seeing us like two old fogeys, too lazy or too tired to change, as is generally the case with couples of long standing," wrote de Beauvoir of herself and Sartre, "people should have seen that our shared experiences allowed us to feel infinitely happy and at ease with each other." What extravagant self-conceit to maintain that only two philosophers could possibly share experiences that bring them close together, while all other old couples have to be content with sitting in a rut! One wonders what can be understood of human politics and history, wars and revolutions, if it is not recognized that most people care enormously about the fates of their parents, children, spouses, brothers and sisters....

But to return to Hélène.

"I grew up with Hélène," Bobin goes on. "I accompanied her in her walks and games.... I looked at the world through her eyes, and learned that the whole infinite universe was contained right there — in the pupil of an eye, in the fine flower of a laugh." Here, you can see Kundera beginning to scowl — ah yes, he'd been waiting for that laugh, and for that "infinite universe in the pupil of an eye"; now he shrugs his shoulders dismissively and turns his back on Christian Bobin.

Kundera's back being turned, Bobin is free to make a rather astonishing statement: "This gaze upon the child is the source of all my words, the origin of all my wealth."

What does he mean by this? He means, I think, that children have taught him to love what is fragile and ephemeral about life — the way it slips through your fingers like sand — and that this is what enables him to write; what he finds important to say in his writing. "Everything, absolutely everything departs, moves towards its own end. It is because it departs that everything is literally miraculous, enthralling."

But, one might wonder, how did Hélène manage to convey this profound truth to Christian Bobin? Not by anything she said or asked; no — by falling asleep. It was the sight of "her face, so naked in the approach of sleep" that allowed the poet to grasp — "with difficulty," he admits — "this knowledge that is not contained in books: exhaustion is what creates strength.... The beauty of a face is poignant because of the light that shapes it unawares — a light whose brilliance is inseparable from that of its future disappearance" (*The Eighth Day of the Week*). In other words, it was a sleeping child who enabled Bobin to grasp the beauty of things mortal — and the fact that only mortal things can be truly beautiful.

Of course, the lyrical terms in which Bobin exalts childhood often sound somewhat sickly-sweet or bombastic, as when he claims that "the child is the clearest reflection of God," or that, "having given up the highest form of science, which is the science of childhood, we have lost the strength of clarity, the virtue of simplicity." Yet it is undeniable that his poems often help us to sense these qualities of strength and virtue, and to enter into contact with the miracle of beauty... whereas, increasingly, Kundera's novels tend to hold forth on "beauty" as a concept.

But is the wisdom we derive from the face of a child really the only wisdom in the world? It's rather disheartening, after all, to reflect that "as of our first days on earth, we know everything there is to know," and that "growing up means forgetting what one could not help knowing." Is there really no hope at all for us post-pubertarian dinosaurs? Oh, but Bobin hastens to reassure us: in reality, the childhood he refers to is within anyone's reach — it is an *attitude*. "When I speak of childhood I am speaking, not of a particular age or state, but of play. When I speak of childhood I am speaking of today, of right now.... Childhood is not in the nostalgia we feel for it. Childhood is in the laughter it gives us."

He who laughs last will laugh best, Mr. Kundera.

Peter Handke: The Real Cradle

"All this contributed to the story of the child, and apart from the usual anecdotes, the important thing the adult got out of it was this: that the child could rejoice, and that it was vulnerable."

That Peter Handke has a child is something all his faithful readers know, for he devoted an entire book to the subject (*Story of a Child*), even if, throughout the book, he maintained a certain literary distance by referring to himself in the third person, as "the man." Before *Story of a Child*, however, children were already present as characters in several of Handke's novels (*A Short Letter for a Long Farewell*, for instance), and spoke like neither clowns nor parrots — producing neither, as Bobin claims, philosophical interrogations ("What is beauty?") nor, as Kundera would have it, incomprehensible gibberish, but sentences such as those which real children actually produce, and which are often astonishing.

In his youth, Peter Handke had subscribed enthusiastically to the anti-familial attitudes of Bobin and Kundera. "For most of those who belonged to this generation" (that of the Sixties), he writes, "the traditional forms of life had become 'death.'" Or again, when he becomes a father, "for once the man sees himself forming, with the woman and the child, a family (something he was accustomed to seeing as 'hell.')"

What changed "the man's" mind was the real birth of a real child. The emotion he felt when he set eyes on his daughter for the first time was profound and lasting. "When they showed the child to the adult through the glass partition, he did not see a newborn baby but an already-perfect human being.... The child, simply by being, with nothing to distinguish it, radiated serenity — innocence was one of the forms of mind! — and this was communicated almost furtively to the adult who was standing outside."

Later on in the book, Handke gives an example of the way in which the child conveys serenity to the adult: "A winter evening, the television on, the child crawls around the man — and finally falls asleep on his knees, exhausted. The small warm weight on his stomach makes watching television, for once, a sheer joy." In Kundera's novels, of course, nothing and no one could ever turn watching television into a joy — for the simple reason that every character goes about his or her business separately. Agnès's daughter giggles to herself as she watches ads on TV, her father skims through a volume of Rimbaud's poetry, Agnès herself goes off to hike in the Alps (*Immortality*); they are never a "warm weight" on each other's stomachs. On the contrary, what they all have in their stomachs is an "empty pocket," which is neither more nor less than the "intolerable absence of weight" (*Laughter and Forgetting*).

Describing innocence as "one of the forms of mind" is equally inconceivable in the Kunderian universe, where innocence, a euphemism for ignorance, is something to be castigated and denounced. The memorable passage in *The Book of Laughter and Forgetting* in which two American schoolgirls, assigned to do an exposé on Ionesco's *Rhinoceros*, disguise themselves as rhinos and laugh hysterically until they finally go floating up into the sky (along with their equally hysterical professor) is a hyperbolic demonstration of children's stupidity. In our day and age, warns Kundera, young people (and especially Americans, who are notoriously immature) no longer know how to approach culture, so they resort to idiotic antics. Handke, like Bobin, believes in a wisdom specific to childhood, one which is inevitably stifled and obliterated by acquired knowledge. "Little by little," he writes in *Story of a Pencil*, "children get lost in the language of adults, if only by saying to one another, 'one of Chaplin's best films.'" Or again, when his daughter (now at school) "stood there at home and recited out loud for the next day the length of such-and-such a river or the height of such-and-such a mountain, the man constantly told himself that he must never forget this, and that one would have to transmit to the end of time the way in which the children of this Earth, eyes wide with terror, recited the so-called knowledge of humanity."

Handke quotes Goethe as reverently as Kundera, and yet here he refers to our intellectual heritage as "so-called knowledge." What, then, is real knowledge? His daughter's very first gaze, Handke says, was "real enough to shake the whole universe." As of that instant, moreover, the child became for the writer "the master with whom he could learn."

Here again, one might almost think one was reading Bobin. But whereas the solitary poet found "the source of all his words" in his own "gaze upon the child," for the writer father, it is the child's gaze that changes everything. "Those staring, virtually unblinking eyes which, at half-adult height, saw each person individually, however large the crowd, and kept looking for an answer..., those eyes, all the time, in the throning streets, supermarkets and subways, were his only certainty. He was sure of it...: with each new conscience, identical possibilities opened up, and the eyes of children in the crowd — just look at them! — conveyed the eternal spirit. Woe to him who misses this gaze."

In other words, what a real child can teach us, if we are there to learn it, and if we have not yet closed our own eyes, is not only *mortality* but *vitality* — the fact that the totality of human possibilities are renewed with every birth, and therefore hope as well. Far from being the "tiresome droning of the species" (Beauvoir) or its clone-like "multiplication" (Kundera), a child is the unpredictable *par excellence*: a confounding mixture of genetic determinism and individuality, the ponderable and the imponderable. To live totally cut off from this *wisdom of possibility* is to renounce the most essential of all poetic traits, namely the capacity for wonder; it is to inhabit the petrified, cynical universe which Handke contemptuously calls "modern times." (How apt that this should also be the title of the intellectual journal founded by Sartre and de Beauvoir after the war!) In Handke's view, the *a priori* dismissal of childbearing (and not, of course, the personal decision not to have a child) is the worst form of "innocence." "Later, he would often have dealings with childless people.... As a general rule, their gaze was scathing and they lived from day to day in a terrifying state of innocence.... He cursed these narrow-minded, self-satisfied prophets — they were the dejections of modern times.... How did these modern people live, and with whom? And what had they forgotten, once and for all, that made them able to understand only the language of pettiness, which has such a big mouth and is anything but objective?"

A knowledge that belittles and rejects the living can only be a sterile knowledge. Handke incites us, not to regress to childhood, not to renounce artistic striving, the beauty of rigour, the search for formal perfection (and one might point out that his own, considerable literary output has by no means diminished since he became a father), but simply, sometimes, to look down. He tells us that looking down — towards the child, the body, everyday life — is not something lowly or inferior; that *it is still looking*. To reiterate Flannery O'Connor's crucial observation, the novelist begins where human perception begins.

It would be possible, of course, to study the works of many other men with many other Cradles — the Belgian novelist Eugene Savitskaïa, for instance, whose exquisite book *Marin My Love* describes how a "giant" rediscovers the material world thanks to the gaze of his "dwarf" — or, in a very different vein, Raymond Carver, whose short stories pitilessly dissect the mean and monumental conflicts that tear families apart. It would also be fascinating to study, a few decades hence, the ways in which real fatherhood has influenced men's writing (by "real fatherhood" I mean the fact of living with and taking care of small children, as opposed to purely legal and economic fatherhood such as as that portrayed in *Le Père Goriot*). Finally, it would be instructive to compare the aspirations to eternal life of non-fathers with those of non-mothers (contrasting, for instance, Kundera's *Immortality* with de Beauvoir's *All Men are Mortal* and Virginia Woolf's *Orlando*, two novels by childless women which recount the adventures of an immortal).

And what about novels on motherhood? Though the Western literary tradition has endlessly glorified and vilified mothers, depicting them as madonnas and martyrs, virgins and vampires, mothers themselves have written amazingly little about their experience with young children. (Apart from Sigrid Unset, Doris Lessing and Colette — or, in the present generation, Toni Morisson and Yûko Tsushima, few exceptions come to mind.) There are two reasons for this. The first and obvious reason is that creation and procreation, until fairly recently, were seen as being mutually exclusive, so that novelists who also happened to be mothers wanted nothing more, in their books, than to escape from the domestic activities which supposedly devolved "naturally" upon them. The second reason, less obvious but I think just as powerful, is that a human experience doesn't really receive its *lettres de noblesse* until men have lived through it. Coline Serreau's film *Three Men and a Cradle* showed young men holding a baby girl in their arms, anguishing about her runny nose, following her least gesture and grimace... the film was an huge success. *Three Women and a Cradle* would have been a non-event. A woman's ecstasy at holding a child in her arms — a woman's mad rage against a child — a woman's heart-rending fear for her child... these are age-old images, that is to say clichés — the very opposite of art.

Mothers and fathers still have everything to say about the complex, staggering phenomenon of bringing works of the flesh into existence and following them as they grow. The presence of children in an artist's life, far from being merely a distraction from his or her creation — exhaustion, worry, endless everyday hurly-burly — can lead the artist to the very heart of beauty.

It's not the only way there, but it's definitely one of the ways.

"Beauty is everything that moves away, after having grazed us...."

We shall let Bobin have the last word.

(1992)

The Limits of the Absolute
Marguerite Duras

Duras's voice has left its mark on this literary half-century, in France and the world over. What kind of a voice is it? Demanding. Uncompromising. Solemn. It resounds like the steps of a priest on the flagstones of an empty church or crypt. It blazes and dazzles like lightning, leaving a sense of burning in its wake. It forces you to close your eyes, give up the reins of reason, allow yourself be hypnotized by its singular syntax, rocked by its rhythms as by the sea....

In many ways, the literature this voice produced is religious literature. It approaches the mysteries of sexuality and death through constant reference to absolutes (All and Nothingness, paroxystic suffering and ecstasy), and eschews dealing with everything specifically human (society, diversity, boredom).

A number of Duras's peremptory, enigmatic phrases are engraved in our memories like the words of God on stone tablets:

destroy, she said
sublime, necessarily sublime
let the world go to the dogs; that is the only politics
my mother has become the flow of my writing
I went mad in full possession of my senses
I give you the torturer along with the rest
learn to read, these are sacred texts

Her characters also stay with us. They *exist*, in much the same way Biblical characters exist. What they have done is done; there is no undoing it. (She says: if I discover that in fact my character is in love with someone else, I don't change the beginning; I add on at the end.) Her manuscripts are irremediable, incorrigible, irrefutable. When she reworks a text, she says, she almost never changes the sentences. Only, sometimes, the *order* of the sentences. Once their dictation had been taken down, the Evangelists didn't ask God if He had any corrections to make. No. The Writ was Holy.

Again like the Bible, or like Greek mythology, Duras's novels engender endless commentary, rival interpretations. (I've heard people arguing over her characters in Dubrovnik, Vancouver, Toulouse.... In American universities, she's become so fashionable that numerous French professors have stopped accepting her as a subject for doctoral dissertations....)

How does a woman go about achieving such (quasi-divine) authority?

At birth, her name was Marguerite Donnadieu (gift of God). It had been father's name. Indeed, she published a first book under this name — a scholarly book full of maps, graphs and statistics — about the French empire, the situation of France's colonies throughout the world. But then... no. False start.

Her name would be Duras, she decided: the father's *region* rather than his name. The father's landscape. The father's vineyards.

Perhaps, also, because Duras contained the word *dur*. Hardness. Durability. Lastingness.

A name destined to last, as if engraved in stone. (Obsessively, Duras would endow her characters with names of metal and stone: Lol V. Stein, Stein, Aurélia Steiner, Yann Andréa Steiner, the Sailor from Gibraltar, Max Thor....)

Where does a women get such a need for hardness, stoniness?

Her childhood in Indochina: hunger, fear, her father's death, her mother's descent into madness, and the other people, those who surrounded the family, cruel, always, and threatening, staring at you, incomprehensible, always these bodies without words, without a common tongue, and then the sea, always, its ceaseless murmur, so close to the bed which is the scene of crime love rape and violence....

The war in occupied Paris: pain, mourning, horror, hunger again, the death of her beloved younger brother, a first child dead shortly after birth, "the horror of such love," the resistance movement, hatred, learning how to torture, her husband arrested, deported, starved half to death, returning "not dead in deportation," the atomic bomb, the God of nuclear love, *Hiroshima mon amour*, and then the fear, fear again, the fear of madness growing worse and worse, alcohol, coma, *delirium tremens*, writing, fear.

She is hard. I do not wish to be hard on her.

Writers do what they can. Duras was able to do a lot.

All writers lie. They lie by selection. In order to create a world for themselves within the world, they include and exclude. They chop, hew, break, smash. They push aside what they consider useless, futile, secondary, insignificant. Like sculptors armed with chisels, they choose the contours of their lies from amongst the infinite number of possible lies. A realistic novel is no more "true" to reality than a *nouveau roman* or the theatre of the absurd. Yet it is always interesting to take a look at what has been left out, knocked off, systematically omitted from a person's work.

Duras's choice was to exclude *life*. Like God, she cast a benevolent gaze on the pettiest of human affairs, the most banal situations. But all her characters — whether they were soccer players, maids, sailors, criminals or children — expressed themselves in the same style — her style. Even the way they said yes was Durassian.

Any subway car at nine o'clock in the morning contains more human diversity than a novel by Marguerite Duras.

Poverty, destitution, and more generally the entire "social" dimension of existence, from starving Cambodian children in *The Vice-Consul* to leprosy in *India Song* to Christine Villemin's chillingly ordinary house* — all of this becomes metaphor in Duras's writing. Close to the writer herself are all those who live on the margins of society: nuns, criminals, prostitutes, persecuted Jews and Arabs, perverts, murderers, ... all the real

---

*See previous, essay entitled "Novels and Navels."

and imaginary victims and perpetrators whom she met, interviewed, and turned into characters.

Not much laughing goes on in her books. Again like God, she seems to lack a sense of humour, fancy, variety. What she has to tell us is extremely serious, let there be no doubt about that. When she refers to "great shouts of laughter in" her conversations with Yann Andréa, we have no idea where they might have come from.

And despite the omnipresence of dialogue in her novels (to say nothing of her plays), there is no real dialogue. No otherness. No actual, interesting, explorable, finite, speakable difference. Questions and answers are interchangeable.

What fascinates Duras is intersidereal solitude, whether one is physically alone or not. What also fascinates her is her own unending effort to overcome this solitude through writing. "The minute we call out, we become, are, already the same. The same as who? As what? As what we know nothing about. And in thus becoming no one, we leave that desert known as society…. The first word, the first cry, we don't know how to utter it. We might as well summon God. It is impossible. Yet we do it" (*Le Navire Night*).

Society is a "desert." We must therefore leave it. We must drink at the fountain, the original source. Keep only what is essential. And for Duras, what is essential is invariably the worst. The most pared-down, the closest to the bone, to the skeleton, to death. Limit experiences.

"As of the first days [in the camp]," wrote Robert

Antelme in *The Human Species*, "it seemed to us impossible to bridge the gap between the language at our disposal and the experience most of us were still pursuing in our bodies."* The idea of something inexpressible, an experience "beyond language," is central to all of Duras's work. Her goal is to give voice to the unspeakable — silence, screaming, rage, madness, hunger. Depression. Non-communication. Non-encounter.

Duras chooses the worst, and turns it into a form of perfection.

Thus, differences of language, culture and social milieu — everything that creates a distance between individuals, and was a source of terror and danger to Duras during her childhood, contribute, in her fiction, to "love." The social dimension is abolished. Duras sees: political violence. She writes, invents: sexual violence. Far from subscribing to the feminist precept of the 1970s according to which the personal is political, she ends up convincing herself that the political is personal.

Otherness is reduced to fantasy: often a *topographical* fantasy. For instance, you can become another person by renaming yourself Duras, after your father's lands. To love another person is to love her name of Venice, Calcutta deserted, Lahore, Battambang. Your name is Hiroshima; mine is Nevers.

The more foreign you are to me, the more I love you. In her foreword to *Hiroshima My Love*, Duras spells it

---

*See previous, essay entitled "Erotic Literature in Post-War France."

out: "Between two people as geographically, philosophically, historically, economically, racially etc. different as it is possible to be, HIROSHIMA will be the common ground (perhaps the only one in the world?) in which the universal givens of eroticism, love and misery will stand out in an implacable light."

Just what are these "universal givens"? Given her personal friendships with Georges Bataille and Michel Leiris, Duras was of course aware of the theories expounded by these writers on the subject of literature and eroticism. Literature as bullfighting; eroticism as religious sacrifice. Now that the cosmos no longer reverberates with the voice of the invisible eternal Spirit, our task is to make it reverberate with something else, and that "something else" is the body, in particular the female body, the fertile body, bearer of life and death, abject object, "thing" *par excellence.*

Duras describes Bataille's heroines in exalted terms: "Edwarda and Dirty are God. Bataille tells us so," she wrote in 1958 in the journal *Ciguë* (Hemlock). Why are they God? we might ask ourselves. Here is the answer: "Edwarda and Dirty are possessed by dispossession. Whereas Dirty still loves and prefers one person in the world, Edwarda no longer loves or prefers anything. Her prostitution has penetrated to her very heart." ("Everything in a woman is sex, including her intelligence," wrote Jean Paulhan in his preface to *The Story of O.*) Or again, this rather dizzying prophecy: "Edwarda will remain sufficiently unintelligible throughout the coming centuries for an entire theology to be based upon her."

Total prostitution, according to Duras, is the only way in which a woman can approach divine status, become grandiose, impenetrable, as "unintelligible" as God. Virtually all of Duras's heroines will aspire to being similarly "possessed by dispossession." She will deprive them of mind, language, intelligence and reason. "All the women in my books," she writes in *Material Life*, "no matter what their age, derive from Lol V. Stein, which is to say from a certain self-obliviousness. All of them have light-coloured eyes. They lack wisdom and foresight. All of them are the cause of their own unhappiness. They are very fearful; they are frightened of streets and squares, they do not expect to receive anything like happiness. All the women in this procession of women in my books and films are alike...."

In other words, all of them are at once similar and dissimilar to Duras herself, who possessed the same traits (especially agoraphobia), but who also possessed a trait that cancelled out or at least compensated for the others, and which none of her heroines possesses, namely: *writing*. Literature was her sacrament; and she performed the uncommon feat of playing both roles in its religious ritual: she was at once the all-powerful creative and destructive god, and the sacrificial victim. Her books give us a "procession" of women who are vulnerable, abject or mad, lost to themselves, forgetful of themselves, forever given up to violence, be it the violence of the world (like the beggar-woman) or the violence of men (like Anne-Marie Stretter).

By writing about them, Duras puts them at a distance, and proves to us how very different from them she is.

In *The Sea Wall*, Duras's first fictional version of her childhood, it is implied that the young girl's entrance into the world of desire and language kills her mother. In the final version, *The Lover*, we learn that Duras's mother, far from giving up the ghost when the Chinese man fell in love with her daughter, actually encouraged the affair between them because the man was rich. The same novel shows Duras realizing, as a young girl, that writing was the only way she could stave off her mother's madness.

Her mother was against this choice, and this choice was against her mother.

Killing her mother is what allows a daughter to write? One of Duras's dreams, recounted in *Green Eyes*, says so in as many words: "*Eden Cinema* was playing at the Orsay Theatre. And one night, after the end of the show, I dreamed I was walking into a house filled with colonnades, inside it there were wide verandahs giving onto gardens. As I entered the house, I heard Carlos d'Alessio's music, the waltz from *Eden Cinema*, and I said to myself, hmm, Carlo is here, he's playing. I called out to him. No one answered. And then my mother emerged from the place the music had been coming from. She was already in the grip of death, she was already putrefied, her face was already greenish and filled with holes. She was smiling very faintly. 'That was me playing,' she said. 'But how is that possible?' I asked. 'You were dead.' 'I just let you think I was,' she said, 'so you could write all your books.'"

In real life, neither her daughter's eroticism nor her

writing brought about the death of Duras's mother. When this death finally occurred, however, in 1957, it coincided with Duras's discovery of masochistic pleasure. "We made love again. We couldn't speak to each other anymore. We were drinking. Very coldly, he would strike me. On the face. And certain parts of the body. We could no longer approach one another without being afraid, without trembling. He took me up to the top of the park, to the castle entrance.... My mother hadn't been put in her coffin yet. Everyone was waiting for me. My mother. I kissed her icy forehead... He was waiting for me in the park" ("The Night's Last Client," in *Material Life*).

The same experience was to give rise to *Moderato Cantabile* and *The Man Seated in the Corridor*.

The barracks commander, wrote Antelme in *The Human Species*, "knew we could sit there without moving and watch a friend being beaten, and that along with the urge to trample the beater's face, teeth and nose, we would also be feeling, mutely but deeply, delight in our own body's good luck: 'I'm not the one who's getting it.'"

Contemplating another person's suffering and being delighted it is not our own — such is the pact Duras establishes with the reader in *The Man Seated in the Corridor*. It is the man who acts, strikes, and looks, whereas the woman lies on the ground with her eyes shut. A third entity is present, however: "I", "me" — and this entity is also looking. The more her heroine is annihilated, the more Duras insists on the gaze of this "I". The female character "cannot see the man." "She will have said nothing, looked at nothing.... She knows that he is looking at her, and can see everything. She knows it with her eyes shut, just as I know it, I who am looking." Again and again, the female character's eyes "flutter open unseeingly, then close again." Where hearing is concerned, on the other hand, the narrator is sometimes conflated with her character: "We hear footsteps, she and I."

Here is the end of the story, in the 1981 version: "I see that the body continues to let itself be struck; it is abandoned, beyond all pain. I see the man insulting and striking the woman.... And then I see... I see... I see that other people are watching.... I see the man lying on top of the woman, in tears. All I can see of her is her immobility. I don't know, I have no way of knowing if she is asleep." The original version of the story, published in a literary journal in 1962, left no doubt as to the heroine's fate: in the final lines of the text, flies are eating her arm.

A similar, invisible "I" is present in *The Malady of Death*. Here, too, it is endowed with the faculty of sight. This "I" says "you" to the man who has hired a "she" in order to tame her body. He weeps as he penetrates her, wants to murder her — meanwhile "she," as usual, is half-asleep, smiling, absent.

What is Duras's definition of love? It emphatically precludes any form of exchange, give-and-take, listening, sympathizing, trying to understand. On the contrary — love is wanting to kill, wanting to die, wanting to commit suicide. It is furtive, secret, criminal, absolute and marginal. It is sublime and sublimated. Love, to Duras's mind, is Christine Villemin's decision to murder her own son. It is her own interminable wait for her husband's return in 1945 — when, she says, she was "sealed to God." It is Emily L.'s letter to the guard, in which she tells him she has a sense of "waiting for a love, perhaps a love for no one as yet, but waiting for this and this alone: love. I wanted to tell you that you were this waiting."

In order that a person be "loved," they have to be eliminated, absent, fast asleep, in a coma, in a concentration camp, dead, anonymous, a foreigner, as far away as possible. Yann Andréa was never as violently attracted to Marguerite Duras as when she was in an alcoholic coma; she felt it; he confirms this; so be it. Amen.

The distinctive tone of Marguerite Duras is the restrained superlative. *(I know the ultimate truths; I shall say no more....)* First I create a world, then I declare it to be the world. As it is now, was before and ever shall be.

Mind is for men, matter is for women. "As a rule, men do nothing for children," writes Duras in *Material Life*. "Nothing concrete.... Women may be writing a good deal more, but with respect to men they haven't changed. Their basic aspiration is still to care for the family, keep it together."

Adventures are for men, love is for women. "Men think of themselves as heroes, just like little boys," writes Duras in the same book. "They love war, hunting, fishing, motorcycles and cars, just like little boys. You can tell this when you watch them sleep — and that's the way we women love our men. We shouldn't lie to ourselves about it. We love our men innocent and cruel; we love hunters and warriors; we love children."

"The female landscape is essential, not to say essentialistic," Duras said once in a radio interview. "It is the landscape of mad love, the way a musical note is held, for decades. *That* is a woman's life. Excruciating and admirable."

Women abdicate willpower, reason and language. And what rises up out of their silence is... *Duras's writing*. She alone among women is endowed with this sacred power. She alone escapes the age-old malediction that strikes women who dare to write. The "Captain," Emily L.'s husband, threatened by the opaque beauty of the poem she is working on about the light of a winter afternoon,* tosses it into the fire. And the young woman's literary dreams are dashed forever.

"The way I write is the way people should write," says Duras, again in *Material Life*. "I write for nothing. I don't even write for women. I write about women so as to write about myself, myself alone throughout the centuries."

And so it is that Duras — *myself alone throughout the centuries* — is the single woman in Duras's fictional universe to have access to mind — that "gift of God" (Donnadieu) — without ever losing it, abdicating it, allowing it to be damaged or confiscated by men.

In the fifty years that separate *The Impudents* from *That is all*, Duras's style, rather than evolving towards complexity, grows increasingly spare and simple, describing a series of concentric circles closer and closer to herself. I am — she who is — myself — writing —

---

*For those who might have wondered, it is Emily Dickinson's poem n° 258.

myself alone — in the beginning — the Word — sex — myself all alone — death — alone —

That was what she really wanted to convey to us. And she did so... absolutely.

(1998)

Good Faith, Bad Conscience
Tolstoy and Sartre

"Fiction is so very much an incarnational art..."
— *Flannery O'Connor*

Tell me a story!

All right, with pleasure! Let me lead you down the garden path....

It's a story filled with coincidences and contrasts — the tale of two great men — Leo Tolstoy and Jean-Paul Sartre — who, though very different from one another, came to symbolize not only their respective countries but virtually their respective centuries. Both these men sought and in many ways managed to embrace the totality of human experience — by writing works in almost every existing genre from theater to philosophy, but also by teaching, lecturing, speaking out publicly to improve the human race, making examples of themselves and ceaselessly putting themselves into question, on the line, in the limelight. It is also, to a lesser extent, the story of the women with whom these men shared their lives — Sophie Tolstoy and Simone de Beauvoir.

So... to begin at the beginning. Once upon a time, two little boys were born — Jean-Paul and Leo. Their families were affluent and the babies were coddled, cared for, spoiled.

However, as happens in nearly all fairy-tales, they were orphaned at an early age. Leo lost his mother when he was two, and his father seven years later. Jean-Paul's father died before his first birthday; he would have no memory of him at all. The young boys were then raised by close relatives — in Jean-Paul's case, his maternal grandparents and, later, his mother and stepfather; in Leo's case, his grandparents and a number of aunts. Interestingly, as of early childhood, both boys found themselves ugly. A significant difference between them, however, can already be mentioned: whereas Jean-Paul was an only child, Leo grew up surrounded by three older brothers and a younger sister. Moreover, Leo was in love with nature and deeply rooted in his land — the domaine of Iasnaya Poliana which had been in his family for generations. He would remain forever nostalgic about his childhood. In a letter to his biographer Pavel Birioukov dated 1903, he describes it as having been "so luminous, so tender and poetic, so filled with love and mystery.... Yes, it was a marvellous period." Little Jean-Paul, on the other hand, was totally indifferent to the charms of the countryside and would later write, "The reader will have understood that I detest my childhood and all that remains of it."

The two boys had another point in common: both of them loved to read, and dreamed of doing extraordinary things when they grew up. Their dreams were strikingly similar. Leo says in *Adolescence*: "I often imagined myself as a great man, discovering new truths for the good of all humanity, and I contemplated other mortals with a prideful awareness of my own value." Jean-Paul says in *Words*: "Sacredness then entered *belles-lettres* and the man of the pen materialized, an ersatz of the Christian I was unable to be.... Earthly immortality offered itself as a substitute for eternal life." In other words, both youths aspired to use the immense power of their minds to become great men. Before they could do so, however, they first had to become men.

Now, two things, as we know, can help turn a boy into a man — love and war. Our heroes were to experience both, but in reverse order and in strikingly different ways. In a word, it could be said that in both these enterprises, Tolstoy "joined the fray," whereas Sartre witnessed events from a distance, as a brilliant spectator and commentator.

Upon emerging from adolescence, the young Count Tolstoy's life was extremely dissolute. He gave up his university studies, squandered his money on gambling, and abandoned himself to "debauchery," contracting venereal disease and enormous debts, whereas Sartre led a serious, tidy, well-behaved existence, moving quite naturally from the Lycée Louis-le-Grand to the Ecole Normale Supérieure just down the street, invariably getting the highest grades of his class and eventually coming in first in the notoriously difficult *agrégation* examination. Whereas at age twenty-three, in the cafés of the Latin Quarter, Sartre was beginning to work out his concept of freedom as the defining characteristic of human beings, Tolstoy at the same age enrolled in the Danube Army in order, as he wrote to his aunt on 28 January 1851, "not to be free anymore.... I've been free in all ways for too long and it seems to me that this excess of freedom is the principle cause of my defects — and indeed, an evil."

The following year, Leo published *Childhood*, an autobiographical novel which was highly successful in Moscow; Jean-Paul's first novel *Nausea* didn't appear until he was thirty-one, but it had an immediate and powerful impact on the Paris intelligentsia. Leo was now at the dawn of his literary life, whereas Jean-Paul was already at the dusk of his — *Nausea*, as it turned out, would be by far his best novel, perhaps the only one destined to outlive him.

For eight long months, Tolstoy took part in the defence of the city of Sebastopol besieged by French and English troops; he had numerous brushes with death; following this, he worked for four years as a war correspondent (1851-1855). Upon resuming civilian life, he began writing stories rooted in the intense reality he had just experienced. At thirty-four, he married Sophie, who was seventeen years his junior.

As for Sartre, he met the woman of his life when he was twenty-four (de Beauvoir was two years younger), and it was only ten years later that he found himself confronted with war. He was drafted into the French army in September 1939, took part in the "Phony War" as a meteorologist (because of his poor eyesight), was taken prisoner, escaped, and spent the rest of the war working on his great philosophical opus *Being and Nothingness*, as well as its fictional counterpart, the trilogy *Paths to Freedom.*

For the rest of their lives, that is, for the next five decades, our heroes' life and work were conducted at the side of their respective women — and these women did everything in their power to assist, support and encourage them in their Titanic writing enterprises. They didn't do so symmetrically, however; in fact the differences between Sophie and Simone are far more salient than those between Leo and Jean-Paul.

Sophie embodied what was considered in her day to be a model wife — she wished for nothing more than the happiness and accomplishment of her genius of a husband. She submitted to him in all matters and, though shocked by his youthful follies (which he confessed to her shortly after their wedding), she loved him passionately, believed in him and venerated him; she bore his children and copied his manuscripts. Since Tolstoy was a man of indefatigable physical and mental energy, this meant that Sophie had a large number of children and manuscripts to deal with — she was pregnant no fewer than fifteen times and gave birth to thirteen children, and she copied literally everything he wrote, almost as quickly as it flowed from his pen, often many times over, including his enormous *Journal* and (six times) the fifteen hundred pages of *War and Peace*. Though not herself an intellectual, she was an intelligent, reasonable woman and a devoted mother. De Beauvoir, on the other hand, was an intellectual. She, too, was convinced that the man she loved was the genius of his time, and though she had a horror of cooking and housework, she was able to do Sartre favours of a literary nature (translating whole novels by Faulkner or Dos Passos, for instance, so that he could include them in his teaching curriculum at Le Havre). This being said, her intention was to become her man's equal — or, as she liked to put it, his "twin." Having children was something she would not be caught dead at. Times had changed, and de Beauvoir advocated the liberation of women through access to contraception, abortion and education — indeed, she eventually became the most famous feminist in the world. She read Sophie Tolstoy's *Journal* as soon it was published in France, and her attitude towards the Russian countess was one of pity mingled with contempt. To her mind, Sophie was her antithesis, not to say her nightmare — she embodied the condition from which she, Simone, had escaped, thanks to the power of her intellect.

Now, Tolstoy and Sartre had another trait in common, namely a strong ambivalence towards all things female. Tolstoy, having been raised in the tradition of the Orthodox Christian Church, experienced this ambivalence primarily as guilt. He lusted after Sophie (perhaps more than he actually loved her), and at the same time he was ashamed of his lust; he considered physical love to be base and bestial, especially for a man of his intelligence and moral excellence. Nonetheless, year after year, he went on making love to Sophie, who gave birth to one baby after another. And indeed, Tolstoy had enormous veneration for motherhood! He simply wished that women could become mothers without the intervention of men — that is, without copulation, eroticism, enticing glances, tempting hips... all those things which, despite his perpetually-renewed efforts at asceticism, he simply could not resist. It drove him mad. He describes the phenomenon admirably in *A Case for Conscience*: "Within him, there has always been a double personality — two diametrically opposed beings have always existed simultaneously in his heart: the first is passionate, blind to all but its own well-being, a man who loves life and gives himself up body and soul to the passions that possess him. The other, on the contrary, is extremely demanding of himself and others, and aspires to moral perfection with the whole force of his intelligence." The conflict between these two "personalities" would only worsen with time, but in Tolstoy's case it seems to have been conducive to the production of literary masterpieces. He wrote *War and Peace* between the ages of thirty-five and forty, and *Anna Karenina* between forty-five and fifty — two of the greatest novels in the history of world literature.

Sartre did not believe in God at all — or only sufficiently to feel that he should vituperate Him from time to time, or gibe at Him by telling Him he didn't believe in Him; thus, instead of being torn, like Tolstoy, he was serene. His own ambivalence towards femininity was of a different nature. What he valued more than anything in the world was the life of the mind: words, sentences, ideas, books, conversations. According to his philosophy, femininity was associated with everything that frightened and repelled him, namely, "immanence," "contingency," the passive and uncontrolled proliferation of "nature," which was constantly threatening to ensnare, engulf, and swallow up his beautiful, immaterial thoughts. This did not prevent him from getting along with women — on the contrary. He enjoyed the company of women, especially young and attractive women. But what he liked about them was his own ability to seduce, dazzle, educate, assist and support them, and especially to oversee their erotic and intellectual initiation.... He invariably remained in control of the situation, never allowing his precious consciousness to be swept away by fleshly embrace.

Whereas Tolstoy was moved and fascinated by the phenomenon of motherhood — many of his novels and short stories contain detailed descriptions of difficult pregnancies and deliveries (*Married Life*), birth itself (*Anna Karenina*), infanticide (*The Power of Darkness*) and the relationship of adults to small children (*passim*), this dimension of human existence was utterly foreign to Jean-Paul Sartre. Vis-à-vis the phenomenon of birth in particular, he never got beyond the "Yuk!" stage which, in the rest of the population, generally reaches its peak at about age twelve, then gradually diminishes. Throughout his life, he would have a puerile-heroic conception of what it means to be a man — not *having* but *severing* connections to other people, especially biological (family) connections. In his fiction, it is the capacity not to give life but to inflict death which proves a character's "freedom" and thus his humanity: Mathieu calmly drowns a batch of kittens (*The Age of Reason*), Roquentin toys with the idea of suicide (*Nausea*), Orestes murders his mother (*The Flies*), and so forth.... Having children, in Sartre's eyes, meant succumbing to "immanence" — how fortunate that he chose to link his destiny to that of de Beauvoir, who didn't want children either!

One result of Sartre's aversion towards nature, femininity and family life is that his fictional characters bear a far vaguer resemblance to actual human beings than Tolstoy's do. *Nausea* may be an interesting novel, but its protagonist is a man whose solitude is so extreme as to verge on the absurd — he has no biological or emotional connection to any other person in the world. Not only is he deprived of brothers, sisters, and children (as was Sartre's own case); he is also (which is more original) miraculously unencumbered by parents — in other words, there is no one in the world whom he can ask to tell him a story..... Given this, it is hardly surprising that he goes through life scratching his head and wondering what it's all about.

An aside: despite their rejection of biological reproduction, Sartre and de Beauvoir were constantly having imaginary children. As of 1935, they systematically referred to Olga Kasaciewiz, one of their lovers and protégées, as their "adopted child." Every time de Beauvoir published a book (and, like Sartre, she was to publish many), she announced the event in her letters to her American lover as the "birth" of a "child." Both Sartre and de Beauvoir referred to their friends on the editorial board of *Les Temps Modernes* as "the family." And their "family" life was far more rigidly structured than that of the average parent — appointments, routines, letters, confessions, lunch with A, supper with B, bed with C, each event of the day organized in advance, planned to a T, and recounted in great detail by each to the other — a far cry from the bohemian spontaneity which people often assume to have been their lifestyle. Finally, when they started growing old, both Sartre and de Beauvoir chose "daughters" for themselves (young women who were by no means lacking in biological parents) and made these women their legal heirs by adopting them.

To return to my story.... Tolstoy and Sartre were now famous writers in their prime. They were published, read and revered all over the world; the wildest dreams of their childhood had already come true.... And suddenly, both of them underwent a crisis. Spiritual, mid-life, existential, call it what you will. But a serious crisis. To put the problem in a nutshell, both of them felt that it was immoral to go on writing fiction when so many people in the world were suffering from hunger and oppression.

In Tolstoy's case, the crisis occurred relatively late — he was fifty years old when, virtually overnight, he decided that his whole life had been a huge mistake. He was increasingly obsessed with social injustice and poverty, shocked by the moral and material abjection of the Russian people, and disgusted with his own wealth. And it wasn't only his material wealth that bothered him (the luxurious family property, the servants, chauffeurs and tutors, embroidered linen tablecloths, crystal glasses and silver cutlery, the piano...); it was also his intellectual wealth. Literature *per se* had begun to make him nauseous, as he couldn't help noticing that it was a prerogative of the affluent classes, and thus intrinsically dependent on the misery of the poor. As he put it in a preface to the works of Maupassant in 1894, "That period, the year 1881, was a time at which I inwardly reworked my whole perception of reality, and in the course of this reworking, the activity known as art, to which I had hitherto devoted all my strengths, not only lost a great deal of its importance in my eyes but became frankly repulsive to me — because of the inordinate amount of space it took up in my life and, more generally, in the conceptions of those who belong to the wealthy classes."

Sartre's crisis was less dramatic, more gradual. He had never had a taste for luxury; material possessions meant nothing to him. He lived in hotels, ate in cafés and tended to give all his money away to friends. Things might have gone on in this way indefinitely.... But because of World War II and the deep guilt feelings it instilled in France's intellectual milieu (we'll come back to this later), and also because of the influence of Marxist discourse now prevalent in this milieu, the man who had always denounced "bad faith" began to be tormented by a bad conscience. And as he would put it in a 1977 documentary film about him: "At that time, numerous modifications occurred within me, and in particular I realized that I'd been subject to a genuine neurosis... this neurosis being, basically, that... I felt there was nothing more beautiful or more important than writing, that writing meant creating works which would last, and that the life of a writer should be understood on the basis of his writing. At that time, in 1953, I came to see that this was a perfectly bourgeois outlook, and that there were many things in life besides writing."

Having thus thrown into question the goals of their youth, Tolstoy published a book called *What is Art?*

(1898), and Sartre a book called *What is Literature?* (1948). Interestingly, the contents of these books and the subsequent behavior of their authors form a perfect logical criss-cross: whereas Sartre attempted to define a social role for literature, but would henceforth avoid indulging in it himself, Tolstoy, though he now disavowed the very notion of art, simply could not stop creating it.

Another aside is necessary at this point, to recall the obvious fact that the novel (unlike music or painting, for example) is made up of words and thus lends itself more readily to didactic or political uses than other artistic forms. In 19th-century Russia, the debate between "art for art's sake" and "politically committed art" was already raging (though in a slightly different vocabulary); indeed, when *War and Peace* was first published, as M. Aucouturier tells us, quoting from the writer's rough draft of the epilogue to his novel, Tolstoy had thought of apologizing to his artistic and intellectual readers for having "disfigured my book by inserting reasonings into it." For all that, neither he nor Sartre had ever considered the novel as a pure object of formal beauty; from their earliest youth, they'd been motivated by the desire to teach, and preoccupied by the artist's responsibility to the world (Sartre had explicitly stated that his intention in writing *Nausea* had been to combine Stendhal with Spinoza). Now, however, it was no longer a matter of *tension* between aesthetics and ethics (a tension inherent to the novelistic genre *per se*); more radically, it seemed to them to be a matter of *choice*.

They made the same choice. Tolstoy decided that from now on, instead of being a great novelist, he wanted to be nothing but a spiritual guide for his people. He converted to a highly personal form of Christianity, based on strict conformity with the precepts and lifestyle of Jesus. He longed to become poor. In an effort to share the fate of simple folk, he began carrying water from the well, chopping wood, tilling the fields at the side of his own peasants — even dressing up, sometimes, as a mujik.

Given that he couldn't bear the sight of chlorophyll and had never owned property of any sort, Sartre could scarcely set about chopping wood or ploughing fields with the French peasants. He did what he could, however, supporting the creation of a far-Left daily newspaper (*Libération*), and handing out copies of the government-censored Maoist rag *La Cause du peuple,* in front of the Renault factories in Billancourt.

Both men went to ludicrous lengths to shed their privileges and bring themselves down to the level of the "wretched of the earth." But (here, as with femininity) Tolstoy felt torn — because he also *loved* his privileges. He loved eating, hunting, playing the piano, and locking himself away in a comfortable study to write. Thus (again as with femininity), he went from one extreme to the other, bemoaning his weakness, making drastic resolutions only to break them a few days later, and despising himself for being incapable of living up to his ideals. Moreover, though now in his late fifties, he could not stop entering his wife's bedroom, making love to her and getting her with child. Sophie complained about this, but not too loudly.

Sartre tended to stay away from de Beauvoir's bedroom; it had been ages since his last visit. De Beauvoir complained about this, but not too loudly. And, thanks in part to the contraception and abortion championed by his life companion, Sartre found it easy to refrain from having children. He also found it unproblematical to stop inventing characters. Up until 1960 he continued writing novels and plays, all devoted to the theme of moral responsibility, the individual's obligation to make choices in the face of History; then even this didactic literature disappeared and Sartre gave up fiction altogether.

In the last twenty years of his life, he wrote only philosophical treatises, literary biographies, political articles and pamphlets. He comes across in these works, as an impassioned and generous man, anxious to put his moral authority at the service of what he sees as the best possible cause. Even in his most abstract moments, his artistic gift is apparent in the form of concrete examples, which stand out on the page like so many shining nuggets of fiction — but never again would he attempt to create minds and personalities different from his own. De Beauvoir, far from bemoaning the fact that her free artist had turned away from his art, applauded, imitated, and some say even surpassed his efforts to capture human reality in a net of theoretical constructs.

Sophie Tolstoy, on the contrary, with an aptness of judgement that might seem surprising in a woman with no diplomas, was grieved to see her husband forsake —

no, betray — his true vocation, which was literature, and write moralizing speeches instead. She hated them. She couldn't bear to copy them — they bored her stiff. Refusing to go along with her husband as he embarked on one crazy crusade after another, she consistently deplored his incursions into genres other than the novel and short story — sermons, lectures, political pamphlets.... As she wrote to him in a letter dated 27 October 1884, "Your taste for music, your impressions of nature, your wish to write — all of this is you, the real you, the one you're doing your best to kill, but which nonetheless remains alive, marvellously poetic and kind — the one who is loved by all who know you! And despite your all efforts you *shall* not kill it."

And she was right — despite all his efforts, he would not kill it. For, just as he couldn't help making love and babies, however desperately he tried to restrain himself, Tolstoy couldn't help writing fiction. In his novels as in the marriage bed, he kept engendering *other people*. It was an irresistible impulse. Seated at his writing desk — after, before, or even *during* the composition of his political and religious tirades — characters would materialize in his brain and begin to talk, gesticulate, *live*. He did his best to manipulate them, turn them into mouthpieces for his ideas — but it simply didn't work. His characters escaped him. They were free, independent, headstrong — truly something *other* than himself! Frighteningly, uncontrollably, like the roots of Roquentin's chestnut tree in *Nausea*, they kept growing, proliferating, and turning into WORKS OF ART!

At nearly sixty, for instance, Tolstoy wrote *The Death of Ivan Illitch* (1886), a stunning short story in which a man on his deathbed comes to grips with the frightening emptiness of his existence. Ah yes... because, you see, in a father's life time passes — there's no getting around it — and in novels time passes too; that's one of the laws of the genre, notwithstanding Roquentin's desperate attempts to bend and break this law.

A man who remains childless, and who thinks of himself exclusively as the son of his works, can go on telling himself that time does not pass. As the French psychoanalyst J.B. Pontalis has pointed out, if Sartre's screenplay project on the life of Freud never panned out, it may well have been because the research led him to see that "eliminating the father can imply spending one's entire life as the mere child of words." This, indeed, was the fundamental theme of Sartre's final "literary" work, *Words*, a magnificent if incomplete autobiography, giving an account of his life from birth to age eleven. In this book (the first section of which is entitled "Reading" and the second, "Writing,") Sartre demonstrated firstly that he had no father, secondly that his mother was his sister not to say his friend, and thirdly that his grandfather was nothing but an immense library. In other words, having miraculously engendered himself through the consumption and regurgitation of language, he had inherited nothing from, and therefore owed nothing to, any living person on this earth. "There *are* no good fathers; this is the rule," he wrote in this book. "It is not men who are to blame, but the father-child relation itself, which is rotten." One wonders what life experience could possibly have allowed this fatherless, sonless man to make such a sweeping generalization!

As Pontalis also points out, however, "the advantage and disadvantage of words is that they are connected only *among themselves*. Those who refuse to receive and transmit will forever fear that they are mere charlatans, verbal creatures, sleight-of-hand artists." Having feared exactly this during his crisis, Sartre now decided to publicly recant. Confronted by the members of his "family" at *Les Temps modernes*, who were in many ways his political superego, he apologized for having put a premium on artistic beauty. Years later (in the film *Sartre*, 1977), one of them needled him about it again: "When you wrote *The Words*, you did, I mean, how shall I put it, you did try to write it in the most beautiful prose possible, so that it would become — I despise this word — an art object, or at least, let's say, a book that would make an impact," and Sartre shamefacedly explained that he had wanted his farewell to literature to be as completely and superbly "literary" as possible. Now, he promised, it was over and done with. He had seen the light and would sin no more. Never again would he attempt to *épater les bourgeois*.

The gulf between Tolstoy and his children, as between Tolstoy and his characters, grew wider and wider. Sophie was not taken in — she *couldn't* be; she was witness to Tolstoy's life in its smallest details, as de Beauvoir was to Sartre's. On 25 July 1897, she wrote in her journal, "Today I recopied Lev Nikolaïevitch's essay on art. He speaks with indignation about the exaggerated importance given to love ("the erotic craze") in all works of art. And then this morning, Sasha said to me, 'My, papa is merry today! And because of him, all of us are merry!' If only she knew that her father is always merry because of that very love he wishes to deny!"

But Time, which continued to pass, was turning Tolstoy's own daughters into women. They were moving away from him, falling in love, making plans to marry. This he found intolerable. He firmly forbade his youngest and favourite daughter Sasha to marry, for he wanted her to be his spiritual heir. His attacks on physical love grew increasingly virulent; he now preached absolute chastity, even within marriage. He wrote *The Kreuzer Sonata*, a long short story whose hero, Pozdnychev, makes a mockery of those very stirrings of first love which Tolstoy himself had portrayed so movingly in *War and Peace*. Pozdnychev tells how, bound to a wife he detested more with every passing day, he murdered her in a fit of jealousy. Throughout the first section of the story, the hero is under his creator's thumb and can do nothing but spout Tolstoy's ideas: the only way to overcome the obscenities and humiliations of erotic desire, he says, is to abstain from sexual activity altogether. "You object that this would bring about the end of the human race?" Tolstoy wrote, in a letter to a friend, as he was working on *The Kreuzer Sonata*. "What a marvellous mishap! Antediluvian animals vanished from the surface of the earth, and the human animal will vanish, too.... I feel as little pity for this two-legged creature as I do for the ichtysaurus...." Gradually, however, Pozdnychev manages to escape his author's influence, put an end to his boring tirades against women and speak in his own voice — a voice which allows weakness, misery, and humanity to show through. The speechifying gives way to stunningly realistic scenes, the pace quickens, and the story culminates in an unforgettable cry from the heart.

Even after writing *The Kreuzer Sonata*, Tolstoy went back to Sophie's bedroom. The minute he emerged from it, he rushed to his writing-desk and wrote in his diary, "What if there's new baby? Oh, how ashamed I would be, especially in front of my children! They would compare the date [of conception] with that of my writing [*The Kreuzer Sonata*]!" Tolstoy was sixty-one at the time, and Sophie was forty-four. One can't help being puzzled by the fact that de Beauvoir, in her two-tome feminist opus *The Second Sex* ("Twins!" she told her American lover), repeatedly describes Sophie as someone who found physical love utterly repulsive. Having already given birth to thirteen children, surely Countess Tolstoy must have been capable of rejecting the advances of her over-ardent husband! The fact is that she did not. "All his coldness and severity melted away," she noted in her own journal, "and it all ended up in the same way, just as it always does! Now he's charming, joyous and tender again.... If present and future readers of *The Kreuzer Sonata* could catch a glimpse into Liovochka's love life, if they could see what it is that makes him so sweet and merry, they'd knock their deity off the pedestal on which they've placed him." It would seem doubtful that a rigid, frigid, abstemious wife could have made Tolstoy so "sweet and merry." Why, then, did de Beauvoir choose to depict her in this way? Could she possibly have been... jealous? On 4 March 1952, when she herself had reached her mid-forties, she wrote to her ex-American lover, "It makes me comfortable to think that my love life ended when it decently had to end. Because I hate the idea of aging women with aged bodies clinging to love!"

Tolstoy and Sartre had another thing in common: they mistreated and overworked their bodies, treating them as if they were negligible quantities. Both were workaholics who tended to write day and night; in addition, Tolstoy carried weights that were dangerous for his age and embarked on crash diets invariably followed by attacks of bulimia; as for Sartre, he consumed mind-boggling amounts of cigarettes, alcohol and amphetamines; neither listened to advice from friends about the need to take better care of the poor beasts whose job it was to trundle around their peerless souls. Predictably, both of them fell ill. Tolstoy, in 1899 (aged seventy-one) spent several months on death's doorstep; Sophie cared for him selflessly and managed to nurse him back to health. Sartre, as of the early 1960's, was increasingly physically diminished. He began to go blind, and suffered from numerous other ailments.

When a great man falls ill, he naturally starts thinking about his mortality — and, just as naturally, about his posterity. Despite vehement protestations from Sophie, Leo now allowed himself to be convinced by one of his disciples, a certain Vladimir Chertkov (aided and abetted by Tolstoy's youngest daughter Sasha), to reword his will so that all his royalties (and not only those dating from after his conversion in 1881, as had been stipulated in the first draft) would go to the Russian people instead of to his family.

De Beauvoir knew the story of Tolstoy's bamboozlement by Chertkov — in fact she devoted a lengthy passage to it in her book *Old Age* (1973). This didn't prevent Sartre, at the end of his life, from meeting up with a "Chertkov" of his own — a political activist by the name of Victor Louis (aka Benny Lévy). Despite vehement protestations from de Simone, Jean-Paul allowed this disciple (aided and abetted by Sartre's adoptive daughter Arlette Elkaïm), to publish books and interviews in which he repudiated virtually all of his past work.

Neither Sophie nor Simone were allowed to approach their partners as they made their final, momentous decisions. And neither would be with them at the moment of their deaths. Sophie, to her despair, was physically prevented by Chertkov and Sacha from attending Tolstoy as he agonized in the train station at Astopovo; as for de Beauvoir, she and Arlette Elkaïm took turns sitting at Sartre's bedside in the hospital — but when he entered a coma in the middle of the night, Arlette refrained from calling Simone and he was dead by the time she arrived the next day. It was the adopted daughter who inherited all of Sartre's personal belongings including his manuscripts, refusing to give de Beauvoir so much as a single souvenir of their five decades together.

Thus, in the end, both Sophie nor Simone were held at bay, kept in the dark, deprived of their moral rights.

Neither had any say about what was to become of their dear genius's work — a work they had generously and unstintingly helped to bring into being over a period of half a century.

On a psychological level, the moral of the story is twofold: firstly, it shows that freely-chosen relations can be every bit as brutal and unpredictable as those which are biologically "imposed." Secondly, it suggests that having (or raising) children and inventing characters, though not "the same thing," imply a similar acceptance of proliferating, uncontrollable human *life* — a similar "passivity," one might say. Of course, you don't need to be a parent in order to write good novels (such a claim would be absurd). On the other hand, it is possible that a systematic, theorized, permanent attitude of hostility towards nature, childbearing, children, the passage of time, the life-and-death cycle... may tend to sterilise the literary imagination.

The driving forces of this tale, however, are historical as well as psychological. That Tolstoy and Sartre were similarly tempted by didacticism, but that Sartre alone allowed himself to be reduced to it, cannot be chalked up to a mere difference in *temperament*; it is also due to a difference in *temporality*. Though their sojourns on Earth overlapped slightly (Sartre was born in 1905 and Tolstoy didn't die until 1910), they were anything but contemporaries; the world they aspired to comprehend and improve was not the same world. To put it briefly, as the 19th century shifted to the 20th, two major traumas took place — the death of God and the massacre of an entire generation of young men in World War I, throwing into question all the traditional values of Western civilisation (family, state, church). Age-old certainties collapsed. Links between generations were severed. There were no more fathers, no more bearings. A clean slate was made of the past.

A new literature emerged in Western Europe. Joyce... Kafka... Beckett... Musil... Sarraute.... Authors whose purpose was no longer to *observe and describe* people's lives, but rather to *reflect upon* them. The territory (brilliantly, meticulously, allegorically) staked out in their books was no longer the outer, but rather the inner world.

In many ways, World War II exacerbated this tendency. Perhaps because churches, monarchies, all historical forms of oppression had come disguised as beautiful stories, people grew wary of narratives and representation *per se* (a wariness theorised by Nathalie Sarraute in *The Age of Suspicion*). In other words, they no longer wanted to be led down the garden path.

"Our task is cut out for us," wrote Sartre in *What is Literature?* — "namely, to create a literature that reunites and reconciles the absolute of metaphysics with the relativity of historical fact." The problem is that literature doesn't arise from "shoulds," "musts" and "tasks cut out for us." As Romain Gary pointed out in *For Sganarelle*, what matters is not whether a novel is "art for art's sake" or "*engagé*, "what matters is whether it is *good*. To be good, it has to create a world the reader can believe in; other genres are available to those who seek instruction.

"There's a certain grain of stupidity," wrote Flannery O'Connor at about the same time, "that the writer of fiction can hardly do without, and this is the quality of having to stare, of not getting the point at once. The longer you look at one object, the more of the world you see in it; and it's well to remember that the serious fiction writer always writes about the whole world, no matter how limited his particular scene."

In France in particular, since World War II, the intelligence of Writers has tended to replace and obliterate the precious "stupidity" of novelists. Stories, the Writers decided, were for children. And it was of the utmost importance that we not be children — that we leave childhood behind and prove ourselves to be mature, rational, responsible human beings.

Today, twenty years after his death, Sartre still has considerable numbers of emulators in France — educated, eloquent men and women who care passionately about the common good and are convinced that it is possible to reconcile a literary vocation with involvement in teaching, journalism, philosophy, reportage, public debates, political activism — almost anything, in fact, except parenthood! Consciously or not, the paths followed by these emulators often resemble Sartre's own, starting out with novels, then moving on to plays, then essays, finding themselves increasingly enslaved to intelligence and maturity, and finally spending all of their time thinking, making speeches and driving their truths home to the rest of us — even in those books which they label "novels."

In other parts of the world, and even in some parts of Western Europe (Ireland, Great Britain, Sweden, Norway...), the novel continues to thrive in an impressive variety of forms. Faulkner never turned his back on storytelling — nor do Coetzee, Marquez, Morisson, Roy, McEwan, Lindgren, Ondaatje.... Fortunately for all their readers — including the French! — all these writers and many more have preserved their faith in characters and plots.

The truth (which common mortals generally recognize but which Writers tend to forget) is that there is a *tension* between solitude and solidarity — between the individual and the various groups to which he or she belongs — and that *this tension generates stories.* Were we devoid of social connections, extensions of ourselves in time and space, ancestors and descendants, no narratives would be possible. Tolstoy, partly because of his numerous offspring, but also because he frequented and studied every layer of Russian society (peasants and noblemen, prisoners and whores, soldiers and children...), experienced this tension every day of his life. This is what made him, against his own better judgment and even against his will, a giant of world literature. To the extent that he allowed his characters to invade and overrun him, he was a master; conversely, every time he insisted on dominating them, forcing them to mouth his own ideas (as in *Resurrection*, for instance), his writing lost its power. At sixty-seven, he performed the extraordinary feat of seeing himself from the outside, as if he were someone else, and turning himself into a character — *Father Serge*, a prideful man whose longing for moral perfection had something hateful and inhuman about it.

Sartre, whose connections and preoccupations were almost exclusively intellectual, was able to go on believing all his life in the preeminence of will and freedom. The following passage from *What is Literature?* illustrates this belief: "The writer is primarily a mediator," writes Sartre, "and his form of commitment is mediation. He may be Jewish, Czech, and of peasant stock, but he is a Jewish *writer*, a Czech and rurally-rooted *writer*." In other words, between a quality given at birth (peasant stock) and a freely-chosen quality (writer), the latter is more precious and important because it implies the intervention of the will. This is unquestionably true in a political or legal perpective — one should not be punished for a trait that is independent of one's free will. But it so happens that imagination, writing, and art obey a different logic, and it was just this difference that Sartre was unable to fathom. *Citizens* should be neither helped nor hindered by their religious, social or sexual appurtenances. But if *writers* cut themselves off from their childhoods, their roots, their physical, imaginary and ancestral memories, they deprive themselves of almost everything that contributes to art. It is precisely these "contingencies" — these vulnerabilities, these forms of "immanence" — that empower them as artists. "The thing that prevents you from writing," Marina Tsvetaeva once said "— that is your true *creative* biography."

It is clear, I hope, that my purpose in telling this story has not been to "sing the praises of the family." Rather, it has been to make a plea in favour of narrative by recalling the literally infinite wealth and potential of individual reality. And this reality necessarily implies *relationships*, both familial and social — for these are what form and deform, delight and damage every one of us. Instead of simplifying through analysis and ratiocination, we need to leave room for complexity and contradiction — and take up the exhilarating challenge of the fact that other people truly do exist, both inside and outside of us.

(2000)

DESTROY, SHE SAID
*Elfriede Jelinek**

*"I wield my axe with all my might,
so that not a blade of grass can grow
where my characters have tread."*
— Elfriede Jelinek

I think that in all my reading life, I've never encountered an author less convivial than Elfriede Jelinek. What do I mean by convivial? "When you read Nabokov," writes Martin Amis, "he welcomes you into his home, gives you his best armchair, makes sure that you are comfortable, pours you a glass of his wine and tries to make everything as agreeable as possible. If you go to Joyce's place, he'll shout to you from the back of the kitchen to come on in, *Have a seat*, he'll tell you, he'll be in the midst of preparing some disgusting punch — *Here, taste this* — and if you throw up it will be fine with him. It is not a matter of courtesy but rather of love for the reader, and the writers I appreciate have that love."

To enter Elfriede Jelinek's "house," you need an iron nerve. The place is crowded and noisy, it's almost impossible

---

*This is a chapter of my book on nihilism in contemporary Western European literature *Professeurs de désespoir*. It was published in September 2004 — i.e., just before Elfriede Jelinek received the Nobel Prize.

to understand the floor plan and, far from making sure that you are comfortable, the hostess spends her time aggressing you and shoving you into around. Meaning is shredded, syntax is chaotic, and it is hard to remain unaffected by the violence the author exerts in all directions, attacking not only the reader but her characters and language itself.

Elfriede Jelinek was born in Mürzzuschlag, in the Austrian province of Styria, in 1946. She was an only child. At the time of her birth, her father was forty-six years old and her mother, forty-two. There is an explanation for their decision to found a family so late in life: "My father," says Jelinek in an interview with Adolf-Ernest Meyer, "only dared to have a child once he was certain that the war had been lost." And why was this? Jelinek's father was Jewish, and the Nazi regime had spared him from deportation because he'd agreed to carry out research contributing to the war effort in his field, chemistry. Just what this implied is not known. It didn't necessarily imply that he invented the formula for Zyklon B, but "contributing to the war effort" says what it says.

His objective collaboration with the government that was carrying out the extermination of his people was to leave an indelible imprint on Friedrich Jelinek. In the early 1950s he became mentally ill, withdrawing into total silence and washing himself obsessively.... Questioned about her father's illness, Elfriede would later describe it as a "powerful neurotic disturbance, a progressive cretinism." "My father was like a heavy shadow weighing on the family," she said. "He was unable to play the conventional father's role, but his silence shaped our family life in important ways." When Elfriede reached adolescence, the situation grew untenable — she and her mother had the father committed to the psychiatric clinic of Steinhof, where he would remain until his death.

As for the mother... she was at least as disturbed as the father; in fact, if everything Elfriede says about her is true, she was something of a monster. To get some idea of what *kind* of monster she was, it suffices to read Jelinek's seventh novel *The Pianist*, which gained world-wide fame a quarter of a century after its publication thanks to the fact that Michael Heineke turned it into a "major motion picture" starring Isabelle Huppert.

Elfriede has quite a bit in common with the novel's heroine, whose name is Erika. Like Erika, as of early childhood she displayed an exceptional gift for music, and her mother put her on a strict regime of piano and composition lessons. Indeed, Elfriede's mother seems to have been convinced that her daughter had an exceptional gift for just about everything, and she organized her days accordingly. All forms of pleasure were forbidden — going out, having friends, playing, taking part in life. She had the right to do one and only one thing: work. "Everything that might have brought me the least amount of physical pleasure, however harmless, was denied me," said Elfriede later on.

Seeing that her daughter was going to be tall, and dreading the awkward movements that might result from this, Mrs. Jelinek forced Elfriede to take ballet lessons between the ages of three and sixteen. In classical ballet, as Elfriede points out, "you're never relaxed. Even the most relaxed movements are the result of a ferocious discipline." Fortunately, the young girl was allowed to play in a chamber music group and an orchestra — these were her only moments of interaction with other people. "That saved my life, emotionally," she says. One shudders to think what might become of her without it.

Despite her ballet lessons (or because of them?), the little girl developed a strange way of moving: "I ran around all the time," she says, "and it drove people crazy. It's a way of moving that is often found in autistic children. I'd spend hours running back and forth from one room to another; it frightened not only my mother, but even the pediatrician." Later on, her writing would be characterized by just this autistic form of hyperactivity. Her novels and plays are an unstoppable outpouring of words which — like her daily life as a child — never leave space for breathing or relaxation. "What interests me," Jelinek would later say, "is the fact of not-having-learned-how-to-live. All we learned were strategies for avoiding and bypassing life." Elfriede would treat her characters exactly as she herself was treated as a child, doing everything in her power to *prevent them from living*.

When Elfriede reached adolescence — the age of flirting, blushing, and dreaming about love — her mother tightened the screws even further. There was no question that her daughter should enter the world of sexuality. Consequently, Elfriede would see all of her experiments in this area as transgressions; pleasure, in her mind, would henceforth be inextricably linked with guilt. Again like Erika, the main protagonist of *The Pianist*, Elfriede became a self-proclaimed masochist. "The transgression of my mother's sexual taboos certainly fed my masochism, if it didn't create it in the first place," she says. "Thanks to those taboos, I am a masochist and I enjoy it."

The most irrefutable proof of Jelinek's masochism is that, apart from a brief parenthesis of married life, she would continue to live alone with her perverse, cruel mother until the latter's death in the 1990s.

In 1964 she published her first poems and began studying theater and art history in Vienna, but had to leave school after a few semesters for reasons of mental fragility. In 1968, she locked herself away in her mother's home and lived there as a recluse for an entire year. The following year, however — "liberated," perhaps, by the death of her father — she launched into political activism. For Elfriede as for many other disoriented young people of the time, theoretical dogma was a convenient putty that filled up the fissures of a threatened identity. She immersed herself in readings in politics, psychoanalysis and structuralism. Sigmund Freud became one of her major references; indeed, she would often show surprising servility with respect to Freudian theory.

In 1971 she received her diploma as an organist — with distinction — from the Vienna Conservatory. Over the next two years, living now in Berlin, now in Rome, she wrote her first radio plays... 1974 was an important year in her life: at twenty-eight, she married Gottfried Hüngsberg (a close collaborator of Fassbinder's), joined the Communist Party (of which she would remain a member until... 1991, two years *after* the fall of the Wall), and published *Women as Lovers*. Now that she'd gotten started, there would be no stopping her.

Her marriage was shortlived; once it was over she became a homosexual and peremptorily declared (oblivious to the counter-examples rampant in our day and age): "For a woman, no serious artistic life can be compatible with having children." Given that leading a serious artistic life was what she cared about more than anything in the world, motherhood was out of the question. She wrote frenetically, churning out dozens of novels and screenplays, translations and plays, and meeting with success in all of these different genres: virtually all the German literary prizes were bestowed upon her: the Henrich Böll Prize in 1986, the Büchner Prize in 1998, the Heine Prize in 2002...

What, exactly, was being thus rewarded?

It is impossible to characterize Elfriede Jelinek's literary works as anything but works of hatred. Even typographically, they are aggressive; the reader strives in vain to grasp the logic behind the different paragraph indentations and print types. The predominant tone of voice is that of devastating irony. And the main subject: the war between the sexes.

Jelinek's vocabulary is permeated with the Marxist, psychoanalytic and linguistic concepts she absorbed in her youth — they serve as a pretext for her destructiveness: "My texts are close to those of [Roland] Barthes," she claims in her introduction to *Lust*. "They purport to do nothing but destroy myths, that is, restore the history and the truth of things."

Elfriede Jelinek's texts do not, in fact, "restore the history and the truth of things"; what they do is demonstrate the impotence of women. The same message is driven home over and over again: man is the norm, woman is the Other; men take up all the room; they direct, create and transform reality, whereas women can only look at the world from the outside, like children or extraterrestrials. Jelinek deprives women (herself excluded) of all forms of initiative and freedom. To write, she says, is to attempt to become a subject; but whereas "men disappear into their works, women, despite all their efforts to disappear, reappear." It is unfortunate that an author of Elfriede Jelinek's prestige and influence should formulate a theory of female creativity so inferior to the one advanced by Virginia Woolf almost a century earlier. Again, the only exception to the rule is apparently Jelinek herself — "People resent me," she says, "because of my phallic insistence on making art and thus turning myself into a subject."

Let us examine how this works in *The Pianist*, which, of all Jelinek's novels, is the one that has sold the most copies and been translated into the most languages. As of the book's opening chapters, an implacable logic is set up according to which the heroine, aggressed by an invasive mother, has no choice but to aggress herself. One of the characteristics of Jelinek's texts is that they move without transition from descriptions of reality to descriptions of fantasy (both equally sinister). "Mother, without prior notice, unscrews the top of HER head, sticks her hand inside, self-assured, and then grubs and rummages about. Mother messes everything up and puts nothing back where it belongs. Making a quick choice, she plucks out a few things, scrutinizes them closely, and tosses them away. Then she rearranges a few others and scrubs them thoroughly with a brush, a sponge, and a dustrag. Next, she vigorously dries them off and screws them in again. The way you twist a knife into a meatgrinder."

Erika, the little girl thus mistreated by her mother, responds by conducting experiments on her own body with a razor blade. At first she contents herself with incising the back of her hand: "For an instant, a slit gapes in the previously intact tissue; then the arduously tamed blood rushes out from behind the barrier." When she reaches adolescence, the girl attacks her own genitals; significantly, it is now mentioned that the razor blade belongs to her sick father: "She is very skilled in the use of blades; after all, she has to shave her father, shave that soft paternal cheek under the completely empty paternal brow, which is now undimmed by any thought, unwrinkled by any will. This blade is destined for HER flesh.... Like the mouth cavity, this opening cannot exactly be called beautiful, but it is necessary.... It's still in her hands, and a hand has feelings too. She knows precisely how often and how deep...."

I will not quote the remainder of this passage which, to me, is unbearable.

Erika grows up to fulfill her mother's wishes and become a pianist, or at least a piano teacher. Her life is split between the lofty and the shabby, between exquisite classical music and sordid sexuality. Even as she holds forth on the subject of counterpoint in Bach, she goes to peep-shows and watches anonymous couples fucking in the city's wastelands.

As she describes a few weeks in the life of her pianist character, Jelinek goes through all the mandatory stations of nihilistic philosophy. She rants and raves against good health: " Health — how disgusting... Health always sides with the victors; the weak fall away." She describes Austrians as alcoholic, petty, self-satisfied and smug. She despises families, which of course transmit nothing but repression: "Young mothers begin their daily march behind the bars of the Castle Garden. The first 'Prohibited' signs are hurled down on gravel walks. From their heights, the mothers drip venom." She has a saintly horror of "crowds," and is convinced that to become an individual, one must be a great artist (like herself.) "People can barely make it alone, they have to move in packs.... Such are the thoughts of Erika, a loner. Nocturnal slugs, shapeless, spineless, mindless! .... They stick to one another with their skins, which are never agitated by a puff of air."

In this passage, Erika is mentally addressing her student Walter Klemmer, whom she will later ask to bind, gag and rape her. Given this project, it is interesting to see how *she* victimizes the "third-class audience" of this piano concert: "One has to tyrannize them, one has to suppress them and oppress them, just to get through to them. One should use clubs on them!... They want shouts and shrieks, otherwise they would have to shout and shriek all the time. Out of boredom."

The surest sign of nihilism, not only in *The Pianist* but in all of Jelinek's writings, is the perception of passing time as a catastrophe. The minute we are born, death begins its work of undermining; life is synonymous with decomposition; only works of art remain pure and sacred, outside and above this universal rotting process. "Erika compulsively sees people and food dying everywhere.... Such are Erika's thoughts. And everything confirms them. Only art, she reflects, can survive longer." Nothing embodies putrescible flesh better than the female genitals; it is unusual, and rather dismaying, to read such a horror of femininity penned by a woman: "Rot between her legs, an unfeeling soft mass. Decay; putrescent lumps of organic material.... Striding along, Erika hates that porous, rancid fruit that marks the bottom of her abdomen." Here again, "Only art promises endless sweetness."

Far from being the origin of life, the vagina is the very image of death: "Soon the decay will progress, encroaching upon larger parts of her body. Then she will die in torment. Dismayed, Erika pictures herself as a numb hole, six feet of space, disintegrating in the earth. The hole that she despised and neglected has now taken full possession of her. She is nothing. And there is nothing left for her."

Readers might be surprised to learn the age of the woman who is obsessed by these dark thoughts: thirty-six. An old lady, the author tells us repeatedly (when she wrote the novel, she was ten years younger than her heroine). "Erika's face is starting to get marked by its future decay.... Erika's decay knocks with scurrying fingers.... Maybe he's the last man who'll ever desire me, Erika thinks furiously, and soon I'll be dead, only another thirty-five years, Erika thinks angrily"; as for Walter Klemmer, the piano student whom she wants to become her lover-torturer, he "thinks about how far he has gone on his mountain streams, but he has never come across such a woman! He won't seek new shores with her: smelly old sewer, he calls her joylessly." He jeers at Erika, tells her that she is old and that she stinks.

Given the fact that in Jelinek's universe, man is to woman is as master is to slave, the only way for a woman to become a master is to *desire* her position as slave. This is why Erika asks Klemmer to torture her: "Did he get it right: By becoming her master, he can never become her master? So long as she dictates what he should do to her, some final remnant of Erika will remain unfathomable." Sexuality being always and only a power game, women need to use lies, wiles and manipulation, pretending to be martyrized when in fact they are in control. "The woman wants to choke on Klemmer's stone-hard dick when she is so thoroughly tied up that she can't move at all."

Klemmer ends up "losing it"; he comes to Erika's place and beats her to a pulp, breaking her nose and one of her ribs, then raping her and leaving her in a bloody heap with her clothes torn to shreds. After the angry lover's departure, Erika's mother cleans her up, tends to her wounds, comforts and consoles her. Towards the end of the book, overcome with love, Erika "throws herself upon Mother, showering her with kisses," even as she thinks to herself, half in tenderness and half in revulsion, "She is flesh of this flesh! A crumb of this maternal cake!"

Once she has recovered from the attack, Erika goes out into the city armed with a knife to look for Walter, but she ends up plunging the blade into her own shoulder.

This, briefly summarized, is the most universally admired of Elfriede Jelinek's novels.

The others are of the same ilk. Sometimes the author finds her inspiration in news items. Such is the case with *Wonderful, Wonderful Times* (1980) — a novel which describes how a young boy murders his entire family. The middle-class family in question is perfect for the author's needs. The father is a former Nazi who has become a photographer; he spends his time making pornographic photos of his wife while calling her "you whore" and "you slut"; he does close-ups of her genitals while noisily complaining that she hasn't washed her pubic hair as he told her to.

This father character is worth taking a closer look at. In an interview published at the end of the novel's French edition, Jelinek speaks at length about the Nazis in Austria and about the poetess Ingeborg Bachmann. "We children born right after the war," she says, "have to face up to the fact that Nazi crimes .... didn't arise out of nowhere, nor did they vanish into nothingness; these crimes can't simply have disappeared after 1945. And Bachmann gives us an answer: *the family*, in which women and children are pariahs or niggers, and in which the man (the father) is the criminal."

Though Ingeborg Bachmann did indeed denounce the oppressive structure of the Austrian family, and though one of her female characters (in the novel *Malina*) said that "fascism" was the first element in any relationship between a man and a woman, her poetry and short stories show complex and sometimes magnificent relationships between men and women (including fathers and daughters); their moral universe is quite at odds with the Manicheism that characterizes Jelinek's work.

Jelinek reduces Bachmann's thinking on the subject to the simplistic terms of her own. Even her description of the typical Austrian family — woman and children as pariahs or niggers; man (father) as criminal — is far less accurate today than it was half a century ago, when Bachmann was writing. More interestingly, it is in flagrant contradiction with what we know about Jelinek's own family. There, as she herself admits, "the father was always the oppressed one; it was the mother who dominated." Isn't not strange (to say the least) that Elfriede, herself victimized by a powerful woman, should feel the need to endlessly repeat that women are everywhere victimized by men?

By setting up an utterly despicable character as of the first pages of her novel (a former SS involved in pornography — what more could you ask for?), Jelinek gives herself a stamp of moral superiority in her readers' eyes, which then allows her to do whatever she wants, including give us detailed descriptions of scenes as perverse and cruel as pornography.

The couple's twin children, Rainer and Anna, are in their early teens. They've read smatterings of French existentialist theory (what they gleaned from Jean-Paul Sartre was essentially the idea of nausea). Anna shares a number of traits with the heroine of *The Pianist*. "Constantly," like Erika, "she is on the verge of exploding with rage"; she's an accomplished musician (with a marked preference for Bach), and already, at the age of fourteen, a past master of self-mutilation: "She is sitting naked on the floor, legs apart, trying to deflower herself with the aid of an old shaving mirror and a razor blade, to rid herself of a membrane that is supposedly down there. But she knows nothing about anatomy and cuts into her perinaeum by mistake. Which bleeds fearfully."

What is shocking about this sort of passage is its icy irony — "she knows nothing about anatomy"; "which bleeds fearfully" — in other words, the author's prideful, contemptuous indifference to a character who in all likelihood resembles her. The reader has no choice but to join her in this ironic stance. There is no way we can get close to that little girl, take her into our hearts or even attempt to understand her; the author's sarcasm keeps her (and everything else) at a distance.

Rainer and Anna despise their parents. More than anything, Anna hates her mother's body (she gluts on the works of Georges Bataille...): "Once, when she was still a child, she watched Mummy in the bathtub.... Revolting.

A body such as that is simply an appendage to a person, and one that easily spoils. It isn't the main thing."

As the story unfolds, Anna grows increasingly mute and anorexic. This is one of the unavoidable side effects of nihilism on women — you hate your mother, you hate the body you most closely resemble; it's only natural that you end up hankering after non-existence: "Sometimes she stopped talking and sometimes she stopped eating; nothing crossed her lips, not even soup, and if it did, she would stick her fingers down her throat and bring back the perfectly innocent soup in a powerful jet of vomit."

Again, Jelinek's response to suffering is to make fun of it; she undertakes to destroy everything in the smallest detail. "The perfectly innocent soup" is a phrase that an S.S. officer could well have pronounced with a snigger, before delivering a blow to the head of a Jew who had just brought up his lunch.

The entire book is written in the same tone of voice. Rainer ends up killing the three members of his family (including his adored twin), attacking them first with a gun, then with an axe, and finally with a bayonet. The author give us the details with great gusto, and the passage ends with the usual tone of fatigued sarcasm: "Now, at last, he is through. The bleeding heaps of humanity are not making a sound. Nor can they be told apart anymore. After all, Death the Leveller annihilates all distinctions. The sexes of the bodies can still be just about made out, but nothing else. You have to take your bearings from that if you want to decide which corpse is whose."

In the interview published at the end of the novel's

French edition, Jelinek says, "Rainer reminded me a great deal of my own diabolical family structure, the dark atmosphere which reigned in our apartment, and I very much identified with him, except that I was saved by writing."

It may be true that writing saved Elfriede Jelinek from madness or criminality. The question nonetheless remains: what obliges us to say that what she writes is great? Is this is really the literature we believe should be read and rewarded? How much violence are we prepared to inflict on ourselves in the sacrosanct name of art? What on earth is going on, if we give our aesthetic approval to this meticulous, methodical trampling of all that is human?

For centuries, novelists and playwrights had the extraordinary privilege of giving birth to human beings in the form of characters — endowing them with life, and inviting their readers to engage in that intrinsically moral activity known as *identification*. (What is moral is not to identify with a "moral" character but identification *per se*, i.e., the ability to put oneself in another person's shoes.)

With Jelinek (as with nihilistic writers generally), identification goes down the drain. It is considered old-fashioned. Kitsch. Over and done with. Let's get rid of the vermin. (One of Romain Gary's most frightening quips comes to mind: "You start out by excluding the character from the novel, and you end up by murdering six million Jews.")

"I refuse to create life on stage," Jelinek bluntly

declares. "What I want is just the opposite: *to create what is not alive.* I want to make all life disappear forever from the stage of the theater. I do not want theater. I wield my axe with all my might, so that not a blade of grass can grow where my characters have tread."

Once you've decided to mistreat people in this way — to *prevent them from living* — it's easy to find theoretical justifications for your decision. Jelinek's books teem with references and quotations; at the beginning of *Malady, or Modern Women*, for instance, she thanks Baudrillard, Barthes, Gœbbels, Bram Stocker, Joseph Sheridan and others from whom she has borrowed scraps of wisdom... Ah! thinks the reader. She must be a knowledgeable lady indeed! But Jelinek never quotes these writers to help us think something through; she quotes them sarcastically, to prove that our brains are garbage cans. "I can't repeat myself often enough," she says: "originality is impossible in our day and age; everything has been said; all we can do is repeat and quote." Just as, in her opinion, individual differences have faded into insignificance in the modern world, ideas, phrases, emotions and stories are all stereotyped; literature has said it all; the best we can do is juggle with clichés until they admit to being clichés.

Jelinek doesn't seem to realize that her disenchanted reflections on "modernity" are in fact old saws. In his book on the modern novel *Pour Sganarelle* (1965), Romain Gary already deplored "the pitiful joke about 'it's all been done before,' as they were saying two thousand years ago under King Solomon. A truly pathetic excuse.... Whether human beings change a little or a lot…, the relationships among individual identities and their milieus are constantly changing, and the sum of these relationships is modified from day to day, giving the novelist his point of departure, an inexhaustible wealth of novelistic material that only God could embrace, with no conceivable limit because it is in perpetual kaleidoscopic movement, the kaleidoscope itself being different with every novelist."

This is the magnificent challenge which novelists worthy of the name try to meet. But it's so much easier to sigh, "Nothing new under the sun"…

"Jelinek's plays are not psychological," the French publisher of *Malady, or Modern Women* warns us in his introduction to the play. "Her language is… crisscrossed by a sub-language made up of idiomatic or proverbial expressions, alliterations, classic texts quoted like advertising slogans. The characters do not so much speak their language as they are spoken by it. She catches them in her trap."

As one reads the play, this is indeed the impression one gets. But isn't it rather childish to catch people you have created in a trap you have created, and make them seem ridiculous by giving them ridiculous things to say? Given that her plays are "not psychological," Jelinek is free to invent totally unrealistic characters — puppets who illustrate her personal convictions to perfection.

Women are frustrated at being women? Of course they are; Emily, the heroine of *Malady*, says so in as many words: "I'll never be completely immortal," she sighs.

"Too bad — only halfway, like everything our unfortunate sex does."

Men are monsters of brutality and egoism? Of course they are. "May I get rid of your wife's head?" asks Heidkliff. "May I stick her? Here's what we shall do at once…: club them with a weight. They don't deserve motherhood. They're unworthy of the paradise of birth. Let's clean out her head, stuff up her mouth and cunt with garlic. A stake through the heart, pounded in…"

In case we're still not convinced, here is additional proof: "They're nothing but cold warders," says Benno. "Slave guards. And they never put things back in order. Their wombs proliferate! Then they kick it out of the house, there you go! The world is what falls, it's true for everyone!"

Readers may or may not know that *the world is what falls* is a quote from Ludwig Wittgenstein. Apart from the rejection of all possible originality, the use of quotations allows Jelinek to dominate her readers: convinced that they must be "missing" most of her allusions, incapable of following, they feel anxious, stupid and inferior.

In the end, Emily and her friend Camilla manage to break away from the norms of femininity imposed by society. And what do they do, once they are authentically liberated? Just as Rainer murdered his parents and sister, they murder their children.

"Mysterious, filtered light. Emily and Camilla are standing silently in the room… Then the two women leap on the two children like wolves and knock them over. A terrible battle ensues, for the children put up a fight. The women sink their fangs into the children's throats. The baby cries: 'Mommy! Mommy!' The women drink all of the children's blood, as the men look on indifferently.... The children agonize, their bodies trembling. The women merely raise their heads from time to time, briefly, before they go back to sucking..."

Is this Jelinek's idea of a feminist victory? Not even that. At the end of the play, Emily and Camilla — who have become a gigantic "DOUBLE CREATURE," "Siamese sisters" sown into a single garment — are murdered in turn by the men. The murder is committed light-heartedly, nonchalantly, and accompanied by comments whose misogyny turns the stomach.

Jelinek justifies the extreme violence of her writing by describing her work as critical, subversive, radical. Here, for instance, is how (in the introduction to the French edition) she characterizes the novel *Lust*, published in 1989 (we should remember that she was still a card-carrying Communist at the time): "Let's say I start out with the following hypothesis: within the capitalist system, individualism has become impossible.... Given this impossibility, we find ourselves with characters who no longer act in their own names, but are mere revealers of a language. *Of course no one likes to be told that his behaviour can in fact be reduced to a series of structures, but it is the truth.* Thus, sexuality in *Lust* is reduced to power relations in a market economy such as they are exercised everywhere in our society — the appropriation of bodies; the helplessness of those who are 'possessed,' and who possess nothing" (emphasis mine).

Jelinek herself, one assumes, is not liable to be "reduced to a series of structures." Neither are we, her readers. Only "other people" — that is, her characters, who are stand-ins for "other people." Yet on the strength of this very dubious "hypothesis," Jelinek feels justified in inflicting upon us, yet again, the most alienating and abject sexual encounters, out of doors, in abandoned lots, with no words exchanged....

In a word, Jelinek appeals to what is lowest in her readers, namely *elitist gregariousness*. Watching her plays, reading her novels, we think, "I understand that these people are assholes; therefore I myself am not an asshole." Our pleasure comes from our relief at finding ourselves on the "right" side — that is, on the side of the author, at one with her *authority*, her writing power. Forced into this position, we have no choice but to be scornful of the men and women Jelinek is destroying with her pen ("I'm an office murderer," she blithely says); she obliges us to share in her hatred and condescension.

Jelinek says that when writing *Lust*, she finally found the style she had always been looking for, an almost painfully dense style which she describes as "pressed, compressed." "I need this compression, carried to the utmost limit." Sometimes, she acknowledges, "it's too much for the reader" — he never has the least respite. "Of course it is madness; even in Bach's fugues, there are interludes during which the organist can relax and play more freely, before the themes and counterpoints and successive voices resume. But this is just what I find impossible. It would be a solution — a way of winding down after orgasm — with me, orgasm is non-stop."

Here, then, is the humble hypothesis I would like to formulate concerning Elfriede Jelinek: in her books, women are insulted, beaten, raped, humiliated, oppressed, ridiculed, degraded, and despoiled not by men, but by Jelinek herself, for reasons which have to do with her personal history. Having taken her mother's place, she manipulates, directs and controls everything that happens in her texts, forcing the words and characters to do exactly as she tells them.

It is enlightening to listen to her describe the way she uses language: "You don't settle comfortably into the language. You have to force it to acknowledge its lies, even when it doesn't want to... I force language to reveal the ideological dimension of words. I never let it rest — I drag it out of bed. Where that comes from, I don't know."

But in fact she knows quite well "where that comes from," and so do we — she drags language out of bed because her mother dragged *her* out of bed, every morning of her childhood. She hasn't forgotten the little girl she once was, who ran back and forth from one room to the other, indefatigably, for hours on end.... No rest allowed. Frenetic activity: piano lessons, ballet lessons, studying, working. Maniacal supervision of her clothes, her posture, her every word and gesture. Unbearable. Now she imposes the same infernal regime on us, and it gives her pleasure — a "non-stop orgasm."

She knows "where that comes from," and indeed she says so, quite lucidly and detachedly: "It probably has to do with my precarious situation as a child. When a child grows up in the middle of a catastrophe, between its parents and the rest of the world, when it finds serenity nowhere — and when the only powerful authority, that of the mother, is a source not of security but of additional threat — *that child has the feeling of not being born*" (emphasis mine).

If you haven't been born, you've got no choice but to give birth to yourself through words. You are led, Jelinek says, "to force words to be born, and squeeze everything they contain out of them. *Perhaps my writing is the transposition of my maternal instinct.*" This sentence should be read in conjunction with another, where Jelinek uses a very different metaphor to describe her literary activity: *"In writing, I give free rein to my murderous impulses"* (emphasis mine).

Thus, we have come full circle. Destroy, she said. Mothers kill their children. To give birth is to deal death. The powerless little girl is now a powerful writer; the child who received death as her inheritance has turned into a literary "mother," giving birth, over and over again, to words that kill. And what they kill, preferably, is women. Jelinek is a clever lady: on the fallacious pretext of denouncing patriarchal and capitalist society, she manages not only to express her morbidity, her rage and her hatred (including her hatred of herself), but also... to make money.

So then the question becomes: *why do we buy this?*

(2004)

BELONGINGS

Reassuring Strangeness

I went to Europe to look for myself,
but I wasn't there, either.
— *American adage*

It is my accent — slight but ineradicable — which invariably sets off the litany of queries: "Are you American?" "No, Canadian." "English Canadian, then." "Yes, from the West — Alberta." A blank stare; it is clear that this declaration evokes nothing in the minds of the people I'm speaking to, and what's hard to explain is that it doesn't evoke a great deal in my own mind, either. Vague images of landscapes — mountain lakes or wheatfields — float across the silence between us and evaporate; I'm distressed to be unable to come up with words to fill the vaccuum created by the naming of my native province. Of course, there are big cities there, with populations of half a million and more. Of course, I grew up there. But no stories, in the past or present tense, allow me to lay claim to a real *heritage* connected to this background. From my schooling I know that the history of Alberta is that of the American West in general — the subduing of indigenous populations in the 19th century through murder or religion, the construction of reserves for the Indians, towns and cities for the Whites. Both the architecture and the ideology of Western Canada are relentlessly, irremediably modern. And English-Canadian culture is a diluted, somewhat "Britainized" version of American culture. *Voilà*....

How can Europeans fathom the utter absence of what they cherish more than anything else: rootedness? Even as a child, I never felt that tremor of patriotism which is apparently familiar to all children in the Old World; even as a child, I experienced Albertan reality as bland and homogeneous; everywhere I looked, perfunctory kindness and polite platitudes were the rule; neutrality reigned.

Life's roads twist and turn. I left Alberta. The story of my adult life is that of a quest, not so much for *identity* as for *intensity*. My family moved to the Eastern Seaboard of the United States; how does it happen that I had a sense of *recognition* the minute I set eyes on the old houses of New England? How can I explain the *relief* I felt, contemplating landscapes that had been cultivated for more than two hundred years? In New York, a word finally began to attach itself to the representation of this *otherness* I so ardently desired — the word "Jewish." The Lower East Side, which at the time was still a poor Jewish neighbourhood, moved me like a shred of dream that comes back to life during the day — it was my *Unheimlich*, my uncanny, at once mysterious and profoundly familiar. (In Canada, I'd learned of the existence of Jews only because one of my classmates celebrated New Year's at an odd date....)

And then Paris. An exile that was intended to be temporary — a joyfully chosen exile, something like a studious vacation period, gradually swelled until it engulfed my entire existence, my very being. Even now, when I try to explain this, I meet with incomprehension: "When are you planning to go home?" "Uh... never." Which home do they mean? Why should the arbitrary place of my birth have any rights over my present desires? Why shouldn't I invent my own roots? "I don't believe in national determinism."

That is the statement of a person with privilege. Nothing is easier for a young intellectual than to declare herself stateless and antipatriotic. Nothing could be more tempting for her than to write off identity labels as alienating. Especially the one people want to glue onto her forehead right off the bat: "American in Paris," paying nostalgic homage to the Lost Generation, a member of that loosely-knit community that roams around the Place Saint-Opportune, the Rue du Dragon, the Rue de Fleurus and the Boulevard Raspail. Few people elicit my empathy less than these tourists who are too lazy to leave, who talk in loud voices in cafés and strum guitars in the métro. When, addressing me in my mother tongue, one of them asks for directions in the street, I'm as shocked as if they'd exposed themselves (how dare they talk "all naked" like that?); I'm almost tempted to pretend I don't understand them, so obscene to my ears are the sounds of English uttered in a foreign land, so brutal is this eruption of "the banal" in a reality whose thin layer of exoticism I find so precious and so protective.

Mine is a voluntary exile — thus, I have nothing in common with "real" exiles, either — immigrant workers, dissidents, refugees — people who have been forced to leave their native lands for "real" (i.e. political or economic) reasons, rather than on an existential whim. They find themselves in Paris, speak French haltingly or not at all, are often physically different from the French. Oppressed and rejected as a group, they tend to stick together for support. The annual ritual of renewing residence permits is far more humiliating for them, swarthy and stammering, than it is for me, white and bilingual; and when I walk through their neighbourhoods, they almost certainly see me as a Frenchwoman.

I'm not, though. I'm a foreigner and I intend to remain one forever, preserving a certain distance between myself and the world around me, taking nothing about it for granted — neither its language, its values, nor its history. In Paris, I was rapidly drawn to the ancient center of the city, where dozens of layers of history are superimposed; I live in a neighbourhood — the Marais — which contains the vestiges of medieval royalty, the golden aristocracy of the 17th century, the French Revolution and the Second World War. All of these layers refer to a past that is not my own. Yet it is here that I feel at home — in these streets whose every storeowner and tramp are now familiar to me.

There are many different ways of getting to "know" the Marais. If I were a francophile, I'd visit all the 17th-century mansions, drift through the long hallways of Madame de Sévigné's home, become an *habituée* of the Carnavalet Museum and memorize the etymologies of street names. If I were Jewish, I'd attend services at the synagogue on the Rue des Ecouffes, stop to meditate before the monument to the Jews deported to Auschwitz, read the numerous depressing inscriptions over doorways. A plaque above the entrance to my own building bears the name of a 22-year-old Jewish girl murdered by the Gestapo — no doubt she lived here. I say "no doubt" because in fact I'm not absolutely sure of this, and my uncertainty is what guarantees the permanence of my state of exile. I learn French history by bits and snatches, furtively, almost surreptitiously — and forget it as I go along. The stones of these buildings have been here for a very long time — *this* is what impresses me, far more than learning the name of the king who put them here. (Perhaps the solidity of things-that-stay counterbalances my panic about time-that-passes.) I need to be surrounded by signs of History. I need to know that men, women and children have been walking for centuries on these self-same sidewalks, or looking out over this self-same pattern of rooftops... but I also need to *preserve a certain distance* from all these signs. I know they don't belong to me, nor do the fabulous stories they tell — except, precisely, as *stories*, which belong to everyone. Even my own neighbourhood has to remain partially opaque to me. When, walking down the Rue des Francs-Bourgeois in the middle of the night, I stop in front of an wrought-iron fence and stand there alone, dreaming as I contemplate the cold geometry of a garden in the light of the streetlamps, I feel a stolen pleasure. I'm wafted back two hundred years in time... and yet I feel no nostalgia for the monarchy, nor do I bemoan the disappearance of the values which brought forth these beautiful mansions. Of the Place des Vosges, I know that it was built to house kings, and used to be called the Place Royale, but was later rebaptized as a token of gratitude towards the Vosges region, which was the first to pay a certain tax (but I'm not sure which one). To my ears, the word "Vosges" is merely a soft sound, and I appreciate the very vagueness of its meaning. The square itself is associated with the countless people I've gone there to meet and the leisurely strolls I've taken there, under its anonymous arcades, in all seasons....

As for the national celebrations in July — parades, flags, brass bands, fireworks and firecrackers commemorating revolution, independence and the birth of modern democracies — the pretext of July 14th in France is as indifferent to me as that of July 4th in the United States or July 1st in Canada. Still... every year on Bastille Day, the Rue Sainte-Croix-de-la-Bretonnerie is blocked off to traffic and, in front of the *Petit Gavroche* restaurant, the neighbourhood residents dance and play musical instruments until dawn. *This* is what I never had in my own country — and when I found it, I promptly adopted it as "my" tradition. Being myself a bastard, which is to say a mixture, having no traditions other than those I have adopted, I don't mind if they are "impure." If Haitians add their drums and North Africans their spicy sausages to the *bal musette* that purports to take us back to 1789, so much the better! To me, the Bastille will never be that highly symbolic prison whose walls were toppled by the attacks of a frenzied crowd. To me, it's a particularly exhausting subway station — or else the golden statue of a winged spirit which I can see from my window, and which I try to interpret as an allegory of my own spirit when my fingers freeze on the typewriter keyboard. That's the way it is — stories matter more to me than history. I've never much cared for blood-drenched paving-stones — even if, in order for there to be a square with the enchanting name of *Place des Innocents*, innocent people had to be massacred there. The physiognomy of the Marais bears the scars of countless conflicts which mean nothing to me — all I want to do is *graze* these traces, the way you can stroke a loved one's forehead without knowing all about the origins of its lines and creases.

For the past seven hundred years, the Marais has also been the Jewish quarter; and for the past twenty years or so, Sepharadic Jews have come to mingle here with the Ashkenazis. Each pastry has three or four different names, depending on whether you buy it in a Polish, a Russian or a Tunisian pastry shop. I wanted to get away from blandness — well, I got what I asked for. Belonging to nothing, I can be taken for almost anything. It's not always pleasant. A linen maid mutters to me under her breath, "It's awful to have to wash the filth of kikes... Never seen such cruddy sheets in my life." My newspaper seller, with whom I exchange warm greetings every morning, turns out to be a militant Zionist....

Again, I'm aware that these animosities have nothing to do with me. But again, it's easy to be against all forms of fanaticism when you yourself have no History to speak of. In a sense, I'm *condemned to tolerance* — and forced to wonder whether fanaticism, in the final analysis, might not be the origin of intensity. Yes, in these few square blocks of the Marais, these streets rife with contradictions, vibrating with all the tensions of the Middle East as well as those specific to Europe — I found the intensity I'd been looking for since my earliest childhood. And yes, this infatuation of a *shikse* with Judaism is admittedly a bit strange, for of course Jewish schedules and eating habits mean nothing to me. (Why would I buy kosher meat? And why should I remember that everything is closed on Saturdays?) Perhaps I feel a slight sense of "belonging" here because, for centuries, Jewish identity has been connected to uprootedness and exile. I'd rather spend half an hour standing in line at *Goldenburg's* delicatessen, listening to a middle-aged lady *kvetch* to the cashier (as the latter grunts her profound, timeless assent), than buy the same tin of sardines in five seconds at the local grocery chain. When the voice of Sophie Tucker singing *My Yiddishe Momme* wafts up to me from the record store downstairs, I'm moved almost to tears — not because I ever had or wished I had a *Yiddishe Momme*; but because the song is so poignant that it ties my stomach in knots. At such times, does it really matter if the poignancy is borrowed?

It goes without saying that I'll never be fully accepted by my neighbours, never acknowledged as "one of their own"; their affection for me will always be slightly brisk and paternalistic ("There you are dear, it's just a little over the 500 grammes you asked for") — but this is exactly what I want. For I don't identify with French Jews any more than I do with the French in general; rather, I identify *thanks* to them. Contrary to what the American adage suggests, selves cannot be found, they can only be made; and what they are made of is always odds and ends. It's quite possible that when I took the decision to lodge my "self" at the very heart of its *Unheimlich*, I condemned myself to living perpetually in the margins. But, for the time being at least, margins are where this self of mine feels the most... at home.

(1981)

"Reassuring Strangeness" Revisited

As in hallucinations, the verbal constructions [of the foreigner] roll over the void, dissociated from his body and his passions, which he has left behind as hostages to his mother tongue. In this sense, the foreigner knows not what he says.... His language doesn't bother him because it says nothing about his passions: the foreigner can utter all sorts of incongruous things without being in the least disturbed by repulsion or even arousal, so well does his unconscious protect him on the far side of the border.

An analytic cure or, more exceptionally, an intense solitary voyage into memory and body can occasionally bring about the miracle of reconciliation between the original and the acquired identities.
— *Julia Kristeva, Foreign to Ourselves*

A decade or so ago, I wrote a short essay called "Reassuring Strangeness," in which I explored in some detail the advantages of being, not so much uprooted as unrooted. The text bore as its epigraph the American adage "I went to Europe to look for myself, but I wasn't there, either" — whereas I was really saying that, in my case, *I had been there*; that, paralyzed by writer's block when I attempted to write in English, my tongue had loosened up the minute I'd given it permission to use French; that the foreign tongue was more "maternal" to me than my mother tongue had ever been.

I described the great emptiness I saw as being my place of origin, the flat plains of the Canadian West extending as far as the eye could see, and the "irremediably modern" cities in which I'd grown up.... But the truth, I now think, is that I was projecting this emptiness and absence of history onto my childhood. *That*, rather than Albertan soil, was where my increasingly twisted and strangled roots were. (And while it's possible to claim to be "without" a culture or a national identity, no one can claim to be without a childhood... except maybe existential philosophers — cf. Sartre's Roquentin in *Nausea*).

Over the past few years, very slowly and painfully, my childhood has begun to wake up again. Drawing on a Canadian metaphor, I would say that it resembles the thawing of frozen limbs, and as everyone who has experienced cold winters knows, what hurts is not the freezing itself — a frozen leg or foot is numb; so is a frozen memory — what hurts is when, after having gently massaged the limb for hours, you feel the blood slowly beginning to circulate again... For the past few years, then, I've been gradually allowing the English language to ressuscitate and lay claim to its rights within my brain, whereas for so long I had rejected it, describing it as "obscene" ("How dare they talk 'all naked like that'?" I wondered about American tourists in Paris). Yes, I can hear its music again, enjoy its poetry, weigh its specific density, allow it to flow down from my brain into my heart, my guts, my sex, circulate freely again, irrigating my whole being... Come, river, I say to it; yes, go ahead and thaw, I'm ready for spring at last; enough of this "My country is wintertime." Oh! I desperately needed to hibernate in French; for fifteen years I slept there, protected by its ice, reassured by the numbness it conferred upon me, feeding on its dreams. Now, getting to my feet, I shake myself, tiptoe over to the door of my cave — and all the greenery I see, in which I long to frolic and which promises to feed me — all of it is English!

I'm grateful to the French language; it's done a great deal for me. And though I now want to take my distance from it, I'm sure we'll meet up again on a different footing — I no longer want it to be my servant or my imaginary mother; my hope is that some day we can become friends, lovers, and that sap and blood can circulate between the two of us as well.

Because of the prolonged refrigeration of my childhood, it took an enormous detour to get me interested in my native land and force me to admit that Alberta was where I really came from; that I really was its daughter. Yes, as surprising as it may seem, the road from Paris to Calgary took me through... Port-au-Prince. I spent the better part of last year putting together a *grand reportage* for French radio (over forty hours of recording, seven hours of broadcasting) about the Haitian diaspora. Why was I so fascinated by the Haitians? There are a number of answers to this question:

Because my own exile was sweet and theirs brackish;

Because the Haitians, like myself, had learned French in school, thousands of miles away from France;

Because I am what is called White and they are what is called Black and, however inaccurate these terms may be, they nonetheless have sadly predictable effects in reality;

Because, especially, I wondered what the exquisite pain of *nostalgia* felt like. I was jealous of the nostalgia described by other expatriates — jealous, too, of their indignation, their gaeity, their solidarity;

Because when Blacks were imported to Haiti by Whites (to replace the exterminated Reds), they brought with them a religion, voodoo, in which certain chosen people are mounted like horses by the gods — or rather the spirits, loas. They allow themselves to be mounted, they seek to be possessed, and when this happens, with the crowd dancing and rejoicing all around them to the frenzied beat of drums, they buck and caper like wild horses, wholly given over to the joy of abandonment, the acceptance of a force that overwhelms them... whereas in Alberta, where I come from, virtually the one and only cultural originality is rodeo. This is a spectacle in which man demonstrates his superiority over animals, a theatre in which, year after year, wild horses are dominated by cowboys and their bloody spurs, in front of spectators who shout "Yahoo!" from the bleachers;

Because I was fascinated with these people who loved their country (a poor country, a country in which poverty is endemic, revolting and scandalous; a country rife with illiteracy, infant mortality, AIDS and violence; a country that has been worn down, stripped, eroded, emptied out by centuries of colonialism, war, and political corruption), whereas I found it so hard to love mine (a wealthy country, a country in which wealth is shameless, spectacular and arrogant; a country of oil and wheat, giant farms and flourishing industries, a fully modern country devoid of both stories and History — a clean, right-thinking country, as muscle-bound and boring as its cowboys).

Why would people feel nostalgic for hell and not for heaven?

This, perhaps, was the most important question of all, the one that incited me to leave France, my own land of exile, and travel to the Haitians' land of exile, which is my native land. My wish was not to visit Haiti itself, but to try to grasp what I could of the way people inhabit it abroad. Thus, what I explored was not a country but the absence, the loss of a country... a ghost country. And I learned a lot. But even as I learned, I couldn't help wondering, deep down, what all this had to do with me, given that I was neither a journalist nor an anthropologist nor a sociologist, but a novelist. Towards the end of the *reportage*, I received an answer in the form of a beautiful dream:

A person — neither male nor female — had been possessed by Damballah. I asked him/her if it had not been too frightening, and he/she answered that it had not; that if Damballa had come to live in his mind, it was because he knew in advance that he would find enough nourishment there. In other words, he already lived there: "I contained him already — it was not a stranger who broke into my being!" This answer filled me with happiness. *"Come to think of it,"* I told the possessed one, *"that's exactly the way it works with the characters in my novels. They come to me because they know I'll be able to feed them. Yes, they already live inside me. So that's what possession is all about...."*

Now it so happens that Damballa is associated with Saint Patrick, and Saint Patrick is none other than the patron saint of Ireland — the land of my own ancestors. As I explored the "Isle in Exile," I may well have been visiting that other island as well, travelling back in my imagination across the plains of Alberta and the years of my childhood toward that original source.

And where there is a source, there is a myth — in other words, exactly what is necessary for magic to take (its) place.

(1991)

Calgary, France

Next year in Jerusalem.
Last year in Marienbad.
This year in Calgary.

Three expressions for events of dubious reality. Did it happen — will it happen — is it happening? Is there something to go back to, look forward to, clasp in one's arms, one's eyes, one's heart? Some memory to be retrieved and revived, some hope to be fulfilled, some neglected clue to one's identity that might lie buried, waiting to be dis/re/covered — way over there?

This was to be the year of the pilgrimage. The year in which I, prodigal daughter of Calgary, would return home (same "I"? same "home"?) after twenty years of wandering. Longer than Ulysses.

We left in 1968.

We were to have returned in 1988.

Not the same "we"; that much I know. The "we" who left in 1968 was a family of which I was the child. A wanting-to-be-woman child, just a few years too young to belong to the rock hippy peaceful violent crazy politicized drop-out sit-in generation which exploded in the course of that same year.

We'd been living in Northwest — ah! the first time in twenty years I've been able to write "Northwest" — up on 13th Avenue and 24th Street, you know? Facing the Singer Apartments? I used to run across the Singer parking lot to catch the bus that would take me down to Queen Elizabeth High.

Yes?

Somebody actually knows what I'm talking about?

There's a Queen Elizabeth Junior High, too, isn't there? And a Queen Elizabeth Elementary? A long and venerable line of buildings right across from our "old" house on Sixth Avenue. One weekend my brother and sister and I, instead of walking the half-block to the gate, scudded under the steel-link fence to play on the school swings and our father punished us: one spank for my little sister (for going under the fence), two for my big brother (one for going under the fence and one for setting a bad example) and three for me (one for going under the fence, one for setting a bad example and one for tearing my dress). First experiences of injustice are ineffaceable. Archetypal.

That was back in 1962 or thereabouts.

In 1963, my stepmother decided not to attend the Queen Elizabeth Elementary Gray Cup party because John F. Kennedy had just been assassinated. I took the bus up Nineteenth Street to my piano lesson, wondering whether I, too, was overcome with grief. Eaton's and The Bay put Kennedy posters in their display windows saying that they were.

Once a week the family drove down to Southwest to attend church and/or Sunday School at the Cathedral Church of the Redeemer.

The Vietnam War was beginning to rage full blast.

In 1966, my father took me to my first anti-war

demonstration, a little straggly one made up mostly of his friends from university or the church. We concocted a banner together at home, saying "Great Holocausts from Little Brush-Fires Grow." (This was long before the film *Holocaust.*) I didn't much understand what was going on.

By 1967 I was a budding flirtatious heavily made-up gum-chewing cigarette-smoking hip-wiggling thirteen-going-on-fourteen-year-old teeny-bopper. Passing easily for sixteen, I landed my first full-time job: washing dishes at the Village Inn coffee shop — somewhere up near the Sears shopping centre, as I recall. It was owned by a lewd, loud Englishman named Mike, who shocked customers by singing, as he pounded ground beef into patties, all the dirty drinking songs he could remember from his youth in London pubs.

When I forgot to be sexy I would play tackle football with the Lehman gang from the top of the hill. Or metamorphose into a Girl Guide and go hiking along the Bow River, pretending to be an Indian. I also joined Junior Achievement, of which my older brother was already a member, and learned the ins and outs of capitalism by manufacturing and marketing products such as paper flowers or candles-in-brandy-snifters, under the benevolent eye of nice guys from Molson's.

It was a strange existence, come to think of it. Part of it spent in prayer, part collecting Beatles cards, part doing heavy necking in cars despite the impediments of padded bras, and part selling doughnuts door-to-door.

At the dawn of 1968, my history teacher entered the classroom one day, pale and shaken. That was the first time I understood that even a far-off political event like the Tet Offensive could be relevant to people in Calgary, Alberta.

Then Bobby Kennedy was assassinated, and then Martin Luther King. Somewhat to my embarrassment, my father made me take a day off from school and read everything the Periodicals section of the Calgary Public Library had on each of these men. Shortly afterwards, he announced that we were moving to the United States. My friends were aghast. The United States, of all places! And now, of all times! But he had found the teaching job of his dreams in New England.

And so it was that I got up secretly in the middle of a sweltering July night — the last night of my life in Calgary — and painted gold and silver doodles, rhymes and smart-ass slogans all over the blue converted schoolbus he'd bought to make the move. The next morning we loaded up — two adults, four kids, two cats, one dog, plus every shred of our belongings — and drove away.

Twenty years later, this year, the other "we" was to have returned, the only element common to the two "we's" being the "I." An "I" now accompanied by an Eastern European husband, our Paris-born daughter, his North African adopted son, and an Extreme Oriental bird. An "I" returning to her native city with a gaze altered by fifteen years in Europe and a native tongue grown clumsy from disuse.

And then it became impossible. The "I" changed yet again, evolving gradually into another "we": just when I had planned to be introducing my new family to my old stomping-grounds, I shall be giving birth to another child.

So it will not come to pass.

But would it have come to pass?

What would I have recognized? What would have silently but solemnly proclaimed "Welcome Home"? I don't even ask "who" — no Penelope awaits me; no forlorn father is fattening a calf in the hope of my return.

The city's population has doubled in the intervening years, its skyline has thickened and sharpened, its oil industry has waxed and waned, its urban planners have made short shrift, not to say mincemeat, of my memories. The Cathedral Church of the Redeemer may still exist, but probably not the Singer Apartments — perhaps not even the two houses in which my old family lived.

Do I really want to know?

For years, I have superciliously denied feeling the least twinge of nostalgia for the scenes of my childhood.

But suddenly, last January, as we were driving home from the Bois de Vincennes, there was a half-hour programme of country and western hits on the radio and I found myself turning up the volume, tapping my foot and rocking with laughter at the lyrics of these formerly-derided "bumpkin" songs.

And then suddenly, in February, the word "Calgary" was splattered across the front page of every newspaper in Paris; each time I saw it I would feel a jolt, and then a small warm wave of pride. My home town is in the papers, not because of wars, riots, massacres or terrorist attacks, but because of the snow. And for the first time in my life, I could use the word "Chinook" in French and be understood. I found myself turning on the TV set for the news every evening — though few things interest me less than the Winter Olympics — just to see if I might recognize the inside of MacMahon Stadium, or a little piece of foothill or forest, and be able to point to it excitedly and say, "You see? I was born somewhere!"

And so it was that, Mohammed not having gone to the mountain, the mountain came to Mohammed: at long last, Calgary has arrived in France.

(1988)

Singing the Plains

Bilingualism: "I speak with forked tongue."

"London is a privileged place for creation," said British novelist Angela Carter in one of the last interviews she granted to the press before her untimely death, "because this city is in an incredible state of disorder, it's full of anger, rife with dissent, distress and suffering — and all of this is the raw material for writing."

"What about you? Where are you from?" people have been asking me regularly, inevitably, for the twenty-odd years I've been living in France. And of course I answer their question. But to myself, inside myself, my answer has always been "strictly from nowhere." I come from a place which is rife with only very moderate suffering, a place where distress and anger are muffled and mild, a place of relative order and harmony — in other words, a place deprived of stories and of History. That place is Western Canada.

In a recent issue of *The Massachusetts Review* devoted to contemporary Canadian art and literature, there is a wonderful piece by Bruce Russell entitled "True North"; the paragraph "Identity" describes my grandparents' generation to a T:

"They hardly exist anymore, nearly extinct: these tall, thin, stiff, tidy, quiet, well-groomed gentlemen. Like defrocked priests who still have something of "the Cloth" about them, they have a regimental air. Perhaps no one could absolutely come home from Dieppe or Vimy Ridge. Indeed, they always seemed to never really be completely present, at least for long. Short attention spans: a tendency to drift. They all wore mustaches, had very good posture, if a slight tendency to stoop their heads, and dressed very carefully. In the world they were honest and a trifle conservative, regardless of their politics. Fair play. Hard work. Charitable. They loved their families, but never really seemed to know them. Their children thought them kind and dull. Their wives were either very independent or very disappointed. The independent ones, some so independent that they had never married them, had careers and causes, or simply tea parties and card games, or religion. The disappointed ones were shadows, and sometimes widows, and they could have religion too. All these adults were Canadians, the only Canadians there ever were. It takes a lot of winters to chill a human being enough to make a Canadian. In those days Canadians could be French or English or Scottish or Lithuanian or anything else. Being Canadian was a noble calling, if a faint one. Canada required a lot of concentration because it existed in the future. It is possible that there are some Canadians of my generation. I think I might have met some, although they are still too young for it to be certain. But I very much doubt if there could be any younger ones. That future the Canadians were waiting for has passed."

More specifically, I come from the gigantic and minuscule province of Alberta: 660,000 km² as compared with France's 550,000; 1.8 million inhabitants as compared with France's 55 million — in other words, three Albertans per square kilometer as compared with one hundred French.

Even within the colourless country of Canada, Alberta is a particularly colourless province. I couldn't help noticing, for instance, that of the forty-seven authors included in Michael Ondaatje's recent anthology of Canadian short stories, twelve were born outside of Canada and none in Alberta. Saskatchewan, yes. Manitoba, yes. But Alberta — not one.

And yet, some three or four years ago, after having denied it for such a very long time, I realized that having grown up in that place *did* matter to me. In the most unexpected places, at the most incongruous moments, a strange nostalgia would overwhelm me. One Christmas, for instance, standing at the butcher's counter of a supermarket in Saint-Amand-Montrond — that is, in the heart of the Berry region which is the heart of France which is the heart of Europe — I saw that they were selling buffalo! I asked a few questions about it in a trembling voice, and the butcher handed me a list of recipes for the preparation of this delicious meat. My head began to spin. Here I was, convinced that this animal had been extinct for the past century, and now the Berrichons were calmly munching on buffalo steaks and roasts! I was deeply shaken.

Or again, driving in Paris of a Sunday afternoon or late at night, I'd be fiddling with the dials on the radio and stumble on songs like *Alberta Sunrise* or *Rocky Mountain Music*, or even *Alberta's Child* –

> *Well up north it's saddle broncs and it's hockey and honkytonks*
> *Old Wilf Carter 78s*
> *Dumb stuff like chores when it's twenty below*
> *They're the things that a country boy hates*
>
> *Too much damn wind and not enough whiskey*
> *Drives them ol' northern boys flat wild,*
> *And he may go to Hell, or even Vancouver*
> *He'll always be Alberta's child.*

– and my heart would start flip-flopping and my feet would start tapping and my fingers snapping and before I knew it I'd be humming along, and my astonished husband would say "Hey! Hey! I thought you hated country and western music."

And I would blush, for that indeed is what I'd been saying for so long, to anyone who cared to listen — I hated country-and-western music, cowboy movies, cowboys, rodeo, juicy steaks and everything that might put me in mind of Calgary, that hick town of a half a million inhabitants where I happened to have been born. But now, since my heart was racing madly and my cheeks had turned bright red, it was clear that there was love involved. So, screwing up my courage, I dared myself to turn that place into, as Angela Carter says, "the raw material for my writing."

I thought about it for a long time. The challenge seemed daunting, not so much because I was ashamed of my origins (in fact I've never understood how people could be either proud or ashamed of something so totally beyond their control as their place of birth), but because they bored me to death.

I talked the problem over with my dear friend the South African writer Denis Hirson, over the course of one of our literary teas. A literary tea is a cup of tea sweetened by friendship into which one dips the biscuit of literary complaint. Denis and I take turns — sometimes he brings the biscuits and sometimes I do. That day, my biscuit was boredom. "Here, taste it," I told him. "You see? Totally insipid. Every time I think about Alberta, I feel like falling asleep." And Denis answered, in substance, "Well, there must be something pretty intense in there, if you have to protect it with all that blandness, boredom and somnolence." And then he gave me some good advice. "Try to dig in under the boredom," he said. "Look behind it, beyond it — there's got to be a treasure there." Naturally, he was right. Somnolence was my system of defense.

A few weeks after this conversation, the first page of *Plainsong* came to me... in my sleep. Or rather, it came to me during a bout of insomnia one night after my baby woke up. I recommend parenthood to anyone who wants to become a writer — you often get your best ideas in the floaty state halfway between waking and sleeping, and babies are continually plunging you into that state.

Here's what I wrote at four a.m. one day in the spring

of 1989 — the first spontaneous spurt of fiction in English I'd had in over fifteen years:

Cowboys! Just look at those men! The sweat and sinew of them! The twine and twist of them! The chest you could bust your fist against! The muscled thighs the pointed boots the spurs with stars the holsters with pistols the hat pushed back or fallen off in the fray with the beast — ah, rodeo! A man alone in a corral with a wild young steer and a rope! Oh dance that dance! Oh twirl that lasso! Oh the man jiving bareback with a frantic arching horse, buck on buck, fuck it man that's what I call a man! Fine honed hard boned blue jeaned bucking fucking man! And such a dust he stirs up!

You choked on the dust, Paddon. You coughed and spat between your legs, under the bleachers...

I rather liked the rhythm of that half-page — but at the same time it filled me with fresh apprehension. I realized that I was not only *bored* by everything that recalled my native culture, I was *allergic* to it. The reason this character Paddon coughs and spits under the bleachers is that his author cannot bear to be in the vicinity of horses, hay, cattle, or anything that even vaguely resembles horses, hay and cattle. I once had a genuine asthma attack in a movie theatre, watching the threshing and reaping of wheat in *The Gates of Heaven*... only to discover during the end credits that the film had been shot in Alberta.

So now, at about four-thirty in the morning, I got out my dictionary and looked up the word *allergy*. And it turned out (as I should have been able to guess) that allergy and energy came from the same rootword *ergia*, action. Energy means "the power of action" and allergy means "the action of the other" (as in allocentric). So, just as Denis had advised me to respond to boredom by looking beneath, behind and beyond it rather than by avoiding it, I decided that what I needed to do in this book was to confront my allergies head-on and turn the action of the other into a power of action.

For a month or so, I even toyed with the idea of physically returning to Alberta during the summer and attending that most quintessentially Albertan (and allergizing) of events, the Calgary Stampede and Rodeo. Perhaps, I thought half-heartedly, it would be a good idea to refresh my memory. But then I remembered the lesson of Mallarmé, "*fleur: l'absente de tout bouquet*" — in other words, literature depends on absence, and sensation often destroys words. I admit to having heaved a sigh of relief. Reconstructing the rodeos, wheat fields and murderously cold winters of my childhood *on the page* would be far more effective than revisiting them in actuality. I didn't want to feel the cold again with my body; I wanted to feel it with my mind.

Thus, the next passages that came to me, several months after the first, were experiments in mental travelling. Though I still had no idea who was telling the story, who was saying "you" to the character named Paddon (or indeed, who that character might to turn out to be), I was sure of one thing: I wanted his life to have spanned the 20th century — that is, the entire history of his province.

I wanted to convey the unbelievable shortness and density of that history.

Just one hundred years ago, what is now Alberta's capital city was still called Fort Edmonton and was basically a trading post of the Hudson's Bay Company; today, the West Edmonton Mall is the largest indoor shopping centre in the world. The year 1838 marked the arrival in Alberta of the first Whites not directly connected to the fur trade; they were missionaries. The first school in Alberta was founded in 1862, also by a missionary. The population of Calgary in 1881 was... seventy-five. Alberta didn't even become a full-fledged province until 1905 (until then it was part of the Northwest Territories); in other words, Albertans are *still* thirteen years short of their centennial!

When I say "Albertans," I am of course referring to white people — to the history of Europeans in Alberta. Like most white people born and raised in North America, I was taught from an early age to feel a mixture of guilt and respect towards the native populations whom "we" had subdued, decimated, and locked up on reservations. As I readied myself to write *Plainsong*, I was aware that the history of the Plains Indians was part of the history of Alberta, and that I would need to read up on this subject — a subject which had scarcely drifted through my mind since the end of elementary school. So I went to the library. It so happened that I was now in the United States, and in the libraries of Boston and New York there were vast numbers of books at my disposal on the history of "native Americans." (That's what we call them now, to be polite. No neutral term exists for the designation of these various peoples, and it's hard to see why they should feel more comfortable with Amerigo Vespucci than Christopher Columbus). Be this as it may, as soon as I started delving into the history of the main tribes in that part of the continent now known as Alberta — Blackfoot, Cree, Blood, Piegan, Gros-Ventre, Sarcee and Beaver — I fell asleep again.

The problem was that nothing seemed to have actually *happened* in Alberta. Oh, there'd been a few little massacres here and there, of Whites by Indians or the other way around — but really, nothing to write home about. The so-called "American" Sioux, after having annihilated General Custer's army of 265 soldiers in 1876, fled north to Canada with their great chief Sitting Bull. They crossed the Forty-ninth Parallel to hide from the mean old Whites who intended to murder them (and who eventually *did* murder them, at Wounded Knee in 1890). Even then, they knew that nothing could happen to anyone in Alberta. As for the famous "Northwest Rebellion" of 1884, one of the most colourful events in Canadian history, in the course of which the revolutionary Métis Louis Riel and his friend Gabriel Dumont incited the Indians and Métis of Alberta to take up arms against the government — even that rebellion was quashed in Batoche, just on the far side of the Saskatchewan border. Every time I got my hands on something that sounded like great human drama — "anger, distress, suffering," as Angela Carter puts it — it turned out not quite to have occurred within the confines of my native province.

I must admit to having felt a bit discouraged, waking

up day after day from my hard pillow of Albertan history books at the Columbia University Library in Manhattan.

Then help came from a wholly unexpected source. It so happened that as I was gathering this banal stultifying documentation for this hopelessly plain and ordinary novel, I was also preparing a series of radio broadcasts on Haitians in exile. Haiti — now, *there* was a country you could feel strongly about. Everything you could ask for — massacres, slavery, black revolution, political corruption, starvation, voodoo, assassination — a fascinating country if ever there was one.

As I explored the history of Haiti, I came across a book that was like a blinding flash of light to me. The book was *Beyond Geography*, by Frederic W. Turner. It is a brilliant description of the way in which the Christian, European conceptions of land, wilderness, progress, conquest, and paradise had brought about the destruction of the native American peoples. As I read this book, I realized for the first time that Haiti and Alberta were part of one and the same history. Haiti was the bloody, violent starting-point of the conquest of America, and Alberta was its soft, mushy, flabby, attenuated ending-point. By the time the Whites finally got to Alberta, the West coast had already been settled and it was just a matter of hooking things up — "manifest destiny," as the Americans call it. There was no longer any point in murdering Indians; we knew they could be subdued much more courteously with smallpox, religion, alcohol and false promises, and this would also entail fewer casualties on our side.

For some reason (which I still can't say I fully understand), the possibility of connecting two places which had hitherto been antithetical in my imagination, suddenly made Albertan history interesting to me. If I could be moved by the fate of Hispaniola's Arawaks, surely I must feel *something* for the Crees and Stoneys of Alberta. Indeed, I saw that the parallels between the two were very strong, in particular as concerns the forced religious conversion of the natives.

God played an important role in Albertan history — not only for Indians and missionaries, but for the homesteaders and their wives. God — along with horses, hay and cattle — was another aspect of my upbringing to which I had grown violently allergic, and to which, over my many years of living in France, I had avoided giving much thought. Now I had no choice but to make Him a character in the novel — and gradually, as I worked with Him, I began to feel a begrudging sort of liking for the guy. He is everywhere in *Plainsong*; the book begins and ends with an evocation of His dastardly deeds.

And so it was that, thanks to the unhoped-for assistance of boredom, allergy, Haitians in exile and an old tired God, I was able to write about my country at long last.

(1992)

Towards A Patriotism of Ambiguity

In the summer of 1993, just before the simultaneous publication of Plainsong *and* Cantique des plaines, *I returned to visit Alberta with my husband and two children. I was forty years old. I hadn't seen Calgary since my departure in 1968, at age fifteen.*

July 4th, 1993
I'm haunted by the fantasy that I shall grow suddenly and spectacularly old in the course of this trip, now that the past has caught up with me...

The distances are impressive: eight hours in the air, ten hours on the ground, four hours in the air. Odd pains at the back of my head throughout the flight, like a razorblade in the brain, momentary but powerful winces.

An airplane documentary on Calgary's chuck-wagon races. My five-year-old son stares open-mouthed, listening to the commentary in French over his headphones. I listen in English. With no advance warning, my eyes flood with tears. Another film, presenting the city of Toronto, cites Peter Ustinov's quip that it is "a New York run by the Swiss." Why do I despise this young man standing in front of the Toronto skyline and blathering about the merits of his city? What do I hold against him? He's too healthy, I think that's it. Too healthy and too wholesome; his English is accentless and therefore, to my ears, bland, transparent.... It's as though I could see through him, as though there were nothing to sink my teeth into.... For me, blandness is the terrifying quintessence of English Canada.

While I was getting ready to embark on the writing of *Plainsong*, I asked everyone in my family, insistently and probably rather annoyingly, "What does it mean to you to be Canadian?" The question had suddenly become important to me. Is it possible to identify (especially positively) with blandness? What, exactly, does one lay claim to when one declares with pride, "I'm a Canadian"? Smoked salmon? Maple syrup? Grandiose landscapes? A certain conception of democracy?

The question had begun to obsess me when I undertook a reportage for French radio on the Haitian diaspora. In the course of my interviews with Haitians in Montreal, New York and Miami, I'd been mesmerized by the beauty and intensity of Haitian patriotism. Despite the fact that according to all sorts of objective political and economic criteria, Haiti was one of the worst places in the world to live and Canada one of the best, Haitian exiles expressed a heartfelt love for their country and did their best to recreate Haiti wherever they went — whereas, in my own heart, Canada and "Canadian-ness" took up virtually no room at all.

July 5th
Calgary. I'm reeling. I can't believe it. The bank teller who sold me traveller's checks this morning went to Queen Elizabeth High School. She remembers Mr. Wannacott

the principal, and Mrs. Reeves the formidable French teacher.... Childhood memories in common — something so simple — something I've been deprived of for decades. I could have wept (tears are never far away, these days).

When we leave the hotel to take a walk in the streets of downtown Calgary — astonishingly empty for a weekday morning — my son Sacha (in a bitchy mood) flatly declares, "There's nothing to see here." I resent his saying it, but deep down I agree with him. Let me try to examine the constituent elements of this "nothing."

Architecture
No love of the past, no respect for history. The Anglican Cathedral Church of the Redeemer, where I took Communion every Sunday of my adolescence — and which, in my memory, was comparable in size to Canterbury Cathedral — is diminutive. It's not just that I myself have grown. The surrounding lawns and gardens have been nibbled away by pavement, the metro tram stops directly in front of the church, and monstrous, characterless skyscrapers have shot up all around it, dwarfing it.... Similarly, throughout the downtown area, only fragments of the old sandstone buildings remain; everything else is metal and glass. Eighth Avenue has been rezoned for pedestrians — a sure way to kill a street. We could be in any city in the American Midwest, or even in a German city rebuilt after the war.

Iconography
What lets us know that we're *not* in Germany are the

ubiquitous images of cowboys on bucking broncs — advertisments for the great Stampede celebrations which will begin a few days hence. At this, I might (should?) feel a shiver of nostalgia, but the images — mediocre, vulgar cartoon-style — are too ugly to allow anything of the kind.

Language
We're in a highly regulated universe. Everywhere you look, you're given benevolent orders, instructions and advice. Upon entering the little park across from our hotel, we're confronted with a sign saying, "This Park is for Passive Recreation Only," followed by a long list of things we're not allowed to do here (running, playing ball, and so forth). Later, we break apart the flaps of a half-gallon milk carton and are greeted by "Thank you for buying a Beatrice product." It's not enough to have paid for the carton of milk, you must also put up with its talking to you.

I feel aggressed by the matter-of-factness of this language. It's far too positive, geeky and simpering for my taste — there's no room here for irony, perversion, tragedy. The only tragedy that took place here has been smoothed over, smiled away, flattened into yet another publicity stunt — in the display windows at *Holt Renfrew's*, the mannequins are set off by a group of pseudo-Indian teepees.

But this evening, reading *The Bible Thief* by the great Swedish novelist Göran Tunström, I come across a passage that disturbs me. The narrator, Johan, returning to his native town of Sunne after several years' absence, is every bit as aghast as I am here in Calgary: "To my mind," he says,

"Sunne had lost its character. The obsequiosity, the servility of the architecture made me nauseous. This occurred when the new pharmacy stared at me with the gaze of a stranger. It had no reason for being there. It disturbed the spatial unity of the street. It was as though someone had gone rummaging in the wastebaskets of cities, extracting sketches of rejected ideas and buying them at a reduced price. This pharmacy was not in its place here; it had not been built in accordance with the possibilities of the site. Its façade could not enter into dialogue with the neighbouring houses.... The decision to build it must have been taken far away from here, by somnolent bureaucrats who were utterly ignorant of the relations between things, and of intimacy — even in their own beds."

And yet, Johan goes on to say,

"The tiny pig-eye windows of the pharmacy stared at me, telling me that I, too, belonged to the ways of thinking that create monstrosities of this sort. We do not exist outside of our era. Time makes me possible and I make time possible. Collective wishes are fulfilled in the concrete actions of a few."

The question therefore became: what have I done to allow — or even foster — the ugliness that surrounds me?

How have I taken part in its creation? How have I contributed, even unconsciously, to calling it into being? When you see the loving care with which Italian villages repair their houses, replace roof tiles on their churches, craft the surrounding landscape so that the eye can rejoice in its harmony, you can understand that children born in such places remain deeply attached to them. Though they may leave to seek their fortunes elsewhere, they will be moved every time they set eyes on this bell-tower, this slow curve of a narrow street, this square paved in red brick, this line of olive-trees.

How does it happen that, in the New World in general and in Alberta in particular, we are so oblivious to the aesthetic aspect of life? How can we care so little about transmitting beauty to future generations? How can we think it's all right to fill our children's brains with a chaotic jumble of fast-food restaurants and gas stations, unsightly buildings and shopping centres? Do we really believe that this ugliness will have no impact on their souls? What sort of nostalgia will an adult born and raised in Edmonton feel, evoking his or her childhood memories of the West Edmonton Mall?

July 6th
T. and the children keep banging into things in our camping-car. They're covered with bruises. I feel at once amused and guilty — is T. starting to wonder whatever came over him to marry a Canadian? Moreover, I'm behaving like a true pioneer-wife — I've taken over all the kitchen and cleaning duties (not exactly my style...)!

What I cook — steaks, hamburgers, pancakes, corn-on-the-cob, hot dogs — is the basic food of the entire North American continent. When we eat out in restaurants, the menu is a hodge-podge of dishes from Italy and China, Germany and Mexico. Not a single Albertan specialty, of course. Does such a thing exist?

The countryside around Drumheller is outlandishly beautiful — but it doesn't *give itself up to you* the way the French countryside does; its beauty is restrained and distant. Everything is grandiose: the fields of canola (the new, politically correct name for what used to be called rapeseed), the flat-bottomed, high-piled clouds, a rainbow arching dramatically behind the grain silos, to say nothing of the badlands themselves, those gorgeous sensuous seams of earth that fold and unfold as far as the eye can see... You can understand why the dinosaurs chose to live here rather than in the plains — the landscape must have been excellent camouflage for them! The bases of these hills look exactly like ridgy rilled grey dinosaur toes digging into the ground. And the tops are flat — flattened at exactly the same height wherever you look, as if to reach up and meet the flat-bottomed clouds halfway.

In fact, of course, the badlands are just the opposite of mountains. Their "summits" are level land (hence their flatness), hollowed out over millions of years by the Red Deer River and its tributaries. Today, after a rainfall, the silt forms were standing mud. Grey, slippery dinosaurs. We're steeped in paleolithic lore.

Is it possible to be "attached" to such a landscape? Contemplating it, I feel exalted and crushed by turns, but not moved. The Group of Seven tried to do justice to Canadian nature, developing new techniques of painting that would enable them to convey its immensity. But is it possible to "proudly lay claim" to... a plain? A Rocky Mountain?

You can't absorb anything in this culture without also involuntarily swallowing a dollop of advertising. At Drumheller's Reptile Museum, there's a sign over almost every glass case: "This display sponsored by XXX Ice Cream" or "YYY Coffee-Shop".... I wonder why I so resent this perpetual reminder of how capitalism works.

July 7th
I'd forgotten there could be seagulls in Southern Alberta. I'd even forgotten the thousands of pick-up trucks! And how sheerly wonderful old freight-trains can be — how passionately I used to love them (after twenty years of living in Europe, that memory must have been obliterated by Auschwitz). And the way kids in cars suddenly pinch their noses and say "Pew!", all the while rocking with laughter, as an overpowering stench of manure hovers in the air for a few seconds.

We're camping out at Kinbrook, an island in a lake near Brooks. On the phone last night, my father told me that Brooks used to call itself "The Best Town in the West by a Damsite" — the lake, in other words, is man-made. Along the artificial sand beach are artificial heaps of stone — the stones are real, of course, but they've been imported from somewhere else and scattered along the water's edge with ostentatious nonchalance, in imitation of rocky seasides in other parts of the continent. This is a civilized place indeed: you decide there has to be a lake on this spot, with stones piled at its edges; you pay for it, and you get it. I ain't complainin', but the effect is rather strange. The island's location, for instance, must have been calculated so that the campsites would face due west and catch the setting sun in its full glory.

But how did they manage to convince the seagulls to come along as well?

July 8th

The French are proud of their vices in exactly the same way as the Canadians are proud of their virtues. I guess that when you come right down to it, French vices are probably every bit as hypocritical as Canadian virtues. (There's been endless debate about the repressed violence of the Puritans — why does no one wonder what happened to the repressed goodness of the libertines?)

In bed this morning: visions of myself, the gal from the Plains, entering Europe's majestic libraries, museums and cathedrals... ascending all those marble staircases so hungrily, so assiduously, so repeatedly — for what? What was wrong with just lettin' our hair fly as we bombed down a dirt road in a pick-up truck with our beer-drinkin' boyfriends at our sides? Last night, as the sun set so aesthetically over the artifical lake, a gang of kids (from Brooks, I assume) materialized before us with resounding rap music and roaring motorboats — the guys making the boats rear up then literally fucking the water with them in a rhythmical vroom vroom vroom, the girls oohing and ahhing from the beach — all of this was my destiny, all of this is what I so narrowly escaped....

These are the thoughts that fill my long silences these days.

We visit the Siksika (Blackfoot) reserve at Gleichen. The people here call themselves Indians, not "native Canadians," "Amerindians" or whatever. First image: a native family cashing in dozens and dozens of empty beer bottles at the local gas station.

The landscape is both magnificent and desolate.

There is no society; there are only "social agencies." A high-tech Administrative Centre organizes various activities and fosters the rebirth of Indian pride by scheduling meetings of the "Elders Group" and the "Youth Group," selling a "kit" including cassette-tapes of traditional lore, and so forth. These activites cannot conceal the glaring fact that *there is nothing to do here*. They are an ersatz for the real, throbbing life of the community, to which we put an end a century ago.

It's evident that few tourists stop to ask for a visiting permit. Still, I was moved beyond words. Old Sun Community College, with its pitiful collection of Blackfoot artefacts — a "museum" in a single dusty classroom on the third floor of the school, was opened especially for us by an obese Blackfoot with a skinny English vocabulary.... By way of apologising for the meagerness of the exhibit, he told us at least twenty times that there was a much bigger and better collection of Indian artefacts at Calgary's Glenbow Museum. Indeed, he added, most of the Blackfoot themselves were in Calgary right now, getting ready for the Stampede.

Then we were allowed to visit the "historic sites" — Chief Crowfoot's tomb (a triangular stack of white stones) and, a little farther on, a large circle of white stones. Despite the simplicity of the monuments, there is an unmistakable sense of the sacred here which seems sorely lacking everywhere else.

Then Calgary again, and tears again, as we breasted the Fourteenth Street hill next to the Auditorium and coasted down into my old neighbourhood. I'd never visited it with a map before. My daughter Léa was kind enough to take an interest in my memories — stories thirty years old but still shimmering in my brain: the week my brother and I camped out in the garage in the middle of winter because we were tired of doing dishes... the coffee-shops my friend Sandy and I drifted into at midnight, in our nightgowns and bare feet, after having climbed out of our bedroom windows... the hill on which I played passionate tackle football with a gang of neighbourhood boys... the first dances, the first kisses, good old Queen Elizabeth School....

July 9th
The Stampede Parade. Again — the minute the first band marches past us, decked out in red and white, the colours of Calgary, I burst into tears. The uniforms are so smart, and the music so stirring — I used to dream of being one of those marching girls in short pleated skirts, twirling my

baton so fast it was a blur — but, come to think of it, *where are they?* Has feminism gotten rid of them? There isn't a single majorette in the whole parade — all the young girls now play musical instruments.... Almost at once, I dry my tears and resume my cynical pose. Roland Barthes, I tell myself (using French theory to protect myself from Albertan emotion), could have written a "mythology" about this strange event. What unfolds before our eyes for a full three hours, in the freezing rain, is a succession of bands and floats celebrating every ethnic group in the province: Indians of all tribes, proudly dressed in their traditional costumes ("You see, Daddy?" says Sacha. "You told me Indians didn't wear feathers anymore, but you were wrong!"), Ukrainians, Irish, Hungarians, Dutch, Scots, Germans — and the single message conveyed to the enthusiastic audience is: "We are here." Over and over again: "We are here." On the spectators' side, the single response to this message is the endlessly reiterated cry of "Yahoo!" There is no participation, no involvement in the event; strictly nothing happens or is meant to happen — they are there, we see them, and we acknowledge their *there*-ness with our indefatigable "Yahoos!"

After the parade, we rush into Eaton's to warm our frozen hands and feet. Oh, this rich and tasteless world, this nightmare of vapidity. Yes, this is clearly the problem I have with my country: its relentless, distressing, dangerous, damaging, perhaps hopeless modernity. Having effaced its (already short enough) past, it skates on the surface of its present.

We spend the afternoon at the Stampede Rodeo and

Fairgrounds — and, here again, I'm shocked by the ubiquitousness of advertising. Every little event has been sponsored by some product or other and we're not allowed to forget it for a minute. Even the "Indian Village" in one corner of the gigantic Stampede Park was brought to us by Husky Oil, of all things, and no one seems to wince at the irony of it.

"This wild horse saddling race," the rodeo announcer reminds us every thirty seconds or so, "is brought to you by Bull's Eye Barbecue Sauce — it's got the big, bold taste!" Amplified by the microphone, his voice is so loud that the spectators sink into silence and passivity and the whole experience becomes somehow vicarious, as if we weren't really present at the arena but watching it on T.V.. The announcer has a hard time whipping up any sort of audible excitement — he virtually has to force our Yahoos and Yippees out of us.

T. and the children seem to be enjoying themselves anyway. As for me, made drowsy by the antihistamines I've taken to fight my allergy to horses and hay, numbed by the repeated injunctions to purchase Bull's Eye Barbecue Sauce, I allow myself to be gradually overcome by lethargy, and oppose a bloated physical resistance to all the glitzy solicitations of my attention. At last, sitting in the bleachers at the Stampede Rodeo with my little boy on my lap, I fall asleep.

July 10th
The quintessential Anglo-Canadian word is "actually." Here in the laundry room at Calloway Park

Campground, it crops up in almost every sentence of the small talk I overhear. "Actually" connotes deference: not only are you stating nothing but the facts, you're stating them, as it were, modestly — as if they'd taken you somewhat by surprise.... "Did you get a good sleep?" "Yes I did, actually." "Can I help you? Because actually we're closed at the moment...."

As if by magic, my general sense of oppression and affliction lifted quite suddenly this morning, when we drew away from the magnetic field of the Past and moved into the Eternity of the Rocky Mountains. All at once I could breathe again, feel my body, stretch my limbs — I was no longer under the ominous influence of "the-woman-I-might-have-become."

With some amusement and some amazement, I see how things used to work in pioneer days — the sense of virtuousness women must have derived from doing all the cooking and cleaning, and the insidious dependency this instilled in men. Here, I sweep and swipe and wipe and wash, toast and boil and grill and fry, handing my little family plates and cups and bowls full of nourishment... and it gives me a strange new power over T. — a power which, were it to last, we'd both begin to find unpleasant. Just as conventionally, it is he who looks after the driving, the firemaking and the dumping.

"How did the dumping go, darling?"

July 12th
The whole experience of these days in the Rockies is archetypal: rain, gophers, Indian paintbrushes, chip-

munks, wild roses, rain, eternal snows, eternal clouds, the thick carpet of pine needles underfoot, waterfalls, rain, turquoise rivers and lakes, my children climbing behind, next to or in front of me, their legs and hands grappling with stone and root...

and the memories of mountain-climbing with my father,
so fine,
unchanged

July 13th
Yesterday, as we bathed in a swimming pool fed by the Banff Hot Springs, there was snow on the mountainside just a few yards above us.

So few people here seem attractive to me — genuinely, interestingly attractive. There are any number of pretty blondes, but their faces are somehow empty, as if suffering from an excess of innocence. And almost everyone wears clothes made of garish synthetic materials.

July 15th
A "semi-strenuous" ten-kilometer hike to Lake Cirque. Sheer turquoise.... It's so hard for me to find a language for this sort of experience. The words that come to mind are the threadbare clichés of tourist brochures — the "sheer turquoise" of the lakes, the "thick carpet" of pine-needles on the forest floor, etc. Nothing exciting can happen for me verbally in such a perfect natural context. And yet, hovering in the light-and-shadow play of the pines, I can sense the palpable presence of Bear, Moose and Coyote — a whiff of their ancient sacredness.

July 16th

Driving driving driving — ah yes, this I remember — the highway along the Saskatchewan River towards Rocky Mountain House, the signs saying "Next Gas 92 km" or "Recreation Area 65 km".... No houses, no billboards, no churches, no picnic tables, no nothing.... The roads themselves are the only sign of civilization. Ain't nobody in these parts but God... and He ain't talkative.

July 17th

Edmonton. Sitting at the desk that used to belong to Grandpa Kester, who took the initiative of removing the o from his name Koester to make it look less German. During summer vacations, first in Peace River, then in Vermilion, I spent countless hours playing solitaire at this desk: just now, I even remembered to pull out the top drawer for support before lowering the writing flap. The green blotter is worn with age, but handsome still.

Today I rediscovered the exact tone of the Low Level Bridge's hum. And the exact sensation — iron-enclosedness, exhilarating strength — of the High Level Bridge.

We visited the fourth and last of the Albertan houses I remember having lived in. A faint aura of poverty and abandonment hung over the Delton neighbourhood. The rock-garden my brother and I used to race our turtles in was gone. A drugged skinny giggling young woman, twentyish, kept wavering up and down the front sidewalk on high heels. Another marriage on the rocks, I said to myself.

The West Edmonton Mall is far and away the most

popular tourist attraction in Alberta. It contains, among other things, a life-sized replica of the boat in which Christopher Columbus arrived in the New World. My children are goggle-eyed.

July 18th
We are in Balzac, Alberta. The choice of this toponym for our last night camping out is some sort of joke on my husband's part. As far as we can see, apart from its campground, the town boasts a silo, a filling-station, a food store, a community center, a United Church, an Anglican Church, and not a single house.

July 19th
The Rocky Mountains were breathtakingly visible this morning as we drove south towards Calgary for the last time. They gave the city skyline an air of noblesse — as if their summits were the jewelled points of a crown laid gently on the landscape....

We visit the Glenbow Museum at last. On the third floor, we cover the entire history of the province within the space of a few hours: Indians, CPR, ranchers, homesteaders, missionaries, washboards, Singer sewing-machines and old pianos, the discovery of oil.... What comes home to me most powerfully is that the lives of the first Whites in this country were made up of *stories* — tales of persecution, uprooting and loss, desperate attempts to hang onto the old heirlooms, languages, symbols of faith.... Almost all of it dissolved with dismaying rapidity: the roots of the first Albertans, who had come here with such high hopes, were pulverized within two short generations, and their many colourful origins relentlessly mixed together to make white. *The diversity of traditions resulted in the effacement of tradition as such.*

Reflections on the Way Back
How can Albertans be proud of coming from Alberta? All of us *came* here, less than a hundred years ago. We appropriated land, more or less getting rid of those who were already living on it. How long will it take for our guilt about this to fade away sufficiently for us to lay claim to our inheritance? Perhaps, throughout the New World, a certain malaise is part and parcel of the national sentiment of the descendants of colonists. And perhaps this malaise, this acute *awareness of ambiguity*, is in fact healthier than the aggressive, chest-beating patriotism practised elsewhere in the world. Perhaps we could construe the frailty of our connection to our land as an asset rather than a liability?

A case in point: the novelist Romain Gary, born in Moscow, who spent his early childhood in Poland and his school years in Nice, served during World War II in Africa and England, married a British writer, embarked on a diplomatic career which took him from Sofia to Berne to La Paz to Los Angeles, then married an American actress before ultimately returning to settle down in Paris; Gary spoke several languages fluently and wrote novels in two of them. In a radio interview near the end of his life, when asked if he thought of himself as a "world citizen," he rejected the term outright.

"Cosmopolitan, world citizen — what do these words mean, frankly? That you like travelling? Tourism? Or that you sympathise with the suffering of people in Bangladesh and that sort of thing? Sure, you can take it even further and say, 'I'm a human being, a member of the human community', and then nations no longer exist, the world no longer exists, nothing exists anymore. No, if you talk about belonging, you're not talking about Europe, or the world, or cosmopolitanism, you're talking about a little hole in the wall somewhere. To my mind, the human community is the *smallest* human community. So I would say, 'I'm a Baquist' — because I live on the rue du Bac."

In fact, however, Gary did *not* identify with the other residents of his bourgeois neighbourhood in Paris; rather, in both his life and work, he identified with everyone who was marginal, weak or dispossessed, including animals. But he was repelled by militant rhetoric *per se*, and considered "the love of all nations" every bit as suspicious as blind patriotism.

Two factors can contribute to the existence of a powerful national sentiment: *time* and *blood*.

Time is what fosters the slow development of a national heritage — that is, an ensemble of specific cultural traits in four main areas — language, religion, cooking and music — all the aspects of daily life that can be ritualised, raised above the level of need and efficiency, and taken towards beauty and art. Clearly, the "patriotism" which I so admire in the Haitians of the diaspora rests on those four pillars: by speaking Creole in the home, keeping in close touch with the Voodoo pantheon, eating spicy meals and regularly attending Haitian balls, they manage to keep their country alive in their hearts.... To a lesser degree, Americans in Paris also form a community. But English Canadians? What culinary or musical rites could I possibly resuscitate with my compatriots in exile?

Blood is important, of course, because violence binds people together. The longer people fight to defend their territory against outside aggressors, the greater the solidarity amongst them. Here again, Haitian patriotism is comprehensible: blood has been shed on a daily basis in Haiti for nearly two hundred years. It's a safe bet that people in Sarajevo these days are growing more and more patriotic. Or, to take examples from closer to home: being an American Indian or a European Jew will remain a powerful source of identity for a long time to come — despite differences of language, cooking, music or even religious belief among the various Jewish or Native American communities — because the blood of these peoples has been shed in horrifying quantities. I recall the gypsy T. and I met last year in Poland. As we chatted together over borscht and grated carrots, in a restaurant located directly across from the Auschwitz train station, he blithely ran through the list of crimes perpetrated against his people, literally beaming with pride as he quoted the precise number of gypsies murdered by Hitler in each and every European country. These horrors of the past clearly gave him a solid and sufficient sense of his identity in the present — he knew not only *who* he was, but *why*. I had no comparable sense of my own *raison d'être*: how could a mere WASP from Alberta hope to compete with such spectacular hecatombs? How could I even pronounce a sentence beginning with the words, "We Albertan WASPS..."? In Canada, the only outside aggressors were ourselves; and if war there was — well, we won it.

We can't even claim to have been "returning," as many Israelis do, to a land we believed to be holy, and ours by birthright. We calmly and firmly appropriated the holy lands of the Indians, despite all their protest and resistance. We were stronger than they were; it was as simple as that. And we never managed to sacralise these lands in turn. That's the way it it is — the New World is a secular place — and perhaps this isn't something we should regret. At least Canadians don't carry out patriotic massacres in mosque-synagogues.

Should we nourish the hope of being attacked by a foreign army some day, just to bolster our sense of national identity?

There hasn't been a great deal more bloodshed in Québec than in Alberta, but a greater amount of time has gone by. The Québecois have reaped the benefits of what we Albertans so cruelly lack: centuries in which to develop traditions, transmit memories, tell and retell the stories of our ancestors. The problem is that Albertan history will probably never acquire this sacred quality, because it began too late: we grew up in the age of the radio and the telephone, the airplane and the moving-picture, the television and the computer. Never again, at least in the Western world, will societies have the chance to evolve in relative isolation from one another. Distances have been reduced to nothing, with the result that the four pillars of culture — food, music, religion and language — are coast-to-coast, standardized, homogenized. I can eat the same hamburgers, listen to the same rap music and watch the same televangelists in Calgary as I can in Iowa City or Miami.... As for the language, as we all know, English has come to dominate not only Canada, but pretty much the planet Earth.

It's a language I abandoned — almost as radically as I abandoned Alberta — for personal rather than political reasons; a language to which, enriched by a long and loving relationship with a foreign tongue, I've recently returned; a language I now speak, they tell me, with minor errors and a slight accent (in the States, these days, people sometimes ask me to *spell my Christian name*, certainly one of the most common names on the continent!).... I often find it destabilizing not to fully coincide with any identity — but at the same time, I'm convinced that this uncomfortable coexistence in my soul of two languages and two ways of being is what makes me most profoundly Canadian. The two have not the least desire to merge; some days, they refuse to so much as shake hands with each other; they seem to enjoy existing in a state of mutual irony, sometimes even mockery and antagonism. In a word, they lay claim to all the ambiguity of their situation.

Come to think of it, this might be just the wisdom which, if they so desired, the people of this country could best embody — *a patriotism of ambiguity.*

(1993)

On Being Beautiful

I'm beautiful. I have never written about this before, so I thought I would try to write about it. It has lasted quite a long time, this beauty of mine, but it won't be lasting much longer because I'm forty now, as I'm writing this, forty now and probably by the time you read it forty-one, and so on and so forth, and we all know it ends up as worms or ashes, but for the moment I'm still beautiful. More or less. Less than I used to be, despite the regular application of henna to my graying hair and concealer to the rings beneath my eyes. Less than Mrs. Bhutto of Pakistan, who is precisely my age. Less than many of my students now — but still, perhaps, a little more than my eleven-year-old daughter. For another year or two ("Mirror, mirror...").

I'm also intelligent. Less so than Simone Weil. My intelligence, too, is already going downhill — though differently from my beauty — and it, too, will end up as worms or ashes. But still. For the time being I'm quite intelligent.

When I say I'm beautiful and intelligent, I'm not boasting. All I have done is take reasonable care of the beauty and intelligence programmed into me by the dice-toss of my parents' chomosomes. (They were both beautiful and intelligent, too, when they were young; they're considerably less so now, but that probably doesn't interest you as much as the rest of what I have to say.)

How is it possible to boast about things for which one isn't responsible?

We're dealt a hand at birth: some of the cards are genetic (skin colour, musicality, bunions), others are cultural (religion, language, nationality), but all are *given* rather than *chosen*. Later, as adults, we can make a conscious decision to change a few of the cards in our hands — by converting from Catholicism to Judaism, for instance, or by moving to another country, or even by having a sex change operation — but the original deal inevitably leaves its deep and indelible imprint on us.

I've never quite understood people's boasting about their destiny-dealt hand, though it's certainly a ubiquitous phenomenon. Perhaps my own origins are too bland to have instilled in me this sort of pride: it's never occurred to me to derive my self-esteem from the fact that I was born in Calgary, Alberta or that I was raised a Protestant or that I have white skin or that I am female. Likewise, I'm responsible for neither my beauty nor my intelligence, which have been two incredibly salient features of the forty years I've spent on this earth so far — and which, until today, I've never had the courage to write about.

My beauty has gotten me many places, some of which I very badly wanted to go to, and some of which I did not want to go to at all. Over the years, I have watched it attack and corrode borders, then take me with it into foreign territories. Borders are ideas erected between age groups, social classes, all sorts of hierarchical entities, in order that society may function as predictably and as decently as possible. They are not solid brick walls. Beauty eats them away. This is the truth; we've all seen it happen, though it happens differently in different places (I'll be coming back to this).

I was not particularly beautiful as a child. I started getting that way at around age fifteen, when I was a junior in high school (I'd skipped a grade — much earlier, because my intelligence was manifest long before my beauty), and as soon as it happened I seduced and/or was seduced by my creative writing teacher. He was ten years older than I (though younger than the man to whom I'm now married), and, shortly before the end of the school year, he took whatever virginity childhood sex games with my brother had left me. I was thrilled, flattered, crazily in love, and, for a long time, proud — yes, proud, for this was something in which my responsibility was implicated. The love affair was a serious one. It culminated in engagement — an engagement I broke off at age eighteen, when I fell in love with someone else. For nearly three years, then, my life revolved around this man. There was no sexual harrassment involved.

Ah, but was he not taking advantage of his position? Of his superior education? Of the intellectual awe in which I held him? He certainly was, just as I was taking advantage of my youth, beauty, and whatever innocence I still appeared to possess. We wanted the same thing, which was to be in love with each other. Were we equals? Were Socrates and the young men whom he instructed and sodomized... equals? Contemporary American society, it seems, would in all likelihood condemn Socrates to death just as ancient Athens did, though for different reasons.

Let us be careful. Let us be subtle. Let us not be polemical and deliciously angry and righteously indignant. The subject is a messy one, as messy and contradictory as the species to which we belong, so let us not pretend to tie up all its loose ends and get it straight and iron it flat. Would I like the idea of my daughter sleeping with one of her teachers? No, not at age eleven. At what age, then? At an age when she has acquired a will of her own, a desire of her own, and an intellect capable of critical discernment. In other words, at an age when (and *if*, for not all young girls have the same weird penchant for brainy older men as I) she wants it. I tend to think that in her case that might mean something like never, but naturally I don't know.

Listen. Last spring I was at a literary cocktail party in Montreal, standing in a corner drinking wine with my brother and an eminent elderly Québecois writer, and the conversation came around to the cases, currently hitting the headlines, of young boys who'd been sexually abused by priests in Québec's Catholic schools. "The problem with this whole outcry," my brother said suddenly, "is that it will make it impossible for actual love affairs ever to take place in those situations again." I saw the older man do a double take and then — to my utter astonishment — heard him say, "Yes, you're right. I had that experience myself. Of course, I wasn't ten or eleven years old, I was sixteen. But still...."

The man was now in his seventies. It had probably been several decades since he had dared allude to this experience, his teen-age love for one of his teachers, but the memory of it was still vivid enough to make his voice tremble with emotion. Clearly, he had loved that teacher, just as I had loved the one to whom I later became engaged. And because we loved them, we also learned a great deal from these seductive teachers. They fed our intelligence, brought our bodies and our minds to life. I read a hundred books because of mine.

Again, the child's age makes an important difference — and also his or her psychological vulnerability. I'm by no means challenging the fact that students have been, can be, are being sexually manipulated or abused by their teachers, I'm only asking that we not leap from this fact to the grotesque conclusion that bodiliness should be radically eliminated from all pedagogical situations. In my own teaching experience over the years, though it so happens I've never flirted let alone slept with my students, I'm fairly sure that my beauty has contributed positively to the transmission of knowledge and ideas, the stimulation of their brains.

Other borders eaten away by my beauty I would definitely have rather seen preserved. For instance, I could have done without having my thighs stroked by the grey-haired doctor who performed my first gynecological examination, or my eyes longingly stared into by the bespectacled young dentist who removed my impacted wisdom teeth. Probably since the Stone Age, beautiful (and less beautiful) girls have needed to learn to defend themselves — whether through sarcasm, cool rejection or karate chops — against these annoying infringements on their integrity. They can come from almost anyone — including, unexceptionally, women. Again, the only criterion for whether this behavior is oppressive or not is whether or not one is made uncomfortable by it — that is, whether or not there is room and desire for response, interaction.

Still other experiences with borders strike me, so to speak, as borderline. After I finished high school and before I entered college (indeed, in order to earn money to attend college, because the gifts and advantages bestowed on me at birth had not included wealth), I worked full-time as a medical secretary in the psychiatric clinic of an august educational institution. By this time, I was seventeen and really quite beautiful, in my WASPish sort of way. I was also extraordinarily depressed. My depression may indeed have contributed to my beauty (as Bob Dylan pointed out, there's something irresistible about sad-eyed ladies). I was depressed partly because my fiancé was far away, partly because typing psychiatric records was a hell of a lousy initiation into adulthood, and partly because my superior intelligence made it painful and humiliating for me to be working full-time as a secretary. After a few months I was so suicidal that I myself entered therapy with one of my bosses. This is not a joke. The therapy was free, part of my health benefits as an employee of the august institution. The shrink whom I chose to see — regularly, alone, in his office, once or twice a week — was, naturally, the one I'd come to like and respect the most, after months of transcribing his Dictaphone summaries of sessions with his patients. Indeed we'd become rather chummy. He was forty and, like myself, not badly endowed in body and in mind — and I, as I have said, was seventeen. By the time I began lying down on his couch, I had already sat for his children a couple of times, attended some of his lectures at the august institution, and received from him as a Christmas present a wonderful pair of running-shoes (like millions of other Americans then and now, he jogged to work off calories and anger).

I entered therapy with him, and more borders were eaten away. No, he did not rape or maul me; he did not even crush me on the couch with the frightening weight of his body. As a matter of fact, his was a small and unprepossessing body; there was nothing frightening about it. He kissed me, standing up, at the end of every session. I kissed him back. We mostly kissed on the lips. Sometimes on the cheeks or the neck. No tongue work, as I recall. Never the least constraint. I found the kisses comforting and flattering, though not arousing. Perhaps he was aroused — but if he was, he never pressed it upon me. That border, at least, was preserved.

Was this a traumatizing experience? In my case, I think not. It seems to me that other acts performed by irresponsible or immature authority figures have left far deeper scars on my psyche. My first-grade teacher, for instance, who — before I skipped into second grade — slashed her red pen across my imperfect copy-book so hard that the page was torn. I'd rather be kissed than slashed any day.

Still, the question is, why did this shrink feel compelled to kiss me? As I saw it (fairly lucidly) at the time, it was partly because of my beauty and intelligence, and partly because the state of extreme fragility I was in had stimulated his protective male instincts. I say this with no irony whatsoever. In fact, I know it to be the truth because I had dinner with this man last month. I'd returned to teach for a semester at the same old august institution, we hadn't seen each other in twenty-three years, he was now nearing retirement, we still got along famously, and in the course of this dinner he told me that in 1971, when I was his patient and his secretary and his babysitter and his friend, he had longed to cast an invisible mantle of protection over my shoulders as I went out into the world.

And I believed him.

Also in the course of our dinner, he complimented me on having pulled through so well. I could see him casting about for laudatory adjectives to describe me, body and soul, and for intensifying adverbs to describe the adjectives. The compliments he came up with were delightful, but it was hard for me to relish them to the full, as they were almost invariably prefaced by the demurral, "I hope you won't think I'm being patronizing." "Oh, no!" I encouraged him, in my very warmest voice. "More, more!" But deep down I was dismayed. What is going on in this country? I wondered. Can it really have grown as dangerous as that to tell a woman she is beautiful and intelligent?

But I've gotten ahead of my story.

After a year of working as a secretary, I'd set aside enough money to be able to attend college, with the help of a scholarship and a loan. It was an excellent college — thanks, presumably, this time, not to my superior beauty but to my superior intelligence. By now I was eighteen and — due to the free-love ambiance in which all of us were floating in those post-Pill, pre-AIDS years — no longer innocent at all. I'd slept with a frightening number of men (men could no longer frighten me — only their number). I was living with the one for whom I'd left my creative-writing-teacher-fiancé. And I'd decided to study, among other things, creative writing.

Although the writer-professor with whom I studied at this college was not then, as he is now, world famous, he definitely had charisma. There were about twelve students in his class — ten women and two men, if I remember correctly. The men can be dismissed at once. The ten women were all, by definition, exceptionally intelligent. For some unfathomable reason, most of them were also exceptionally beautiful. From the beginning of September until the end of June, all of us competed frantically to please the teacher.

Now, what does "competed frantically to please the teacher" mean? Well, it means that we used our minds and bodies to gain his approval, just as he used his to gain ours. We dressed in a certain way, talked in a certain way, wrote our short stories in a certain way, and walked into his office for our bi-monthly individual "conferences" in a certain way, each of us hoping against hope that he would recognize us as that special person whose body and mind he could appreciate, admire, cherish and caress.

I won.

But then, I may not have been the only winner. Perhaps there were ten winners, and he was just prodigiously gifted at juggling his time schedule to include us all.

At college as in high school, I was an active subject rather than a passive object in my love affairs with professors. This time, however, I knew that the person was not a crucial element in my destiny. Both of us felt fairly rotten about betraying our partners, and found the hotel rooms we went together at once expensive and sordid. We soon phased out the erotic aspect of our friendship — and fortunately so, for had the other students become aware of it, the atmosphere in the classroom would probably have been affected. We remained in touch, however, for a number of years afterwards.

But now my story switches directions.

At the age of twenty, under the auspices of my excellent college, I came to Paris for my "Junior Year Abroad," then went on to spend my senior year abroad, and to do a Master's degree abroad, and now, twenty years and two French children later, I have hit upon the perfect inscription for my tombstone: *Once abroad, always abroad.*

Oddly enough, despite Frenchmen's worldwide reputation for being sexually obsessed, my dealings in France with professors, employers, gynecologists, dentists and shrinks have all been relatively maul-free. Since I did not become ugly overnight upon moving to Paris, I have come to wonder whether my borderline erotic experiences as a young woman were not, at least partially, determined by cultural factors — i.e., whether there was not something specifically American (rather than, say, "modern" or "Western") about them. It seems to me that as a general rule (and with all the usual caveats regarding this sort of generalisation), the French accept the fact that they have, and are, bodies. The prevailing social decorum is not as all-or-nothing as it is in the States, where the alternative seems to be: either overt sexual contact or feigned indifference to all physical characteristics. In France there is an intermediary level of communication based on the continual exchange of glances, witty remarks, hand gestures and the like. Both men and women take part in this exchange. As the French do not attempt to radically rid social existence of physicality, they are not in such a state of patent contradiction and frustration as are the Americans (I think I'm mainly speaking of White Americans here). In a word, they tend to value the art of sublimation.

Americans, it would seem — again, these are the humble observations of a former insider and current outsider who has just spent a few perplexed months back on the "inside" — are taught less to love or enjoy their bodies than to take care of them. As a people, they seem to conceive physicality essentially in terms of health, exercise, self-defense, autonomy, anatomy, and how-to sex manuals. When one roams the aisles of the supermarkets from which they feed themselves, one essentially has the choice between health food and junk food; plain ordinary wonderful unprocessed unimproved unadulterated food is virtually impossible to find. Americans are becoming phobic about what they put into their bodies — no other country in the world diets so much or suffers from so many eating disorders. In the realm of eroticism, analogous extremes are represented by pornography and *The Joy of Sex*. It is as though the American people required that everything erotic and gastronomic be quantified, verbalized, exhaustively described and discussed and dissected.

As a result, they often seem genuinely (or disingenuously?) convinced that the whole aesthetic, interactive dimension of their bodies is non-existent. Taking this dimension into account can imply concealing as much as revealing, modesty as much as brazenness; it is the opposite of "letting it all hang out." I once had a beautiful young long-blonde-haired American female student who came close to getting herself lynched in Morocco by sauntering across a field dressed in nothing but short shorts and a halter-top. A group of Arab peasants tore after her waving pitchforks — and she was not only terrified but totally nonplussed at the aggressiveness of their reaction to her body. She was just being natural! By European standards, beautiful young long-blond-haired American girls who stare men straight in the face are not natural, they are come-ons. By North African standards, they are prostitutes if not witches. No, I'm not defending the *chador*; I'm simply marvelling at American lack of sensitivity to the fact that — and the ways in which — other people, other peoples, might respond to their bodies.

Sexual harrassment, on the job and elsewhere, definitely exists in France, but that's not quite what I'm talking about here. I am talking, rather, about the fact that a certain degree of eroticism is not only tolerated on the social scene but considered to be a normal part of it. Like my own American students of today, I was enraged and humiliated, when I first came to Paris, by the stares, whistles and muttered remarks of men I passed in the streets. My first attempts to take pensive solitary walks in the cities of Southern Italy invariably ended in fits of hysteria and tears. But the native women in these countries know how to handle their men. And the rape rates are far, far higher in the United States, where playful, tacit, intangible erotic exchange in public is increasingly taboo. (I still squirm whenever I recall the time, on a French TV-show with a number of other women writers, I was the only one who claimed she resented these unsolicited displays of male approval. The other guests were overtly nostalgic about the "good old days" when men used to whistle at them in the streets, though it wasn't quite clear whether these days had vanished because they had aged or because feminism had cowed men into silence.)

Admittedly, there have been occasions in France on which I have felt my beauty to be a handicap. Once or twice I have narrowly escaped rape; more than once or twice I've had devastating doubts about whether a person's enthusiasm for one of my books or articles might not be rightfully due to my big blue eyes. This has tended to make me insecure — and even, sporadically, miserable. But I refuse to exaggerate. These are small dramas. My beauty has never made me nearly as miserable as an assembly-line worker, or a crack addict, or a Black mother on welfare.

I have also — calmly, naturally, as every beautiful woman knows how to do — allowed my beauty to bring me minor favours and advantages: faster service in restaurants, increased courtesy in libraries, more humorous and less expensive exchanges with policemen.... The occasions have literally been numberless. They have also been unavoidable — to avoid them, I should have had to disguise myself as an ugly person (as Simone Weil did) by wearing thick black glasses and dressing in frumpy clothes, or indulging in some extreme "eating disorder."

Listen, I would like for once to lay all my cards on the table (I might as well — I'm a novelist now, which means that I can be neither hired nor fired; in many important ways I have nothing to lose). Every human being on this earth is a combination of mind and body, intelligence and beauty, greater or lesser, now greater, now lesser, forever in flux and forever in interaction. But it is quite rare that one and the same person should experience both extremes, being treated alternately as all-body and as all-mind. Having exercised such wildly disparate professions as masseuse and feminist journalist, nude model and

English professor, bar "hostess" and guest lecturer in prestigious universities, I am probably in a better position than most to revolt against the bad faith so prevalent in the United States today (since it cannot possibly be a question of naïveté), which pretends that our minds do not live in bodies, and that we respond to each other's minds independently of each other's bodies, and that what we love in each other when we make love to each other's bodies is not also, in large part, each other's minds, and that professors can teach and students study without their bodies ever being present in the classroom, and that bosses and employees and colleagues and work-mates can interact professionally without their bodies ever being present in the office or factory — and that, moreover, it is possible for these bodies to miraculously burst into existence when, in private darkened bedrooms enclosing one or two or more consenting adults, all systems are suddenly said to be "go," whereas they have been forced to "stop" "stop" "stop" and "stop" all day long in every other situation in which they've found themselves.

These American bodies are no longer allowed to smoke, they're no longer allowed to joke, they're no longer allowed to perspire; all of their sexy ambiguities have been banished to oblivion, war has been declared on their capacity for innuendo; flirting has been outlawed because it presupposes inequality (and this is true — or, more accurately, flirting underlines, renders flagrant and therefore undeniable, the inequality that in fact exists between the beautiful and the less beautiful, the intelligent and the less intelligent, the funny and the less funny)

— oh at all costs let us not recognize these sorts of inequality, let us cover our eyes and pinch our noses and plug our ears in front of them; the work place is for getting work done and schools and universities are for getting an education and restaurants are for eating and bars are for drinking and streets are for striding purposefully from one place to another and none of these places no no no is an appropriate place for bodies, for sensuality, for sidelong glances, for flirting, ah ah ah, flirting leads to rape, the eyes and words of a man on a woman's body are already a miniature version of rape, and all forms of physical exchange between human bodies must be as predictable and safe and contractual as the sale of a house.

Again, let me attempt to be clear and discerning and calm. People who study well and write good papers, whether they are beautiful or ugly, brown or yellow, tall or short, should receive good marks; and people who have appropriate credentials or working records should never need to consent to being sodomized by the powers-that-be in order to get a job or a degree or a promotion. The role of beauty — and every other culturally or genetically inherited factor — in situations such as legal trials, political elections, thesis defenses and tenure hearings should be as close to zero as possible. (Thus, it is outrageous that Californians should currently be discussing the length of a judge's skirt: if judges and lawyers in so many countries wear long black robes, it is precisely to anul or at least neutralize the particularities of their bodies.)

In public life, in other words, modern democratic institutions are rightly required to be blind to physical traits. At the opposite end of the spectrum is love-making, in which physicality attains extremes of intensity. But in between the two there is social existence — life on the job, in the neighbourhood, at school, in the subway — a fascinating, shimmering, shifting mix of public and private, physical and spiritual, proximity and distance, conformity with code and spontaneous invention. What I'm saying is that in the United States, this crucial middle ground (of which, of course, physicality is but one facet among many) is currently being eroded to nothingness by maniacal verbalization and ludicrous legalism. And that the compulsion to aberrant sexual behavior is worsened, not attenuated, when sociality is thus unnaturally invaded by moral imperatives and declarations and calculations.

What I am not saying (I insist, politely banging my fist on the table) is, "Hey, Men! Hunting Season Open All Year!" All forms of sexual coercion are repulsive. But we must be careful or, under pretext of policing them, we shall lose a vast and rich dimension of human existence, namely the language of bodies, the hundred silent languages of bodies, which vary from country to country, social class to social class and milieu to milieu — yes, the complex, moving languages through which, wordlessly, endlessly, men and women ask and answer questions about each other, move, suggest, demur, wiggle, giggle, arch eyebrows, light cigarettes, graze a hand, a cheek, a shoulderblade, manifest wonder, admiration, tenderness, arousal, delight, defiance.... (Is it because these languages are being silenced in America that gays and Lesbians so often resort to grotesquely obvious codes to get their messages of desire across?) But — ah ah ah and then, but then, what if desire becomes aggression? What if it becomes manipulation and threat and blackmail? What if it becomes forcing and pushing, shoving and battering, angry hell? Well then then then, if it becomes that, well then, there are already laws against that. But if it does not become that, then it becomes life. And the very definition of life is: *win a few, lose a few*. Since when does one go running to a lawyer or a journalist every time there is a loss?

What we have a right to in this life, as even the American Constitution acknowledges, is not happiness; it is, rather, the pursuit of happiness, which is a very different thing indeed. In the same way, the concept of equal rights by no means implies that we are or must pretend to be identical to one another. If a deck of cards contains fifty-two fours of diamonds, what sort of passionate poker game will anyone be able to play?

My daughter is also turning out to be beautiful and intelligent — which means that, in addition to teaching her to eschew boasting about it, I shall need to teach her a certain number of things about the treatment she can expect at the hands of the world, just as parents have always prepared their children for the (positive and negative) effects of being Ukrainian, Tasmanian, Jewish, Catholic, dwarves, white, black, haemophilic, red-haired, skinny, knock-kneed, and so on and so forth, including all the possible combinations of these traits.

Though they will have more or less weighty consequences depending on the geographical, historical, political and social context in which one grows up, all these factors are part of the hand one is dealt at life's outset. There is no fatalism involved here; I don't mean that once you get your cards, the game is tantamount to over. I simply mean that all of us play the game according to the cards we have in our hand — bluffing and feinting, discarding and drawing, trying to influence the other players, winning and losing.... The progressive/ liberal/ revolutionary/ existentialist philosophies we have espoused over the past couple of hundred years have tended to blind us to this simple truth, universally recognized by novelists and children, namely that *people deal with what they're dealt.*

(1994)

Of all my essays, this is the one that has been the most widely translated — it exists in thirteen languages including Hebrew and Japanese and was even published in Brail; it sparked off violent controversies in Italy and Spain.... I should add that, a decade having passed since I wrote it, my daughter is now more beautiful than I am, and that this is fine with me.

The Gospel According to Saint Matthew

In memoriam Reverend William J. Huston

Matthew... I can still hear how gentle the word was as my minister grandfather pronounced it, the *th* making his tongue whistle slightly between his teeth, the initial *M* wetting his full lips like honey, the vowels emerging clear and full from his throat (in a voice that sometimes rang but never thundered).... I may be wrong but it seems to me that for whatever reason, the name of that particular Evangelist elicited a special feeling in him.

This man was the child of a couple who could have benefited from a few well-aimed miracles. His father, who was stone deaf and therefore illiterate, was a woodcutter in Ontario (we're in the last decade of the 19th century). In one of the lumber camps where he was employed, he met and fell in love with the Irish cook — who was not deaf, but blind; both, moreover, were already in their early forties. They married and had two sons in rapid succession; the mother, a devout believer, took on a job as caretaker of the Methodist church across from their house. When her sons were in their early teens, she fell ill and died; the elder boy had to give up school to help support the family, but the younger one, my grandfather, was able to pursue his studies thanks to the assistance of his friends in the Church; when the father died in turn a few years later, the Methodists decided to take over all his expenses. He never forgot their generosity and, as soon as he reached adulthood, made up his mind to become a minister in that branch of Protestantism.

He, of course, when he began a sermon or a family prayer service with a quote from *The Gospel According to Saint Matthew*, had actually read the book in question. His own younger daughter would read it, too, and be lastingly affected by it — so much so that she would train as a medical missionary and spend thirty-five years of her life spreading the good news up and down the slopes of the Himalayas.

But to me — to us, his grandchildren, and in all likelihood to most of his congregation as well, *Matthew* was neither a book nor even the author of a book; it was always and exclusively a quote or a series of quotes, a fragment chosen as the point of departure for a moral lesson — which, though we may sometimes have found it boring or insipid, nonetheless left its poetic imprint on us: the King James translation of this gospel is as densely studded with verbal jewels as *Hamlet* or *Macbeth*... In addition to its poetry (and inseparable from it), *Matthew* also left us with a certain image of Jesus — an image which not only continues to accompany me, but is quite simply part of who I am.

For fully fifteen years, in the numerous Protestant, then Anglican churches where I attended Sunday school and Catechism classes, I absorbed homeopathic doses of *Matthew* without ever reading it, without knowing in what ways it differed from the three other official Gospels, without suspecting that there might be other, non-official versions of the same story (the censored, long-suppressed Gnostic Gospels) — and, most incredibly of all, without realizing that Jesus's life was actually inscribed somewhere in the history and geography of the world. To us, Israel and Egypt were like Peter Pan's Neverland or Sleeping Beauty's enchanted forest — how could they possibly be located on the same planet as Calgary, Red Deer and Edmonton? *Bethlehem, Nazareth, Galilee* — these were magical, incantatory names. In many ways, the Gospels were like fairy tales — in both types of story, miracles were performed, demons wreaked havoc, the heavens opened up and disembodied voices made earth-shaking declarations; the main difference being that, unlike the weekday fables peopled with witches and dragons, the Sunday-morning fables were taken seriously by the adults who imparted them to us. However prosaic their other activities may have been — teaching mathematics like my father or polishing silverware like my grandmother — they truly seemed to lend credit to these preposterous tales and, by making them sound serious and deeply ethical, did their best to ensure that we would do likewise.

How does it happen that until the age of sixteen or seventeen, despite my education (undeniably longer and more elaborate than the average education on this earth), I remained unaware that Jesus, the Scribes, the Pharisees, Judas, the Prophets and the Old Testament were (good heavens!) Jewish, and that the Palestine of the Bible had the same geographical location as the Palestine referred to in contemporary news articles (about the 1967 war, for instance)? The answer, clearly, is that religious instruction has far less to do with knowledge than with faith. Pointing Israel out to us on a map of the world, or situating the life of Jesus in the historical context of the Roman Empire, would have dissipated the "mythical fuzziness" that is indispensible to every system of belief. The point was to make us perceive the events of Jesus's life as *true*, but as belonging to a different kind of truth than ordinary facts, banally circumscribed in space and time.

Like all religious dogmas, the Christian dogma comprises four different layers, each of which preserves some elements of the former and eliminates others. The first and most distant layer, now engulfed in the mists of Time, would be the actual words pronounced by a young, charismatic Jew born in Palestine during the Roman occupation, and of whom little can be known with certainty. Next come the Scriptures: between three and seven decades after this man's death — at a time when the Jews, having suffered cruel defeat at the hands of the Romans, were desperately clinging to their ethnic identity and ancient laws — the Evangelists and other authors of the New Testament set out to consolidate the doctrine of a rebel church, one which would be less finicky, and more open to the rest of the world than traditional Judaism. Thirdly, these Scriptures were propagated in countless sermons over the centuries by a huge number of priests and ministers, each of whom condensed, cut, combined and conflated the sacred texts according to his own personality and the political needs of the time.... Fourthly, there is the fraction of these sermons that churchgoers (including myself) retained for their personal use, either because it helped them find meaning in their lives — or, on the contrary, because it gave them something to revolt against.

It is tempting to say that any resemblance between the first and last strata would be purely fortuitous — or else the result of a miracle!

I have just now read *The Gospel According to Matthew* for the first time in my life. And, being no longer a child, and having acquired some experience in reading and judging written texts — having, moreover, learned a few things about the history of Christianity in general and the writing of the Gospels in particular (virtually nothing is known about the author of "Matthew," except that it was not the tax-collector apostle, and probably not only one person), my reactions to this reading are very mixed. Emotion at the profound beauty of some of Jesus's sayings. Indignation at the gospel's internal contradictions. Scepticism vis-à-vis the miracles Jesus is said to have performed. And astonishment at the way in which "Matthew" insists on making every detail of Christ's life coincide with Old Testament prophecy, even if this requires a fair amount of invention....

Gradually, a sort of realization dawned on me. Not for nothing is this fifty-page, two-thousand-year-old text one of the most influential pieces of writing in human history. Not for nothing, but not for any single reason, either. For a plethora of *different* reasons — in other words, not *despite* but *thanks* to its logical inconsistencies. The faces of Christ revealed to us in *Matthew* are not only multiple, they are also mutually incompatible; thus, each can elicit the identification of different group of readers. And if you take the *non*-readers into account, a group to which I myself belonged until just now, and to which the overwhelming majority of Christians have always belonged, then the possibilities for identification become virtually infinite.

Ah yes — a thrilling book indeed. What a story! No matter which Jesus you're looking for, you're bound to find Him in Matthew.

There is the "human" Jesus of the Sermon on the Mount — this was the one my grandfather introduced me to, and whom he did his best to emulate all his life: having been born, like Jesus, in modest circumstances, he never ceased preaching and practising compassion, respect for the humble, and help for the impoverished. Matthew's Jesus is "human," too, because of the fear and doubt that fill his heart in the Garden of Gethsemani: "My soul is exceeding sorrowful, even unto death"; "O my Father, if it be possible, let this cup pass from me" (XXVI: 38-39); J.S. Bach's *Matthias Passion* portrays the same, highly poignant Christ.

There is a Jesus who is "human" in the negative sense of the term — that is, touchy, prideful and vengeful. This version of Christ was inculcated into huge numbers of Europeans, and for centuries they used Him to justify their persecution and destruction of the Jews. Even nowadays, it is not unheard of for schoolchildren in France to turn upon a Jewish classmate and hiss, "You killed Jesus," leaving the child at a loss as to how he could possibly have accomplished such a thing.... In Western Canada, however, no one ever told us that the Jews were to blame for the Crucifixion — if only because there were so few Jews in the vicinity. No: we learned that the human heart (beautifully symbolized in Bach's *Passion* by the choir) could be good and evil, loyal and disloyal by turn. We learned, in other words, that *we* were the ones who had loved, followed, praised and admired Jesus, and that *we* were the ones who had crucified Him (it now occurs to me this was an excellent introduction to crowd psychology). Neither my grandfather nor any of the other preachers of my childhood so much as breathed a word to us about the Jesus who ranted and raved against his enemies (after having enjoined *us*, his followers, to love them, turn the other cheek, and forgive their offenses seven times seventy times!) — the one who calls the Scribes and Pharisees "ye hypocrites" and "Ye serpents, ye generation of vipers" (XXIII:33), and warns them about what's in store for them on Judgment Day: "there shall be weeping, and gnashing of teeth" (*passim*) — or the Jesus who declares, in effect: "Ha! I could summon up twelve legions of angels, if I felt like it!" (XXVI: 53) — like a kid who swaggers and talks tough when he feels under threat.

Another of Matthew's Jesuses is "superhuman" in a positive way. This is the man whose birth and baptism were marked by supernatural events (although, modern rationalists that we are, we cannot help raising an eyebrow when Matthew, after having run through the forty-two generations of ancestors connecting Joseph directly to Abraham, blithely adds that Mary was pregnant before she ever "knew" her husband; thus admitting that Jesus had nothing to do with this illustrious family tree); the miracles, the exorcisms, the confrontations with Satan in person — from which, naturally, Jesus invariably emerged victorious.

Finally, *Matthew* contains a negatively "superhuman" Jesus, who also went undiscussed in the churches I attended. This Jesus entered the town of Bethany, for example, and, feeling hungry, rummaged among the leaves of a fig tree; when he realized that it bore no fruit, he grew angry and caused the tree to *wither up and die* (XXI: 17-21)! This is the man who was capable of feeding thousands of people with a few loaves and fishes? And who admonished us to be as "the fowls of the air" (VI: 26) and not worry about where our next meal was coming from? How, then, could he inflict such drastic punishment on a poor, innocent *tree*?

Even the most apparently straightforward of Christ's sayings can lend itself to disparate interpretations. "The Kingdom of Heaven is at hand," for instance, can be seen as either a promise or a threat. It was definitely intended as a threat by "Matthew" himself — that is, the individual or individuals who, some dozen years after the destruction of the great Temple of Jerusalem (68 A.C.) had a vested interest in proving that Jesus had *predicted* this cataclysm, the point being to make it seem fair punishment for those Jews who had refused to recognize him as their Messiah.

For my grandfather, on the other hand (and for virtually everyone who talked to me about the Gospels in Western Canada), these same words meant something very different. "The Kingdom of Heaven is at hand" — look! All you need to do is stretch out your hand and you can touch it — paradise is right in front of you, here and now!

Even as a child, I remember, I was disturbed by the fact that Jesus contradicted Himself. For instance, he told his followers to "Honour thy father and thy mother" (XIX: 19), but immediately afterwards he declared, "Every one that hath forsaken houses, or brethren, or sisters, or father, or mother, or wife, or children, or lands, for my name's sake, shall receive an hundredfold, and shall inherit everlasting life" (XIX: 29). How were we to reconcile the two demands? There was a third piece of advice on the subject, so radical that no one ever quoted it: "And the children shall rise up against their parents, and cause them to be put to death" (X: 21). Nor did anyone tell us of the day when Jesus's mother and brothers came to speak to Him and He refused to receive them (XII: 46-50). Jesus was generally thought of as a pacifist, because of his famous declaration, "All they that take the sword shall perish with the sword" (XXVI: 52): how, then, could one also justify his saying, "I come not to send peace, but a sword" (X: 34)? And how could my meek and mild grandfather have crossed the Atlantic Ocean in 1916 for the express purpose of killing Germans? Or again: having chosen Simon among all his disciples, renaming him Peter (or "Rock") and founding his very Church upon him (XXI: 18), how could Jesus berate then this same person for his lack of faith, even going so far as to curse him — "*Vade retro, Satanas!*" (XXI: 23)....?

The Jesus we knew had nothing to say on the subject of fornication and eunuchs; these were probably not words that could easily pass the lips of Canadian ministers in the 1950's. What would my reaction have been, had my grandfather begun a sermon with the words: "Whosoever shall marry her that is divorced committeth adultery" (V: 32) — whereas he himself had united in holy matrimony my father and his second wife? More surprising still: "There are some eunuchs, which were so born from their mother's womb" (XIX: 12).... No, that sort of passage would have caused the congregation's mind to wander — better not to even get them started on that line of thinking....

The many visages of *Matthew*'s Jesus have had a powerful influence on non-Christians as well. To take but a few examples from modern history, the Christ figure has served as a positive model for writers and thinkers as varied and unorthodox as Hannah Arendt (the theme of innocence), Simone Weil (purity, chastity, poverty), Roman Gary (altruism), Etty Hillesum (non-resistance to evil), Göran Tunström (love) or Breyten Breytenbach (martyrisation) — and as a negative-model, of course, to Friedrich Nietzsche (weakness, submission, renunciation, servility).

Jesus's multiple personality in *The Gospel According to Saint Matthew* partially explains the diversity of the uses to which he has been put over the past two millenia. Never would he have dreamed, for example, that in his name, one day, more than ten thousand miles away from the country in which he had preached, at the heart of prairie lands undulating with endless wheat or endless snow according to the season, in a small white clapboard church, in a village all of whose inhabitants were white-skinned, before paintings of him as either a baby or a corpse but also, weirdly enough, white-skinned — yes, in his name, an old lady would stretch out a beige-gloved hand and angrily slap her granddaughter's right knee to bring it closer to her left — because, of course, one thousand nine hundred and sixty years after the birth of Christ, it was indecent for a young girl to sit with her legs apart in church, as if she were a young boy.

Nor would he have dreamed that in his name, in Prague, on Good Friday, 1386, thousands of men, women and children would be bludgeoned to death simply because they happened to belong to the Jewish faith. Or that, in His name: murderous Crusades, colonization, the extermination of the Indians, the despoiling of Europe's poor for the construction of sumptuous cathedrals, the massacre of Protestants on Saint-Bartholomew's Day, monasteries of ferocious austerity, corporeal punishment in British public schools, the Lord's Prayer broadcast daily over loudspeakers in American schools, the Papamobile, dollar-hungry televangelists, an interminable civil war in

Ireland, obese tourists sweating and groaning under the weight of the True Cross on Jerusalem's *Via Dolorosa*, miserable little girls in French Catholic boarding-schools being forced to attend class carrying their urine-soaked sheets on their shoulders....

But also, in his name — churches in which the important moments of countless human lives have been given ritual importance — births, weddings and deaths, mourning and hope, in the silence of prayer and meditation or in the deafening fervour of a group singing along with the organ. Painting, sculpture, and music of the highest genius; gifts bestowed with love, comfort provided, meals shared, oppression denounced and injustice combatted, helping hands outheld, words murmured to appease suffering, gestures of love and charity imitated, repeated and spread all over the world, throughout the centuries....

Recalling, all these years later, how very gentle the word *Matthew* sounded on my grandfather's lips, I feel grateful to the Christians of my childhood for having spared me the more noxious aspects of the *Gospel According to Matthew*, transmitting only its most beautiful and generous-minded passages. If perchance I was made the least bit better by my acquaintance with the "Good News," it was thanks to them.

(2001)

The Decline of "Identity"?

"What annoys us is what allows us to define ourselves. Without upsets, there is no identity."
— *Cioran*

"The Lord creates; man can recreate."
— *David Homel*

In the course of a recent trip through Brittany, I accepted the hospitality of a woman whom I knew only slightly, but whose kindness was great and whose generosity was insistent. Having spent much of the day doing intensive tourism, I retired at afternoon's end to the room she had placed at my disposal. There, I did some deep breathing and a bit of yoga, took out my notebook and began, pen in hand, to allow the day's images and impressions to take shape in my mind. About ten minutes elapsed; scarcely had I begun to concentrate than my hostess tapped on the door and burst gaily into the room with a pile of things to "entertain me" and "keep me busy." I don't remember everything the pile contained. Among other things: a special issue of a TV mag devoted to the civil war in Algeria, a large book of glossy photos on Swedish interior decorating, and the most recent novel by one of her favourite authors, who was definitely not one of mine.

Conversation with this woman (a highly likeable individual, I hasten to add) was along much the same lines. It was impossible to remain on the same subject for more than, say, ninety seconds. And have you ever been to Egypt? Oh, it's splendid, absolutely splendid. What about India, have you been there? No, neither have I, but I'm dying to go; I've been doing snatches of reading on Hinduism and trying to get a feel for the place. Yes, I was in New York once but only for two days, that's not enough, it was on the way back from a group excursion to New Orleans, I must say I was a bit disappointed with Louisiana, the bayous and all, I found the landscape a bit desolate. Ah yes, the complete works of Cioran — I bought the book but I haven't gotten around to opening it yet... it's so hard to find the time! But have you read the latest Coelho? And that new Chinese film, uh, what's it called? You know, by the director who made... Oh yes, what's going on in Rwanda is perfectly abominable, but right here in France, in the city suburbs, mark my words, there'll be a civil war one of these days... I don't much care for the music of Pierre Boulez, do you? And Milan Kundera — yes, he writes directly in French now! And just think, in Czechoslovakia, that playwright, what's his name, the one who used to be in prison, he got elected president! And the situation in Sarajevo... to think that it's in the very same city where the First World War began, no I didn't see Bernard-Henri Lévy's film on Bosnia but his wife Arielle Dombasle played in another film I liked a lot, just a minute, the title will come back to me, speaking of which, I'm sure you approve of Ariane

Mnouchkine's hunger strike, she and her theatre company came to town a while ago, they did a play by Molière, it was unforgettable. *The Wings of Desire* is a marvellous film, don't you agree? Wim Wenders was in Portugal for a while — have you ever been to Lisbon? I happened to be there just two weeks before the great fire broke out — what a tragedy! And that earthquake in Japan, I read that it took the firetrucks and ambulances much too long to get there. And David Waco and O.J. Simpson... oh there's so much violence in the world!... But do come outside and let me show you my hydrangeas, they're perfectly exquisite this year!

Now, this is serious.

A century or a century and a half ago (and a century and a half is *nothing*, it's when our grand-parents or our great-grand-parents were born, in other words *yesterday*), writers could still write with an eye to broadening their readers' horizons.

In the middle of the 19th century, readers led lives which, like our own, had their ups and downs; but these lives were *restricted to reality* to a degree which it has become almost impossible for us to imagine. Their reality was *present*, rather than presented or represented. They had no cameras, radios, telephones or cars; still less did they have TV sets in their living rooms or movie houses in their neighbourhoods, not to mention computers, fax machines, video cameras, CD-ROMS or the World Wide Web.

From the minute they got up in the morning to the

minute they went to bed at night, these readers basically knew only what they could see, hear and touch. The streets of their towns and cities were only what they were. Their sights and sounds had never been duplicated, recorded on film or magnetic tape, much less invaded by sights and sounds from somewhere else. In the here and now, their only access to distant times and places was through words — tales and legends handed down from one generation to the next; theatrical productions on feast days; chapbooks; Gospel stories reiterated in Sunday sermons, and finally, for the happy few who had a modicum of education and leisure time, novels (often serialized in the daily newspaper) poetry and plays.

As a general rule, readers of the mid-19th century frequented people from their own milieu; they did not have paid vacations and they did not go gallivanting off to other parts of the world; literature, whether high or low, elitist or popular, was their only form of escape from reality; it alone allowed them to break away from the visible, tangible world, get acquainted with lifestyles different from their own, travel to imaginary lands. (I'm purposely leaving aside two other fabulous forms of escape from reality: music, because it conveys no specific content, and dreams, because they're not a cultural phenomenon.)

Despite the relative monotony of their existence, these readers possessed a number of reassuring certainties. They had virtually no doubt, for instance, that God existed; and very little doubt that there was life after death. Moreover, they had long-established traditions which meant a great deal to them — religious festivals on specific days of the year, winter evening gatherings among peasants, lace head-dresses for women, wild dancing at harvest time or on Bastille Day, turkey and chestnuts at Christmas, Easter cakes baked with time-honoured recipes, the ceremonious gesture of uncorking a bottle of wine.... In a word, each of these readers had a *cultural identity*.

Contemporary readers, on the other hand, have a thousand, which is tantamount to saying that they have none. Even in the least developed, most inaccessible parts of Europe, where ancient customs have survived to some extent, the arrival of television some thirty years ago put a halt to evening gatherings: images replaced words and the TV-set usurped the symbolic function of the hearth, becoming the convivial center around which family members now gather... and remain silent.

So here's what I said to myself, when my benevolent but chaotically cultivated hostess finally left my room: over the past one hundred and fifty years, the role of writers has been radically and irreversibly transformed. Our purpose is no longer to weave magic tapestries in front of our readers' eyes, broaden their horizons, incite them to dream or fantasize about other worlds, multiply and enrich their experiences.... Our readers are every bit as savvy as we are. On TV tonight, they have the choice between a documentary film about West African voodoo, a 1940's American detective thriller, a talk show on AIDS, and a historical panorama of the Bolshoi Ballet; if they decide to turn on the radio they can listen to Harlem rap, Hebrew religious chants, a West Indian *meringue* or an opera by Monteverdi; and, provided they live in a big city and have a bit of money in their pockets, they can get to know Sweden, India or Japan by attending a Bergman, Satyajit Ray or Ozu retrospective; they can take in a play by Brecht or Aeschylus, watch a dance performance from Johannesburg or listen to a concert of experimental music from China; they can drink Manhattan cocktails, eat a Vietnamese meal, go dancing afterwards in Argentina and wind up the night singing bawdy songs in an Irish pub.

Perhaps, I said to myself (having now locked the door of my room so that my hostess would understand that I was sound asleep), the role of today's intellectuals and writers is just the opposite of what it used to be.

To narrow down. To isolate. To build walls. To concentrate. To hold at bay the dizzying dazzling rush of sounds and images, choices, information and influences. To create a void. A silence.

To say one thing, and only one. Or two...

but in depth.

Hmm... universal writers for limited readers and limited writers for universal readers — is that what it boils down to? I admit that this way of framing the problem was somewhat simplistic — as often happens when one is reasoning under the influence of a bad mood. As usual, reality is more complex. Let me attempt, then, to add some nuances to the picture.

Ever since literature has existed, national labels have been stuck onto it. Novels were described as being French, English, German, Russian, Spanish, and so forth — and this was only natural, for they indeed reflected (or rather crystallized) essential aspects of the countries in which their authors lived: landscapes, sensibilities, psychological types, social or racial conflicts, religious and popular beliefs, historical backgrounds, and so forth. When novelists went abroad, their descriptions of the countries they visited were written for their readers at home. (Pierre Loti's "Japan", for instance, is specifically conceived for the eyes, ears and palates of the French; the same can be said of George Sand's "Venice"). Even writers who lived abroad for long periods of time never lost sight of who they were and whom they were writing for: despite the two decades Turgenev spent in France, the plots, atmospheres, characters and dilemmas of his novels remained resolutely Russian.

What is the situation now, at the end of the 20th century? As far as national or cultural identity goes, every conceivable tendency is represented on the shelves of our bookstores, from *wanderlust* (Chatwin, Le Clézio) to glossolalia (Joyce). I should like, however, to take a closer look at three types of contemporary writing identities, which I shall call polarized, pulverized, and, finally, divided.

At one extreme of the identity spectrum, a large number of novelists continue to draw their inspiration essentially from their rootedness in a particular land, history, and culture. Especially in those parts of the world where the novel is a nascent, recent phenomenon, the reference to national identity is still virtually compulsory. Martinique, for instance, is rightly proud of having authors like Patrick Chamoiseau and Raphaël Confiant, whose books display an impressive verbal energy to describe the joys and miseries of the island — its history, traditional beliefs and folktales, natural and human catastrophes. A somewhat analogous situation pertains in French Canada: Québec literature is young and therefore still preoccupied with its identity. (Also as in the West Indies, it has a love-hate relationship with the great French literary tradition, to which it owes much but from which it convincingly proclaims its independence.)

Other "polarized" writers, however (any number of examples come to mind, including Toni Morisson, Russell Banks, John McGahern...) have nothing to prove and nothing to teach; their attachment to a specific group or land is not conflictual in any urgent, present way; simply, within their local universe, they have discovered all the wealth, complexity and contradictions of the human soul, and can thus go on exploring this universe forever, without inflicting boredom on either themselves or their readers.

Of all the novelists of the 20th century, I can think of none who aspired more ardently than Romain Gary to embody the opposite extreme of the spectrum, namely the mad multiplication or *pulverization* of identity. Gary managed the rather incredible feat of going down in history as a French writer — whereas, born a Jew in Lithuania in 1914, raised in Russia and Poland until he moved to Nice in 1928, he left France in 1940 and did not live there again until twenty years later; and even then he continued to be a compulsive globe-trotter, speaking seven languages fluently, writing his books and articles in two of them, translating himself back and forth, and declaring proudly: "All my literary roots are planted in my *métissage*; I am a bastard."

Because of his mother's megalomaniac dreams for his future, Gary suffered as of early childhood from a painful sense of uncertainty about his own existence. He changed names almost as often as he changed addresses (going from Roman Kacew to Roman Kacew-Gary to Romain Gary and signing his books under the additional pseudonyms of Fosco Sinibaldi, Shatan Bogat and Emile Ajar.) His favourite joke was the one about the chameleon: you put it on blue cloth and it turns blue, you put it on red cloth and it turns red, you put it on Scotch plaid and... it goes crazy.

How, then, despite the mind-boggling diversity of his cultural and national roots, did Gary manage to deserve the stamp of "authentic Frenchman?" The answer is that he fought for Free France under the orders of Charles de Gaulle, served as a bomber pilot from 1942 to 1944, was decorated with several military medals and awarded the title of Compagnon de la libération.... In the course of those same two years, moreover, he wrote — in French — a magnificent novel called *A European Education*, which won a major literary prize and became a national bestseller. Yes, there is no doubt about it — even from the unlikely raw material of a Russian-Polish-Jewish wanderer, *that* will make a great Frenchman out of you.

Gary's behaviour after the war was even more dumbfounding. In 1945, when he learned (at the same time as the rest of the world) about the massive extermination of the European Jews, he had two possible identity choices at his disposal, both of them valid, both of them gratifying: he could proudly claim to belong either to the group of *heroes* (glorious French resistance fighters) or to the group of victims (persecuted Jews). It is an indication of both Gary's nobility and his eccentricity that he opted for neither of these choices. Instead, he sat down and wrote a far-fetched futuristic novel about the oppression of Blacks in Harlem (*Tulipe*, 1946), followed by a novel whose hero was a well-meaning, rather likeable Frenchman who had collaborated with the Gestapo (*Le Grand Vestiaire*, 1948).

For the rest of his life, Gary would strive not only to understand but to *become* the human species in its entirety. His novels are set now in the past, now in the present, now in the future; their plots unfold in every one of the five continents; their protagonists are clowns, ambassadors, prostitutes, intellectuals, policemen, rug salesmen, arms dealers, little boys, aristocrats, anarchists, hippies, Jewish violinists...

What Gary was seeking to embrace by means of this prodigal, oceanic oeuvre, was not "humanity" as a universal, abstract entity, but *every particular human being* (which is a very different thing). His own lack of identity, though it caused him intense suffering, also freed him from the narrow, determining frameworks in which most of us are caught up. He didn't see himself as a "man without qualities" (he had powerful attachments to certain landscapes, languages, types of music), but the very multiplicity of his allegiances made it impossible for him to adopt chauvinistic points of view. He was irritated by everything that resembled national, religious, sexual or racial pride.... Such pride seemed to him a trap, a dangerous delusion, and a barrier to communication.

Between these two extremes (polarized and pulverized identities), a new species of writer has appeared over the past century or so, a species which we can call *divided*.

In order to become a divided writer, it does not suffice to change countries (like Henry James) or languages (like Jan Potocki); you have to *suffer* from it. In other words, the displacement must challenge your very sense of who you are, and become the central, painful theme of your existence.

Perhaps the first divided writer in this sense of the word was Franz Kafka, living in Prague and writing his books in German. To him, nothing went without saying: neither his language, nor his national and religious identity, nor his status as a son, fiancé, doctor of law, insurance company employee... not even his status as a human being (was he not, rather, a *bug*?).

Is Kafka a feather in the cap of "German literature" or a jewel in the crown of "Czech literature?" The question is preposterous. In much the same way, it is amusing to watch both France and Ireland laying claim to the work of Samuel Beckett for "their" respective literatures — as if Beckett's books were not fundamentally different from those of Victor Hugo. The truth is that the author of *Endgame* repeatedly proclaimed his disgust for all forms of belonging, even to the human race.

In the course of the 20th century — with its massive displacement of populations and its ever-swifter means of transportation and communication — divided writers have become increasingly numerous. I am thinking, of course, of Nabokov, Stein, Rhys, Rilke; closer to us I am thinking of Rushdie, Ishiguro, Walcott, Ondaatje, Semprun, Kundera, Bianciotti; closer still, I am thinking of poets and novelists whom I know personally: Ying Chen, Linda Lê or David Homel, Leïla Sebbar, Adam Zagajewski, Luba Jurgenson, C.K. Williams, Adam Biro — or again, the many gifted writers of the Haitian diaspora in New York, Montreal and Miami... and, finally, I am thinking a little bit of myself.

These writers are neither rooted nor uprooted; indeed, they frequently describe the very concept of "roots" as an illusion, not to say a dangerous delusion. They are neither sedentary nor nomadic. They are in exile.

According to Vera Linhartova, a Czech writer living in France, for writers who choose to change countries, "the very word 'exile' is particularly inappropriate. For a person who leaves his country with no regrets and no intention to return, the place he abandons is far less important than the one in which he must arrive. Henceforth, he has chosen not to live 'outside of this place,' but to embark upon a path leading towards a 'non-place,' an elsewhere that will remain forever beyond his grasp. Like the nomad, he feels 'at home' wherever he goes."

I find it hard to imagine a statement about expatriation with which I agree less. The place and language left behind by displaced writers are the place and language of their childhood. How can they write anything true, beautiful, or powerful, if they wilfully obliterate all the images and emotions connected with their first years of life, and decide in advance that the place of their childhood is "far less important" than the one in which they must arrive...?

Non-places do not exist — or, if they do, they exist outside of this world, in the cosmos of abstract ideas explored by philosophers and mystics; under no circumstances can they be the territory of a novelist. To claim that writers can be nomads and feel at home wherever they go is to display either denial or disingenuousness. *No one* feels at home wherever they go — not even real nomads! Take a group of Sahraouis out of their desert tents and plunk them down in the middle of a California Jacuzzi party or the Frankfort book fair... they are liable to be more than a little uncomfortable.

At first glance, it might seem that Linhartova's lyrical praise of voluntary exile could be applied to the (extreme) case of Romain Gary. In fact, however, it cannot. Gary explained on many occasions that he had to keep on the move because otherwise he felt "locked up inside myself, bound hand and foot... and hating the limits thus imposed on my appetite for life — or rather lives." Only once, at the edge of the Red Sea, thanks to a sort of suspension of time due to a delayed passport validation, did he manage, "with the help of some haschich, to escape from the penitentiary that condemns one to be only oneself."

Writers in exile, far from feeling "at home wherever they go," are usually at home *nowhere*. People often ask me, "So you're equally comfortable in English and in French?" and when I answer, "No, equally uncomfortable," they think I'm being coy. I'm not. *If you're comfortable, you don't write.* The literary machine only jerks into motion if there's a minimum of friction, anxiety, misery, some little grain of sand to crunch, grind, jam the cogs.

Divided writers are not stateless people. They are not world citizens. They are intimately acquainted, not with one culture (like Jean Giono), not with all cultures (as was Gary's ambition), but with two. Sometimes as many as three or four, but usually two. This means they have the point of view of their original culture on the acquired one, and vice versa. Far from saying "I'm from nowhere, so your little squabbles are of no concern to me," they usually say, "Since I can feel concern about two countries, I feel concern about all countries." As a general rule, however, this does not incite them to leap into the arena of political action. Rarely, at least in their writings, do they practise what Sartre called *engagement*. They tend to preserve a certain distance. The distance is precious to them. It's what makes them suffer... understand... write. "I now realize," says Leila Sebbar, "that whereas division used to torment me, I've grown attached to it and care about preserving it. It's perpetually threatened by unity, or reunification, I don't know what the right word would be. Today, it's this very imbalance that makes me exist, makes me write."

Here then, it seems to me, is what the writers of this new species are saying:

They are saying, first of all, that in a world where people can choose their religion the way they choose a brand of yogurt in a supermarket, and change religions as easily as they change undershirts, it is no longer possible to look to the Beyond for comfort, a sure sense of our identity, and reassurance as to our right to exist.

They are saying, secondly, that our collective self-confidence has been shaken by what we've learned about the infinitely small and the infinitely large, that is, about chromosomes and planets, that is, about the arbitrary, improbable and therefore utterly poignant nature of our presence on the Earth. ("And often and willingly," wrote Pirandello as early as 1904 in his remarkable novel *The Late Mathias Pascal*, "often and willingly, forgetting that we are but infinitesimal atoms, we show one another mutual respect and admiration, and are even prepared to go to battle for a tiny piece of land, or to complain about things which, were we truly aware of our insignificance, would seem to us nothing but silly trifles.")

They are saying, thirdly, that for those who inhabit the industrialized West, there will never again be such a thing as a nice, comfortable, cradle-to-grave identity. The certainties of 19th-century readers may have had their advantages, but they are gone forever. *Je est un autre*, once and for all. All of us are multiple from birth onwards, not only because of the intermingling of populations and languages in the modern world — not only because TV acquaints us with dozens of cultures other than our own — but, more profoundly, more existentially, because we now know that, physically, each of us is the product of two different individuals, and that, psychologically, we are molded by the looks, words, gestures and expectations of our fellow human beings.

They are saying, fourthly, that in spite of this, the differences among individuals (and also among cultures) continue to be extremely interesting.

They are saying, fifthly and lastly, that having two identities, though it may be nervewracking and make you feel nostalgic or spleeny every now and then, is preferable to having only one — and also preferable to having a dozen (poor Gary!).

Melancholy is almost always part of the *Weltanschauung* of this new species of writer. So is self-irony. Even when they smile, you can often detect a faint sadness in their eyes.

"And I'm not even a foreigner," says a character in David Homel's novel *Sonya and Jack*. "I'm from neither here nor there. I'm from somewhere in between."

"Expatriates are like that," writes Pierrette Fleutiaux in *Will We Be Happy?* "The new expatriates and even the old ones: there's this back-and-forth mechanism inside of them which they just can't stop; they're constantly comparing, here with there, there with here, perhaps we should invent a nationality just for them, the nationality of the here-and-there, and of the special mixture this creates and which has no name."

Or again, this declaration by Salman Rushdie in a recent interview: "Clearly the consequences of migration are that every aspect of the migrant's life is put into question....

literally everything about the culture that you bring and your belief systems and indeed your personality is put into question, because... the roots of the self, classically, are thought to lie in the place you come from, in the language you speak, in the people you know, and in the customs that you live with. And when you migrate..., you lose all four of those roots, and you suddenly have to find a new way of rooting your idea of yourself."

Divided writers are rarely as eupeptic as the disciples of what Confiant and Chamoiseau call *créolité*; they may express admiration for the glossolalic theories of Edouard Glissant but will be unlikely to imitate them; similarly, they will tend to be leery of multilingual word play *à la* James Joyce — because for them, the superimposition of languages and cultures is anything but a game. And they are deeply at odds with the "multiculturalist" values currently fashionable in the United States, which are often nothing but a handy disguise for the childishly arrogant, intolerant, supercilious reaffirmation of the narrowest and most visible particular identities.

Division, on the contrary, often induces a sense of inadequacy, not to say guilt. Leading a double existence can make you feel duplicitous — and even, in extreme cases (again, Romain Gary), schizophrenic.

These writers of a new species know that it is absurd to be nationalistic, sectarian, chauvinistic, and enrol one's literary talent in the service of a cause (whether revolutionary, moral or religious), because it is absurd — or miraculous, which amounts to the same thing — to be alive.

These writers are neither heroes nor victims. They try to look at themselves, and at the human species, as lucidly as possible. They're more interested in the weak than the strong, and more at ease with paradox than parable. Except in situations of real crisis, they're unlikely to deliver moral lessons, wave banners or go to war. They're usually reluctant to make speeches or join parties. They tend to avoid chaos, rather than reflecting it in their writings. Their goal is to construct, reconstruct, on the page, a world in which it is possible for them to breathe, live, move. ("Our only nation is imagination," as Confiant once put it.) Their purpose is not to bolster certainties, but to rattle them.

That is what they do. That is the one and only thing they do... but *in depth*.

(1995)

Knowledge Uprooted
A Journey in Six Stages

"There were parts of himself that were so different from other parts of himself that he could not understand how they could all be in his one self. But there they were, and though the disparate parts often surprised him, he'd come to enjoy the merry-go-round that was his soul. What else was he to do?"
—F.X. Toole, Rope Burns

Stage One
How I Fell In Love With Ideas

The exact sciences belonged to my father. As far back as I can remember, my father shared his passion for physics and mathematics with me. First there were little experiments such as showing that the surface of the water could be higher than the edge of the glass, or that a spoon, if laid down gently enough, could float on its back in the soup. Later there were number series, elegant or playful equations, geometric solids and their astonishing permutations — and finally, when I was fifteen or sixteen, abstract studies in the "fourth dimension." I've always preserved a sense of excitement for this type of knowledge — a knowledge which I found exalting because it was irrefutable, and which dealt with the secret harmony of the universe. Why harmony? The question long obsessed my father. Why harmony? (But also: why is harmony sometimes absent? Why chaos? Why will it never be possible to discover a rule for the recurrence of prime numbers? A dizzying question indeed.)

As for my mother, she was of a more artistic bent of mind — a good amateur pianist and a voracious reader, she loved theatre, the opera and the ballet...

For all that, it would be too pat to say that I owe the right hemisphere of my brain to my mother and the left to my father, and that my own sense of being painfully divided between theory and fiction reflects my refusal to choose between these two individuals, who split apart when I was six. No, the fact is that my mother is gifted with a down-to-earth, rational, efficient personality, whereas my father is a dreamer, a man tormented by doubts and spiritual interrogations — he grew interested in physics, he once told me, as a means of understanding metaphysics.

Be this as it may, once the divorce had taken place, it was my father who, with the help of his second wife, raised the three children. In a perfect reversal of the classical psychoanalytic situation, the mother — being far away, reachable only through letters — became a *symbol* (connected to writing), whereas the father, very much present in our everyday lives, belonged to the order of the *real*.

In high school in New Hampshire, I was given my first courses in literature properly speaking, and I've had no better ones since. The wonderful old lady who ran the school read us Dante's *Divine Comedy* out loud (in translation) from beginning to end; our French teacher initiated us into plays by Sartre and Cocteau; our theatre professor had us memorize long soliloquies from *Macbeth* and *Hamlet* and study *Midsummer Night's Dream* line by line, learning to hear its polysemic richness, see and appreciate its verbal pyrotechnics; as for our young English teacher, his enormous library was permanently at our disposal and he introduced us to Tennessee Williams, Robert Coover, Richard Brautigan, Japanese haikus, Anatole France, Jerzy Kozinski, Walt Whitman — and also, astonishingly enough, to our own ability to write. He taught us that literature spoke of death, sex, madness, fear — of *ourselves* — and that, provided we approach any page, blank or printed, with the fullness of our living strengths, it would be within our reach.

Not a speck of literary theory. How was that possible? Nothing but passion, compassion, listening and communicating. When I think about it, nothing I learned about literature in that strange little school in the backwoods of New Hampshire has been belied in the decades since.

Stage Two
A Vague Longing, Doomed To Failure, To Achieve Artist Status

Then began my university career — a checkered one indeed, the details of which I shall spare you. But it included, among other things, a course on "The Literature of the Absurd" (Beckett, Camus, Ionesco) on the West coast of Canada; a course on *Thérèse Desqueyroux* and *Tartarin de Tarascon* in the Bronx, and finally, at a chic, costly little college in one of the cushier suburbs of New York, a course on "The Psychology of Creativity" (readings in Freud, Jung and even Simone de Beauvoir), and a writing course in which, at long last, I discovered writer's block, rivalry, literary impotence, rage and jealousy, and the violent longing (absurd, of course, in a nineteen-year-old girl) to become a Writer with a capital W and give birth to a masterpiece by next week at the latest. In brief, I learned to no longer dare write at all — and also, having failed as a writer, to want to die.

STAGE THREE (A SHORT ONE)
Down With The Illusions Of Art;
Long Live Revolution And Theory

At the age of twenty, I came to Paris for my Junior Year Abroad. A good thing I did, too. Because in France the situation was very different. There, at the time, no one was yearning to become a novelist, which simplified matters. When I talked to my new French friends about my aspiration to write fiction some day, they giggled politely. No, they assured me. That's not at all what is needed. What's needed, then? I asked them. The revolution, they told me. And how does one achieve that? I asked. Why, through theory, of course! they said, in substance. The time for dreaming and making people dream had come to an end — what was important now was to read and speechify. If one absolutely *had* to write, the least one could do was to eschew fiction and write theory. Down with the romantic existential *angst* of petty-bourgeois students. What a relief!

I was thrilled to learn that all my hang-ups and neuroses stemmed from the capitalist regime under which I'd been living up until then — and that, in the new society, not having compromised myself excessively with the class enemy, I'd be allowed to share in the benefits of the dictatorship of the proletariat. Thus, I harnessed myself to a new reading list. No more Japanese haikus, no more Shakespeare, France or Whitman — at top speed, I ingurgitated the complete works of Marx and Engels, but also Foucault and Althusser, but also Derrida and Barthes, Metz and Kristeva, Deleuze and Guattari, Lacan and so forth. On top of all this, in that same vintage year of 1975, new books with new ideas were coming out — books by Hélène Cixous and Luce Irigaray, Annie Leclerc and Marie Cardinal, adding some feminist spice to the already tasty ratatouille of theories. What a marvellous mess! It was all so arduous, so exciting! Especially when you tried to reconcile Deleuze's desiring machines with Lenin's soviets and electricity, or Lacan's mirror stage with Trotsky's permanent revolution, or Barthes's pleasure of the text with Marx's surplus value, or Cixous's white ink with Irigaray's speculum.

What do you mean, you don't get it? Surely you can't be that thick-headed, try again, read through it more carefully, take notes, listen, it'll come, it'll come....

STAGE FOUR
Theory And Fiction In Uneven Alternation
When, in that same year of 1975, Roland Barthes admitted me into his *petit séminaire* at the Ecole des hautes études en sciences sociales, my excitement knew no

bounds. At last I'd entered "real life"; I was hanging out with the greatest thinkers in the country of great thinkers — those theoreticians who, thanks to the irresistible power of their ideas, were going to change the world. All my inner dilemmas had vanished — as had, indeed, my literary ambitions; in the space of two years I'd become a real "left-wing Parisian intellectual" — that is, a woman gifted with a head and a sex and nothing in between, a woman who knew how to talk and fuck because both of these activites could be construed as revolutionary, each in its own way, but who spoke out against marriage and particularly against children, yuk, barf, the family was a reactionary institution, so was the church, so was the novel when you came right down to it, in the post-revolutionary world there would no longer be any need for story-telling. Meanwhile we could go on reading Flaubert and Proust, Baudelaire and Musil if we felt like it, but these authors were kept at a distance in two equal and opposite ways, simultaneously put on a pedestal and knocked off of it. Yes, on the one hand they were idealized and praised to the skies, but on the other hand they were analyzed to death. It is difficult to conceive of a book whose intention is more destructive of literary imagination than Barthes's *S/Z*, which dissects a famous short story by Balzac — not, as our high school teacher had done with Shakespeare, to allow us to hear its richness and explore its depths, but almost on the contrary, to isolate its various "codes" (hermeneutic, symbolic, of action, and so forth), reveal its implicit class prejudices, denounce its ideological assumptions, and ferret out its "myths." Well, I'll be! I said to myself. Who would have thought that Balzac could be expressed as a formula? I was every bit as dazzled as I'd been as a child, when my father's elegant equations revealed to me the hidden harmonies of the universe.

Indeed, though he rejected all things familial, Barthes was in some ways a second father to me ("spiritual father," as we all know, is a pleonasm). Incongruously, I at once set out to translate him! As of 1976, the New York literary journal *Fiction* published my translation of one of his "mythologies" ("Billy Graham in the Winter Cyclodrome"); I also translated, for my own pleasure, the totality of his book *The Eiffel Tower*, and dreamed that he would dub me official translator of *The Empire of Signs* (luckily this dream did not come true). For two years, from 1975-77, I attended both his large seminar (devoted to "A Lover's Discourse"), and his small seminar (on "The Intimidations of Language"; "The Opera" and "The Practise, Function and Ideology of Crossing Out"). In 1977, I attended his inaugural lecture at the Collège de France, then his seminar on "The Neutral" (my lecture notes may still be around somewhere...).

What remains of all this, today? Well, quite a bit, to tell the truth. While Barthes's efforts to turn semiology into a science now seem to me heavy-handed if not ludicrous, I still appreciate his passion for precise words... his reflections on cliché, on the opposition between History and Nature... on so-called "phatic" communication, on performatives, redundance, hysteria, arrogance, stereotypes, and "the doxa." It was thanks to Barthes (and later on, for different reasons, thanks to Todorov), that I was able to free myself of Marxist theory. I was "formed," as the French say, by Barthesian concepts, the Barthesian gaze; these are undeniably a part of what I've become.

But Roland Barthes was not the only influence and I don't want to caricature that period of my life. If I delve into my memory, if I speak without sarcasm, I must acknowledge that those were years of exceptional effervescence, an exhilarating time in which to conduct one's intellectual apprenticeship — it would be hypocritical, today, to say that I regret it, or that it no longer has anything to do with me. My theoretical interests between, say, 1974 and 1979, covered the entire spectrum of the human sciences. It would be an understatement to say that I went along with the fashionable intellectual ideas of the time (in a word: structuralism): I glutted on them. Poetics, linguistics, psychoanalysis, ethnology, anthropology — off the top of my head, here are some of the readings that made a lasting impression on me: Roman Jakobson's work on aphasia, on sound and sense; Genette's *Figures; Tristes tropiques* by Lévi-Strauss, all of René Girard, Denis de Rougemont's *Love and the Western World*, countless tomes of Freud, Deleuze and Guattari, Lacan (whose seminar I also attended in the year 1977-78), Bataille (especially *Eroticism* and *Literature and Evil*; Mary Douglas's *On Impurity*, Marguerite Mead's *Coming of Age in Samoa*, not to mention exciting works in anthropology and linguistics — Mauss, Saussure, Malinowski and many more.

My new life was exhausting and euphoric. While I taught English to earn my living, I was taking an active part in the women's movement and beginning to write in

French. I published articles in several feminist journals and signed my first book contract in 1978 — for a nonfiction book on men and little girls, facetiously entitled *Jouer au papa et à l'amant.*

At the same time, I undertook to rewrite for publication the master's thesis I'd done under Barthes's direction — *Dire et interdire: éléments de jurologie.* I was (and indeed still am) enthralled with the subject of linguistic taboo. And when you look at the titles of my later non-fiction books — *Mosaïque de la pornographie, A l'amour comme à la guerre* — it's clear that they prolong and ramify that first exploration of taboo and transgression. For a good decade of my life, I was absorbed (not to say obsessed) with the idea of "necessary evil" and its direct or indirect connections to the debasement of women.

Not until 1980 (the year of Barthes's death, but also the year that marked the beginnings of my life with Todorov) did I dare to take the leap — at last, without a net — into fiction. It was unthinkable however, after an education like mine, to write a "realistic" novel, *à l'américaine.* I was far too conscious of the artifices, structures, voices and points of view involved in story telling. Thus, I tend (like Kundera and Cortázar in some of their books) to try to draw my readers into the pleasure of my experiments with form. *The Goldberg Variations* is comprised of thirty-two interior monologues. Nothing happens, and everything happens. The writing of that first novel plunged me into a state of unprecedented joy. Genette described it as a "small masterpiece," which flattered me immensely. My path seemed cut out for me.

By this time I was married to Todorov (of whose work,

for some unfathomable reason, I had read not a single line before we met); over the years, he would become (among other things) a true intellectual partner to me. One thing we had in common at the time was the fact that both of us wrote our books and articles exclusively in our adopted tongue, French. More importantly, being himself a serene and rigourous scientific thinker, Todorov gradually freed me from the need to write theory.

As often happens, however (cf. Arthur Koestler's description of his connection to the Communist Party in *Comrades*), before the abandonment, there was an exacerbation of my involvement with theory. This coincided, in a way which might at first seem odd, with another important event in my life, namely motherhood. Nowhere more than in *Mosaïque de la pornographie*, written during the nine months of my first pregnancy (1982), did I deploy my knowledge of literary theory more systematically. I carefully analyzed the literary genre of porn in its "high" and "low" forms, as consumed primarily by men or primarily by women, and conducted a ruthless narratological study of points of view, implicit content, sollicited identifications, and so forth. The book was a total flop.

By this time, I was teaching at American universities in Paris; "Semiology" at my *alma mater*, Sarah Lawrence; and especially, for a good ten years, "Feminist Theory" at Columbia. What exactly was *that*? I don't think I have too much to be ashamed of. What I tried to give my students in the course of that decade was not an ideology, not a doctrine, emphatically not a dogmatic, "politically correct" approach to life and literature. Rather, I used what I had learned from Barthes & Co. to introduce them to a series of important French writers: Sade, Bataille, Duras, Cixous, Irigaray, Kristeva...

Meanwhile, I was writing precious little fiction — nothing but *The Story of Omaya* (1985), which explored the panic-stricken soul of a rape victim.

Threatened, no doubt, by the irrefutable reality of motherhood, tormented, perhaps, by the same fear of engulfment as my own mother, I indulged in voluntaristic, not to say frenetic theoretical activity throughout the early 80's — writing books and articles, teaching and lecturing left and right; in 1983, I even directed a colloquium on "Women and Signs" at the International Center for Semiological Studies in Urbino, Italy. True, my own contribution was distinctly tongue-in-cheek (a play confronting various theoretical approaches to Melville's *Pierre; or, the Ambiguities*) — but still, in order to fool around with those ideas, I farmed out my ten-month-old daughter for two whole weeks!

I should add that in *all* of my non-fiction writing, from *Jouer au papa et à l'amant* (1979) to *Losing North* (2000), far from adopting a classic academic style or trying to sound severely scientific, I use a highly personal tone of voice, always including vignettes about my daily life, my readings, my childhood, and so forth. There is far more autobiography in my non-fiction than in my fiction! Roland Barthes' distinctive use of the first person singular must have been a model to some extent, but this trait was also something I'd picked up from feminism ("the personal is political") and from Lévi-Straussian structuralism ("Who is observing? Who is speaking? What are the hidden assumptions?" etc.) Crucial to me at the time was the question of the *conditions* in which works of art and ideas can or cannot reach fruition.

The *I* which I used so freely in my essays was also, no doubt, one of the effects of my *uprooted knowledge*. A certain shamelessness was made possible by the fact I was writing in a foreign language — partly because, at least in my imagination, my parents did not speak this language, but more importantly because for me, *French had nothing to do with my intimate, inner life*. In French I could say, quite calmly and even with a certain indifference, things it would have been impossible for me to reveal or even think about in my mother tongue.

And then, in 1986, just when my correpondence with Leïla Sebbar entitled *Lettres parisiennes: autopsie de l'exil* was about to be published, I fell ill. Acute myelitis, origin unknown. Numbness of the legs. I could no longer walk a straight line. For the most part, I stayed in bed. Time for reflection. For stock-taking. In my mind, the neurological illness would forever be connected to my new awareness that I was living in exile. I experienced it as a warning: be careful, you've frozen your roots, your tongue, your childhood... A novelist without a childhood can write nothing valid. You're on the wrong path.

Finding the right path wasn't easy, however.

As of 1987, *Thrice September* was a symbolic gesture of return to my origins and to English. This novel embodies an almost perverse linguistic position. Written in French by an anglophone, it is made up almost exclusively of the diaries and letters of a young American girl (ostensibly written in English but extemporaneously "translated" by the girl's best friend, who is French, as she reads them aloud to her mother). Writing *Thrice September* plunged me into insomnia, and sleeping pills led me to the edge of a nervous breakdown.... The first draft of the book was terrible, and my publisher turned it down.

The following year, pregnant for the second time, even as I reworked the novel that had been damaged by my own mental fragility, I embarked on another lengthy book of non-fiction: *Journal de la création*. It is at once a diary of my pregnancy, an attempt to understand the crisis of 1986-1987, and a study of the ways in which a dozen writing couples of the 19th and 20th centuries dealt with what I called "the mind-body problem." The book was published in 1990, and it marked a turning-point.

From then on, I consciously undertook to *uproot knowledge* in my soul, that is, to tear it out by the roots (*déchouquer*, as the Haitians used to say for what they did with Duvalierism). My criterion, now that I'd had the chance to stare my own mortality in the face, had become: "*Does this help me to live?*" It had become increasingly clear to me that neither Lacan nor Foucault nor even Barthes helped me to live. Rilke did; so did Virginia Woolf; and so did André Schwartz-Bart. If I had to summarize in a single sentence this period of theoretical "disillusionment" (without trying to generalize on the basis of my own experience), I'd put it this way: in the final analysis, unlike the theoreticians, *I was more interested in love than in "a lover's discourse."*

This made it possible for me to write novels.

As of the fall of 1989, when *Journal de la création* was at the printers, I began writing *Plainsong*. In English. Though its structure can scarcely be described as traditional (in a spiral-shaped chronology, a young woman "invents" the life of her grandfather using the few facts she has at her disposal and a thin manuscript left to her when he died), it is a book with real characters and a real plot, and its central subject is love. The page had been turned at last.

Fifth Stage
I Prefer Fiction

1990-1993. Total silence for three years. Impossible to find a publisher, either for *Plainsong* or for its French translation, *Cantique des plaines*. With my soul in my shoes, I began a new novel, again in English: *Slow Emergencies*.

"Life begins at forty," says a song I've always loved by Sophie Tucker. In 1993 I turned forty and at last embraced the literary vocation which had been my goal when I arrived in Paris twenty years earlier. For all that, my dividedness didn't disappear — it merely shifted: now, instead of being divided between theory and fiction, I was divided between French and English, for I had come to realize that *translating* my books, whether in one direction or the other, actually improved them.* *Plainsong* and *Cantique des plaines* finally appeared simultaneously in France, English Canada and Quebec. It was my tenth book, and

it marked the real beginning of my life as a writer. In France, I'd finally found a publisher who believed in me. In Canada, the book received the Governor General's prize — but in French, which threw a number of Québecois nationalists into a furor and made me suddenly, unpleasantly famous. Rarely have I felt as schizophrenic as on the day of that prize ceremony — when, on stage in the National Library of Ottawa, in front of a largely anglophone audience, I was required to read in French an excerpt from a book which — *for once* — I had written in English!

At around the same time, fortunately, I discovered the work of another Mixed Mind, another "foreign body in French literature," as he himself put it, an author of multiple languages and identities who was to have an enormous impact on me — I'm referring, of course, to Romain Gary. Between 1993 and 1995 I read his thirty-one novels and his single book of non-fiction: *Pour Sganarelle*. The latter intensified my mistrust of theory and definitively renewed my faith in the novel.

All of this being said... With the exception of *Slow Emergencies* (the only one of my novels to be "pure

---

*A confession: in putting *this* book together, I forgot that "Singing the Plains" had been originally written in English, so I translated it from the French translation "Les Prairies à Paris." When I compared the two versions, it turned out that the twice-translated text was superior to the original. I find this rather frightening. Maybe if I translated my books back and forth fifty or sixty times they'd get *really* good!

story"), all of my fiction bears the imprint of my early involvement with theory. *Instruments of Darkness* revolves around the character of a novelist and the novel she is writing; *The Mark of the Angel* is sprinkled with direct address from the author/narrator, a voice which remains present in order to "keep the reader company" as he/she descends into hell; *Prodigy* is a series of interior monologues, juxtaposed in a polyphony; and in *Dolce Agonia*, the narrator is none other than God himself, the "author" of all things...

Yes, I now lay claim to my status as a Mixed Mind, but I haven't become serene for all that. Some days, I long for the innocence of writers like Beckett or Duras, who never allowed themselves to be "sullied" by contact with academia and its abstract reflections on literature. Other days, on the contrary, I long for Knowledge and scientific certainty. A couple of years ago, Marina Yaguello asked me take part in a conference on "The Mother Tongue," and I took intense pleasure in listening to the other lecturers — on the differences between the English-language poems of Brodsky and Nabokov, for instance, or the cerebral activity of bilinguals when using their native as compared to their adopted tongues. It was such a relief to be with people who *really knew things* and were eager share their knowledge, whereas judgements in the world of literature are so hopelessly subjective!

When I myself am working on a novel, I prefer to read non-fiction. In recent years, rather than the linguistics and anthropology of my youth, I've acquired a taste for popular scientific books in physics (Stephen Hawking,

Stephen Jay Gould), psychology (Alice Miller), and neurology (Oliver Sacks, Boris Cyrulnik).

From time to time, not often, I do still produce a more "academic" piece of writing (most recently, "Good Faith, Bad Conscience" dealing with the interaction between art and politics in the work of Tolstoy and Sartre). But this isn't literary theory — and indeed, if there's one field of thought into which I *never* venture anymore, it's literary theory! This is no accident. Writing a novel and thinking about how novels work are divergent, not to say radically incompatible activities. To write a novel, you must not be overly aware of what you're doing. This leads me very naturally to my final section...

STAGE SIX
A Taste Of My Own Medicine

Yes. As a novelist, the last thing I want to do is understand "how it works" — that is, to attempt to explain, as my readers so often want me to do, *how* and *why* I write what I write.... If I explain it, I'm afraid I won't be able to do it anymore. More than any other field of knowledge, therefore, "poetics" has had to be uprooted once and for all.

Whereas I accept, embrace, *contain* those great theories which shaped my thinking in the 70s and 80s, and whereas I can admire, rather incredulously, an author like the South African J.M. Coetzee who writes great novels and brilliant literary analyses in alternation, I do my best to avoid contact with academic discourse about what *I*, myself, write. Such discourse acts upon me like a poison, causing me to ask myself all sorts of questions about the dominant themes in my fiction, my obsessions, my stylistic mannerisms, the connections between my life and work, and so forth (thus, I declined to attend the conference about myself which took place last year at the Sorbonne.) I feel a real threat emanating from that sort of thing, and I have to protect myself — talk about my work as much as you like, but for pity's sake, spare me your conclusions!

When I read academic analyses of my books (and there's no reason to think they're worse than what is currently being published on other authors, dead or alive), I feel an acute sense of discomfort. Not always, but most of the time, I find them distressingly reductive. (One American literature professor, for instance, advanced the theory that in *The Mark of the Angel*, Raphael who plays classical music represents the elitist, reactionary *bourgeois* class, whereas Andras, who loves jazz, represents the working class.... No "normal" reader has ever come up with such an asinine interpretation!) Artists are floored by this sort of mental aberration. It's as if a woman had lovingly baked you a chocolate cake, and you'd responded by giving her your opinion as to the respective quantities and brands of flour, butter, sugar, etc. she'd used in making it. *But... she would say... but... was it good? Did you like it?* This is all novelists want to know. They don't want you to be clever. They want you to be moved.

The problem is that it is much easier to teach cleverness than emotion. In French schools (as in French hospitals), no one has the slightest idea what to do with emotions... These days, I often observe with despair the way my own children are being taught literature in school (ironically enough, the new trends are largely the result of their own father's theories!!). In many ways, I find their courses far less stimulating and enriching than the ones I took in New Hampshire thirty years ago. I can enjoy listening to my daughter put together a deft analysis of "points of view" in a passage taken from Rousseau's *Confessions*, and of course I'll rejoice with her if she gets a good mark on her exam, but I'm convinced that Rousseau himself would have been horrified to see his work talked about in this way, because when he wrote that passage he was thinking of *nothing of the kind*; and what he was trying to convey to his readers was *nothing of the kind*; and by forcing my daughter to focus exclusively on the structure of the text, her professors allow the true meaning of the scene to go undiscussed. Or again: after having studied, say, *Lorenzaccio* in junior high school, my son will know all about the Medici family in the 16th century, the literary school of Romanticism in the nineteenth, and the ways in which various scenes of the play mirror one another. Any impulse on his part to identify with the young Alfred de Musset, however — existential malaise, a dizzying sense of unreality — will be vigourously discouraged. So what is literature *for*?

To take another example... From my point of view, as the author of *Journal de la création*, I found it valid to invent the neologism *figidity* to describe my state of neurological numbness. Fifteen years later, coming across that term in the table of contents of a doctoral dissertation is no fun at all — I find it profoundly disturbing. And reading a sentence like "Huston had lost all sensation in her genitals and felt herself to be simultaneously rigid, frozen and frigid" makes my skin crawl.

This naturally obliges me to throw into question everything I myself have written, over the years, on the life and work of various writers. Is there any reason why my speculations on Duras, for example, should be less inaccurate, less reductive than the above-mentioned speculations about me? And what about my scintillating descriptions of Sand and Musset, Scott and Zelda Fitzgerald, Sartre and de Beauvoir, Plath and Hughes...? In the dozen or so years that have elapsed since the publication of *Journal de la création*, virtually all my certainties on the subject of art (in particular the idea that art is intrinsically opposed to "life" or "reality") have bitten the dust. How would I feel if a scholar (even a respectful, benevolent, conscientious scholar) published something about the interaction of thought and passion in my life with Todorov? I'd feel terrible. Not only because I'd resent the invasion of our privacy, but because the *main thing* would, of necessity, be missing — that is, life itself — changing, fluctuating, impalpable life, teeming with secrets and contradictions and mysteries.

As far as I know, there's one and only one way of getting at *that* through words: fiction.

(2001)

The Foreign Mother

All mothers are foreigners.

The one I lived inside, and whose voice I felt vibrating long before I could hear it, the one whose body nourished me even as she dreamed yes even as she refused to stop dreaming, the one who rocked me and who, rocking me, went on dreaming about freedom and fulfillment, the one who instructed my ears and my lips so that I gradually came to understand, emit, articulate and decipher the sounds of the English language, even as she went on making plans for her own future, her own success (something which should have been her absolute right but was not, in those days, the days of the feminine mystique and the homemaker fulfilled by her whiter-than-white laundry and her gleaming hardwood floors) — that one ended up throwing in or should I say throwing out the towel, along with the bathwater, the bathtub, the baby, three babies, the husband, the broom, the rolling-pin... and went on to pursue her dream of leading a more adventursome existence in a foreign land.

That one, then — the one of whose flesh I am the flesh — became a stranger to us. She turned into an idea, an absence, an abstraction, a letter, a woman of letters. In the letters she wrote to us, her children, she described at length and in detail the foreign countries she was visiting, or going to visit, and the foreign cities she was living in, or planning to live in, and the languages she was learning,

Romanic and romantic, fabled and fabulous, and the men who, in these foreign tongues, were courting her, our foreign mother. Having most likely fallen in love with (among other things) the breasts no toothless mouths were chewing on, these men invited her (as she told us, her children, in letters mailed to Western Canada from London, Madrid, Majorca) to their home towns, and the following year she would bring us black lace mantillas, and dolls in flamenco dresses, and fans, and daggers, and screams, and murders, no no no she certainly wouldn't have brought us all that, she must have drawn the line somewhere, what is the truth? Our mother's lips, painted bright red, telling us that her favourite colours were now red and black. She'd become Spanish! Her hair was black as night! Her lips, fingernails and toenails were red as blood! Beautiful she was, beautiful, impressive, intimidating and foreign, our permanently absent mother. She would lean down to kiss us good-bye, wipe off the red smudge her lips had left on our cheeks, and climb back into the bus, the train, the boat, the plane, the interplanetary rocket.

The next one, then. The one who came right afterwards. The one who instantly replaced the other, the first one. The second one, therefore. Our mother as well, for we called her "mother" too. Also a foreigner. Proficient — but only proficient, not yet completely fluent — in our mother tongue. Teaching me another mother tongue — her own. Arriving with her suitcases and her memory full of Europe — a different Europe; not Spain but Germany; not flamenco but waltzes by Johann Strauss; not red-and-black but green-and-grey; not mantillas and daggers but porcelain cups and silver cutlery; not mad dreams of freedom but Catholic piety and optimism — we'd never seen anything like it, or even dreamt that such things existed, and also — in the secret, invisible suitcases of this little German girl who had grown up to marry a Canadian, and become a mother overnight to three foreign children — the will to live after, despite and against the memory of a world war. A foreign mother, yes, very, taking our mother's place most gracefully, at the table, in the kitchen, in our father's bed, passing herself off as our mother — oh, sweet, gentle imposture. Kind, light-hearted, laughing usurpation! But nonetheless: lies, devastation and destruction, taboos and prohibitions, day after day, year after year.

The one, as well, whom I *chose* (so to speak) to be my mother, and who simultaneously elected me as her daughter — a mutual adoption you might call it, freely carried out, with no formalities or obligations, for the sheer pleasure of being together as often and as long as possible, despite the five thousand kilometers that separated our respective homes. Yes, a Russian Jew born in the state of New York can be mother to an Irish-German-British Protestant born in the province of Alberta — advisor and confidante, dependable and whimsical, a member and even a pillar of my family — this woman, too, is one of my foreign mothers.

And then comes the one oh yes the one which I myself have become, after having crossed the Atlantic Ocean in turn, a foreign mother, speaking my children's language with an accent, giving them a mother tongue that doesn't belong to me, rocking them with lullabyes they cannot understand, whose strange sonorities wake them up instead of putting them to sleep, overseeing their education with spelling and grammar mistakes, depriving them of a grandmother (which of my one, two, three foreign mothers should be their grandmother, and in what order? A little of each, or none at all?), preparing their palates for unusual foods, their ears for strange vowels, and their hearts for extraordinary journeys. To the flesh of my own flesh I am otherness incarnate, a close and present unknown, an *elsewhere* deeply engraved in their daily lives.

Who are the other ones?

I walk in the streets of Montreal with my four-year-old goddaughter, who was born in China. She leaps and plays in the snowbanks, talking to herself in Québecois, the language she has learned from her adoptive mother, who herself was born in Switzerland.

More, more.

I open my eyes, look around, and realize in astonishment that *all mothers are foreigners*. I see the distance that sets in so rapidly between them and their children — yes, the strangeness, the foreignness which is there, almost from the start; the non-identity, the non-congruency; in the exchanges between them I see not only fusion, tenderness, caressing and caring connection, but all that rubs and scratches, corrodes and currupts; I see the smiles but also the wounded glances, the airs of defeat and disappointment, I hear the cooing but also the voices that screech with impatience, break with exasperation, dissolve into tears, and I begin to see that in fact mothers are just this — our first foreigners, our first encounter with the incontrovertible reality of the other. In other words, what is important about mothers is their *otherness*, their not-too-closeness, their difference from ourselves....

Without difference there is nothing, neither hatred nor love; without the other there is no self; my inordinately numerous and foreign mothers have taught me this much — that chromosomes are less important than the heart, and that what really counts is for the child to feel cherished by its mother *as an other*, and to learn to cherish her, in turn, for the not-me person whom she is.

(2002)

Bibliography

Amis, Martin. interview quoted in the French daily newspaper *Libération* (June 5, 2003).

Antelme, R. *L'espèce humaine.* Paris: Gallimard, 1957. (*The Human Race*, tr. J. Haight and A. Mahler, Marlboro Press, 1998.)

Aucouturier, M. *Tolstoï.* Paris: Seuil, 1996.

Barrett-Browning, E. *Aurora Leigh.* London: The Women's Press, 1978.

Bataille, G. *Madame Edwarda.* Paris: J.-J. Pauvert, 1956.
— *L'érotisme.* Paris: Minuit, 1957. (*Erotism: Death and Sexuality*, tr. M. Dalwood. San Francisco: City Lights Books, 1986.)
— *La Littérature et le mal.* Paris: Gallimard Folio, 1958. (*Literature and Evil.* tr. A. Hamilton. New York: M. Boyars, 1985.)

Beauvoir, S. de.
— *L'Invitée.* Paris: Gallimard, 1943. (*She Came to Stay.* Cleveland: World Pub.Co., 1954.)
— *Pour une morale de l'ambiguïté.* Paris: Gallimard, 1947. (*Ethics of Ambiguity*, tr. B. Frechtman. New York: Philosophical Library, 1949.)
— *Le Deuxième Sexe.* 2 vol. Paris: Gallimard, 1949. (*The Second Sex*, tr. H.M. Parshley. New York: Knopf, 1993.)
— *Les Mandarins.* Paris: Gallimard, 1956. (*The Mandarins.* Cleveland and New York: World Pub. Co., 1956.)
— *Mémoires d'une jeune fille rangée.* Paris: Gallimard, 1958. (*Memoirs of a Dutiful Daughter.* tr. J. Kirkup. Cleveland: World Pub. Co., 1959.)

— *La Force de l'âge.* Paris: Gallimard, 1960. (*The Prime of Life.*
tr. P. Green. Cleveland: World Pub. Co., 1962.)
— *La Femme rompue.* Paris: Gallimard, 1967. (*The Woman Destroyed.*
New York: Pantheon Books, 1987.)
— *La Force des choses.* Paris: Gallimard, 1963. (*Force of Circumstance.*
tr. R. Howard. New York: Putnam, 1965.)
— *Une mort très douce.* Paris: Gallimard, 1964. (*A Very Easy Death.*
tr. P. O'Brian. New York: Putnam, 1966.)
— *Faut-il brûler Sade?* Paris: Gallimard, 1972. (*Marquis de Sade.*
tr. A. Michelson. New York: Grove Press, 1953.)
— Interview with Jean-Paul Sartre in *L'Arc: Simone de Beauvoir*, 1974.
— *La Cérémonie des adieux.* Paris: Gallimard, 1980. (*Adieux:
A Farewell to Sartre.* tr. P. O'Brian. New York: Pantheon Books,
1984.)
— *A Transatlantic Love Affair: Letters to Nelson Algren.* New York:
The New Press, 1997.

Bobin, C. *La Merveille et l'obscur.* Venissieux: Paroles de l'aube, 1991.
— *Le Huitième Jour de la semaine.* Paris: Lettres vives, 1986.

Cixous, H. "Le Rire de la Méduse." In *L'Arc* n° 61, 1975.
— "La venue à l'écriture." In *Entre l'écriture.* Paris: des femmes, 1986.
("*Coming to Writing" and Other Essays*, tr. S. Cornell. Cambridge:
Harvard University Press, 1991.)

Confiant, R., Chamoiseau, P. and Bernabé, J. *Eloge de la créolité.*
Paris: Gallimard, 1989.

Duras, M. *Un Barrage contre le Pacifique.* Paris: Gallimard, 1950.
(*Sea Wall*, tr. H. Briffault. New York: Farrar, Straus & Giroux,
1967.)
— *Moderato Cantabile.* Paris: Minuit, 1958. (*Moderato Cantabile*,
tr. R. Seaver. New York: Grove Press, 1960.)

— *Hiroshima mon amour*. Paris: Gallimard, 1960. (*Hiroshima mon amour*, tr. R. Seaver. New York: Grove Press, 1961.)
— *Le vice-consul*. Paris: Gallimard, 1966. (*The Vice-Consul*, tr. E. Ellenbogen. New York: Pantheon Books, 1987.)
— *Détruire, dit-elle*. Paris: Minuit, 1969. (*Destroy, She Said*, tr. B. Bray. New York: Grove Press, 1970.)
— *Le Navire Night*. Paris: Mercure de France, 1978.
— *L'homme assis dans le couloir*. Paris: Minuit, 1980 (the first, more violent version of this short story was written in 1957 and published in 1962 in the journal *L'Arc*.)
— *La maladie de la mort*. Paris: Minuit, 1983. (*The Malady of Death*, tr. B. Bray. New York: Grove Press, 1986.)
— *L'Amant*. Paris: Minuit, 1984. (*The Lover*, tr. B. Bray. New York: Perennial Library, 1986.)
— *La Douleur*. Paris: P.O.L., 1985. (*Douleur*, tr. B. Bray. London: Collins, 1986.)
— *Emily L*. Paris: Minuit, 1987. (*Emily L.*, tr. B. Bray. London: Collins, 1989.)
— *La vie matérielle*. Paris: P.O.L., 1987.
— *Le Ravissement de Lol V Stein*. Paris: Gallimard, 1988.
— "Les Yeux verts." In *Petite bibliothèque des Cahiers du Cinéma*. Editions de l'Etoile, 1996. (*Green Eyes*, tr. C. Barko. New York: Columbia University Press, 1990.)

Faas, E. *Ted Hughes: The Unaccomodated Universe*. Santa Barbara: Black Sparrow Press, 1980.

Felman, S. *La Folie et la chose littéraire*. Paris: Seuil, 1978.

Fleutiaux, P. *Allons-nous être heureux?* Paris: Gallimard, 1994.

Gary, R. *Les Trésors de la mer rouge*. Paris: Gallimard, 1971.
— *La Nuit sera calme*. Paris: Gallimard, 1974.
— *Pour Sganarelle*. Paris: Gallimard, 1965.

Handke, P. *Courte lettre pour un long adieu.* Paris: Gallimard, 1975. (*Short Letter, Long Farewell,* tr. R. Manheim. New York: Farrar, Straus & Giroux, 1974.)
— *Histoire d'enfant.* Paris: Gallimard, 1983.
— *Histoire du crayon.* Paris: Gallimard, 1987.

Homel, D. *Sonya and Jack.* Toronto: Harper Collins, 1995.

Hughes, T. *The Hawk in the Rain.* New York: Harper, 1957.
— *Crow: From the Life and Songs of Crow.* London: Faber & Faber, 1974.
— *Gaudete.* London: Faber & Faber, 1977.
— *Selected Poems,* 1957-1981. London: Faber & Faber, 1982.

Jelinek, E. — special issue of *Texte + Kritik* n° 117, August 1999.
— *The Piano Teacher,* tr. J. Neugroschel. London: Serpent's Tail, 1992.
— *Lust,* tr. M. Hulse. London: Serpent's Tail, 1992.
— *Wonderful, Wonderful Times,* tr. M. Hulse. London: Serpent's Tail, 1990.
— *Women as Lovers,* tr. M. Chalmers. London: Serpent's Tail, 1994.

Kristeva, J. *Etrangers à nous-mêmes.* Paris: Fayard, 1988. (*Strangers to Ourselves,* tr. L.S. Roudiez. New York: Columbia University Press, 1991.)
— "Entretien sur l'art," *Sorcières n° 10.*
— "Un nouveau type d'intellectuel," *Tel Quel* n° 74.
— *Histoires d'amour.* Paris: Denoël, 1983. (*Tales of Love,* tr. L.S. Roudiez. New York: Columbia University Press, 1987.)

Kundera, M. *La Valse aux adieux.* Paris: Gallimard, 1976. (*The Farewell Party,* tr. P. Kussi. New York: Knopf/Random House, 1976.)

— *Le Livre du rire et de l'oubli*. Paris: Gallimard, 1979. (*The Book of Laughter and Forgetting*, tr. M.H. Heim. New York: Penguin Books, 1981.)
— *L'insoutenable légèreté de l'être*. Paris: Gallimard, 1988. (*The Unbearable Lightness of Being*, tr. M.H. Heim. Boston: Faber & Faber, 1984.)
— *L'immortalité*. Paris: Gallimard, 1990. (*Immortality*, tr. P. Kussi. New York: Grove Weidenfield, 1991.)

Le Guin, U., "Some Thoughts on Narrative." In *Dancing on the Edge of the World*. New York: Grove Press, 1989.

Linhartova, V. "Towards an Ontology of Exile," paper given at a conference entitled "Paris-Prague: Intellectuals in Europe," published in *l'Atelier du roman* n° 2, Paris, Flammarion.

Meyer, A.-E. *Sturm und Zwang: Schreiben als Geschlecterkampf.* Hambourg: Ingrid Klein Verlag, 1995.

Morrison, T. *Song of Solomon*. New York: New American Library/Signet, 1977.
— *Beloved*. New York: New American Library/Signet, 1987.

Nin, A. *Delta of Venus: Erotica*. New York: Harcourt Brace Jovanovich, 1977.

O'Connor, F. "An Enduring Chill." In *The Complete Stories*. New York: Farrar, Straus & Giroux, 1971.
— "The Nature and Aim of Fiction." In *Mystery and Manners — Occasional Prose*. London: Faber & Faber, 1972.

Olsen, T. *Silences*. New York: Dell, 1983.

Ozick, C., quoted in Frieda Gardner, "From Masters to Muses." In *The Women's Review of Books*, vol. IV, n° 7, April 1987.

Paulhan, J. *Les Fleurs de Tarbe ou la terreur dans les lettres*. Paris: Gallimard, 1973.
— *Lettres aux directeurs de la Résistance*. Paris: Gallimard, 1945.
— Preface to *La nouvelle Justine*. Paris: Le Point du jour, 1946.
— *De la paille et du grain*. Paris: Gallimard, 1948. (*Of Chaff and Wheat: Writers, War and Treason*, tr. R. Rand. Urbana: University of Illinois Press, 2004.)

Pétrement, S. *La Vie de Simone Weil*. Paris: Fayard, 1973. (*Simone Weil: A Life*, tr. R. Rosenthal. New York: Pantheon Books, 1976.)

Plath, S. *The Journals of Sylvia Plath*. New York: Random House, 1982.
— *Letters Home*. New York: Harper and Row, 1975.
— *The Collected Poems*. New York: Harper and Row, 1981.
— and Hughes, T. "Poets in Partnership," BBC interview, 1961.

Pontalis, J.-P., Preface to Sartre, J.-P., *The Freud Scenario*. Chicago: University of Chicago Press, 1985.

Raimbault, G. and Eliatcheff, C. *Les Indomptables*. Paris: Odile Jacob, 1989.

Rank, O. *Le Mythe de la naissance du héros*. Paris: Payot, 1983.

Réage, P. *Histoire d'O* (with a preface by J. Paulhan, "Le bonheur dans l'esclavage"). Paris: J.-J. Pauvert, 1957.

Rilke, R.-M. "Lettre à un jeune poète." in *Œuvres I: Prose*, Paris: Seuil, 1972.

Robert, M. *Roman des origines, origines du roman*. Paris: Grasset, 1972.

Ruddick, S. *Maternal Thinking: Towards a Politics of Peace*. Boston: Beacon Press, 1989.

Russell, B. "True North." In *The Massachusetts Review*. Amherst: Mass. Vol. XXXI, n° 1-2, Spring-Summer 1990.

Sade, D.A.F. de. *Œuvres complètes*. Paris: J.-J. Pauvert, 10 vol. 1986-1988.

Sartre, J.-P.
— *La Nausée*. Paris: Gallimard, 1938. (*Nausea*, tr. L. Alexander. Cambridge: R. Bentley, 1979.)
— *L'Etre et le néant*. Paris: Gallimard, 1943. (*Being and Nothingness; an Essay on Phenomenological Ontology*, tr. H.E. Barnes. New York: Philosophical Library, 1956.)
— *L'Age de raison*. Paris: Gallimard, 1944. (*The Age of Reason*, tr. E. Sutton. New York: Vintage Books, 1992.)
— *Saint Genet, comédien et martyr*. Paris: Gallimard, 1952. (*Saint Genet, Actor and Martyr*, tr. B. Frechtman. New York: Pantheon Books, 1983.)
— *Les Mots*. Paris: Gallimard, 1964. (*Words*, tr. B. Frechtman. New York: Vintage Books, 1981.)
— *Qu'est-ce que la littérature?* Paris: Gallimard, 1964. (*What is Literature?* tr. B. Frechtman. London: Methuen and Co., 1950.)
— *Huis clos — Les mouches*. Paris: Gallimard, 1976. (*No Exit and Three Other Plays*. New York: Vintage Books, 1956.)

— *Sartre*, film by A. Astruc and M. Contat. Paris: Gallimard, 1977. (*Sartre By Himself: A Film Directed by A. Astruc and M. Contat.* New York: Unizen Books, 1978.)
— *Lettres au Castor et à quelques autres*, 2 vol. Paris: Gallimard, 1983. (*Quiet Moments in a War: the Letters of Jean-Paul Sartre to Simone de Beauvoir, 1940-1963.* New York: Scribner's, 1993.)

Sebbar, Leïla. *Lettres parisiennes: histoires d'exil* (in collaboration with N. Huston). Paris: Bernard Barrault, 1986; Flammarion "J'ai lu", 1999.

F.X. Toole, *Rope Burns*. London: Vintage, 2001.

Tunström, G. *Le Voleur de Bible*. Paris/Montreal: Actes Sud/Leméac, 1988.

Weil, S. *La Pesanteur et la grâce*. Paris: Plon, 1948. (*Gravity and Grace*, tr. A. Wills. New York: Octagon Books, 1979.)
— *La Connaissance surnaturelle*. Paris: Gallimard, 1950.
— *Attente de Dieu*. Paris: la Colombe, 1950. (*Waiting for God*, tr. E. Cranfurd. New York: Capricorn Books, 1959.)
— "*L'Iliade ou le poème de la force.*" In *La Source grecque*. Paris: Gallimard, 1953. (*The Iliad, or, The Poem of Force*, tr. J. Holoka. New York: P. Lang, 2003.)
— *L'Enracinement*. Paris: Gallimard, 1952. (*The Need for Roots*, tr. A. Wills. New York: Octagon Books, 1979.)
— *Cahiers* I, II, and III. Paris: Plon, 1988. (*The Notebooks of Simone Weil*, tr. A. Mills. London: Routledge, 2004.)

Woolf, V. "Professions for Women." In *Women and Writing*. New York and London: Harcourt Brace Jovanovich, 1979.